INSIGHT GUIDES

CYPRUS

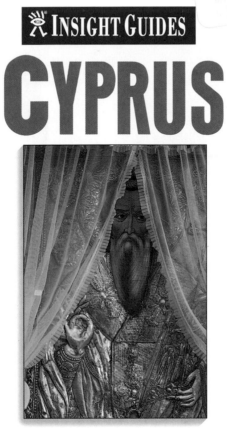

Discovery CHANNEL

APA PUBLICATIONS
Part of the Langenscheidt Publishing Group

INSIGHT GUIDE
CYPRUS

ABOUT THIS BOOK

Editorial
Project Editor
Julia Roles
Managing Editor
Emily Hatchwell
Editorial Director
Brian Bell

Distribution

UK & Ireland
GeoCenter International Ltd
The Viables Centre, Harrow Way
Basingstoke, Hants RG22 4BJ
Fax: (44) 1256 817988

United States
Langenscheidt Publishers, Inc.
46–35 54th Road, Maspeth, NY 11378
Fax: (1) 718 784 0640

Canada
Thomas Allen & Son Ltd
390 Steelcase Road East
Markham, Ontario L3R 1G2
Fax: (1) 905 475 6747

Australia
Universal Publishers
1 Waterloo Road
Macquarie Park, NSW 2113
Fax: (61) 2 9888 9074

New Zealand
Hema Maps New Zealand Ltd (HNZ)
Unit D, 24 Ra ORA Drive
East Tamaki, Auckland
Fax: (64) 9 273 6479

Worldwide
Apa Publications GmbH & Co.
Verlag KG (Singapore branch)
38 Joo Koon Road, Singapore 628990
Tel: (65) 6865 1600. Fax: (65) 6861 6438

Printing

Insight Print Services (Pte) Ltd
38 Joo Koon Road, Singapore 628990
Tel: (65) 6865 1600. Fax: (65) 6861 6438

©2004 Apa Publications GmbH & Co.
Verlag KG (Singapore branch)
All Rights Reserved
First Edition 1991
Third Edition 1998
Updated 2004

CONTACTING THE EDITORS
We would appreciate it if readers
would alert us to errors or out-
dated information by writing to:
**Insight Guides, P.O. Box 7910,
London SE1 1WE, England.
Fax: (44) 20 7403 0290.
insight@apaguide.co.uk**

www.insightguides.com

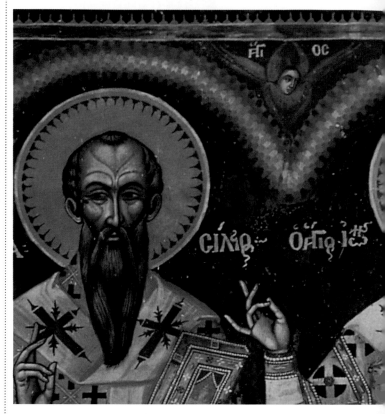

This guidebook combines the interests and enthusiasms of two of the world's best-known information providers: Insight Guides, whose titles have set the standard for visual travel guides since 1970, and Discovery Channel, the world's premier source of non-fiction television programming.

The editors of Insight Guides provide practical advice and general understanding about a destination's history, culture, institutions and people.

Discovery Channel and its popular website, www.discovery.com, help millions of viewers explore their world from the comfort of their own home and also encourage them to explore it first-hand.

How to use this book

The book is structured both to convey an understanding of the island and its cultures and also to guide you through its attractions:

◆ To understand Cyprus today you need to know something of its past. The **History** section explains the complex story of the island, while the **Features** section introduces the reader to the land and its people.

◆ The main **Places** section gives a run-down of all the places worth seeing. Places of major interest are cross-referenced by numbers or letters to specially commissioned full-colour maps.

◆ The listings in the **Travel Tips** section give easy-to-find information on such things as transport, hotels, restaurants, shops and outdoor activities. Information may be located quickly by using the index printed on the back cover flap, which can also serve as a bookmark.

◆ The book is illustrated with photographs selected to convey both the beauty of the island and the character of the people.

◆ Four special **pictorial spreads** provide insight into particularly photogenic areas of interest.

The contributors

The entire book was substantially revised in 2002. **George McDonald**, a tried-and-tested Insight writer and researcher who regards Cyprus as his second home, covered the Republic of Cyprus, while **Katerina** and **Eric Roberts** updated the text for the North, reflecting the many changes taking place in that part of the island. This new edition produced in 1998 was edited by **Julia Roles**, an experienced travel guide editor and past visitor to Cyprus, who built on the original edition by **Hansjörg Brey** and **Claudia Müller**.

George McDonald updated most of the text, injecting new life into sections written by **Klaus Hillenbrand**, **Joachim Willeitner**, **Alexander Laudien**, **Günter Weiss** and **Angelika Lintzmeyer**. McDonald also wrote several new features, as well as the pictorial spreads on *Hellenic and Roman Sites*, *Byzantine Landmarks* and the *Akamas Peninsula*.

Northern Cyprus was covered by **Marc Dubin**, while botanist **Lance Chilton** described the diversity of Cyprus's plant life in the *Island of Flowers* pictorial spread. Veteran travel writer **Paul Hellander** updated the book in 2004.

Bill Wassman and **George Taylor**, as well as several other photographers favoured by Insight for their flair and expertise, made an indispensable contribution.

Thanks go to **Penny Phenix** for proofreading and indexing the book.

Map Legend

– – –	Buffer Zone
– – – –	District Boundary
– • –	National Park/Reserve
✈ ✈	Airport: International/Regional
🚌	Bus Station
P	Parking
❶	Tourist Information
✉	Post Office
† †	Church/Ruins
†	Monastery
☾	Mosque
✡	Synagogue
⌂	Castle/Ruins
∴	Archaeological Site
∩	Cave
⚊	Statue/Monument
★	Place of Interest

The main places of interest in the Places section are coordinated by number with a full-colour map (e.g. ❶), and a symbol at the top of every right-hand page tells you where to find the map.

INSIGHT GUIDE
CYPRUS

CONTENTS

Maps

A map of Cyprus is on the inside front cover.

Routes of walking trails in the Troodos Mountains and Akamas Peninsula are shown on the inside back cover

Introduction

History

Features

A young boy
herds his
goats through
the arid fields
behind Agia
Napa

BETWEEN THE LINES

History has shaped Cyprus and, as the divided island
debates its future, the past is still a potent force

Sunshine, blue sky and beaches are the criteria that determine many people's choice of holiday destination, and in the summer months Cyprus scores a hat-trick. But the island is not only a paradise for indolent sun-seekers: archaeological discoveries dating back to 7,000 BC, medieval castles, remote mountain villages, and inviting cedar forests, orange groves and vineyards attract more adventurous travellers too.

Although Cyprus, the easternmost island of the Mediterranean, is girdled by the Near East, the pervading Eastern culture is matched by a large dose of European influences. The ancient Greeks, Rome and Byzantium, the crusaders and the Venetians, the Turks and the British have all left traces. The English writer Robert Byron, in *The Road to Oxiana* (1937), said of Cyprus: "History in this island is almost too profuse. It gives one a sort of mental indigestion."

Lawrence Durrell had a heartier appetite for history. In *Bitter Lemons*, his impressionistic account of his life on Cyprus between 1953 and 1956, he rejoiced in "the confluence of different destinies which touched and illumined the history of one small island in the eastern basin of the Levant, giving it significance and depth of focus."

Compared with the surrounding countries of Syria, Lebanon and Turkey, Cyprus is prosperous. Evidence of new industry and development is everywhere, although it is not always agreeable to the eye.

But the thin veneer of prosperity hides deep fissures. The war of 1974, which resulted in Turkey occupying almost 40 percent of the island and one in three Cypriots becoming refugees in their own country, is still fresh in local minds despite a recent opening of the "border" that has allowed renewed contact between the two sides. As for visitors, they still face the choice of a holiday in *either* the north or the south as visiting both sides is limited to day trips to the north if visitors are in the south.

So Cyprus is much more than sunshine, blue sky and beaches. This Insight Guide will acquaint you with the many different aspects of the island, both positive and negative, and provide you with a true insight into the nature of the place and its people. ❏

PRECEDING PAGES: writing on the wall, Kolossi; inside Limassol's castle; the church of Agia Paraskevi in Geroskipou; sunset over the Rock of Aphrodite near Pafos.
LEFT: door in Alsancak.

Decisive Dates

9000–7000 BC Stone tools, kitchen waste and other items, found in the Kyreneia Mountains and at Kataliondas, indicate that Cyprus was inhabited during the Mesolithic period.

7000–3000 BC Neolithic period. Traces of settlement at Choirokoitia.

4500–3500 BC Traces of Neolithic settlement in Sotira. Ceramic production begins.

3500–2300 BC Chalcolithic Period. Copper used for making tools and jewellery. Red-on-white ceramics predominate.

2300–1050 BC Bronze Age. Copper production increases. Trade with Syria and Egypt.

1900–1625 BC First fortifications. Ceramic art developed further.

1625–1050 BC Egkomi becomes the centre of the metalworking industry and the export trade.

1500 BC ONWARDS Cypro-Minoan syllabic script used.

1400–1200 BC Economic prosperity.

1200 BC ONWARDS Aphrodite cult in Palea Pafos.

1200 BC Egkomi and Kition destroyed by "Peoples of the Sea".

1050 BC Egkomi destroyed again, along with most Late Bronze-Age settlements. Salamis re-founded.

1050–750 BC Iron Age. Phoenicians settle the island. Temple of Astarte in Kition. Royal Tombs at Salamis.

750–475 BC Archaic Period.

700 BC Assyrian king Sargon II subjugates the city-kingdoms of Cyprus.

650 BC Royal Tombs at Tamassos built.

560–540 BC Egyptian rule by Ahmose II.

540 BC Persian rule begins.

498 BC Every city-kingdom except Amathus joins the Ionian Revolt. Persians tighten their grip on the island.

480 BC At the Battle of Salamis (in Greece), Cyprus joins the Persians against the Greeks.

475–325 BC Classical period. Cyprus becomes a Persian naval base.

411–374 BC Pro-Hellenist King Evagoras I of Salamis unites the island, despite Phoenician resistance.

325–358 BC Hellenistic Period. Cyprus incorporated into the empire of Alexander the Great.

333 BC Alexander the Great, with Cypriot kings' support, defeats the Persians at Issos.

323 BC After the death of Alexander, Cyprus becomes embroiled in the various wars of succession.

312 BC Zeno of Kition founds Stoicism in Athens.

311 BC Nicocreon, King of Salamis (and the last in the line of rulers of the independent city-kingdoms), commits suicide.

294–58 BC Ptolemaic rule. Cyprus becomes a province of Macedonian-ruled Egypt, with Pafos the capital. Tombs of the Kings at Pafos built. Economic and cultural upswing.

58 BC Cyprus becomes a province of Roman Empire.

AD 45 Apostles Paul and Barnabas arrive on the island as missionaries.

AD 115–116 Jewish uprising culminates in the expulsion of all Jews.

313 Edict of Milan grants Christians freedom of worship in the Roman Empire.

3rd–4th CENTURIES Mosaics at Pafos created.

332 and 342 Pafos and Salamis destroyed by earthquakes. Reconstruction of Salamis, which, renamed Constantia, becomes the island's capital.

395–647 Early Byzantine period.

5th CENTURY The island's Church becomes autocephalous – independent of the Patriarchate of Antioch.

5th–6th CENTURIES High point in the construction of early Christian basilicas.

647 First of a series of devastating Arab invasions.

730 Iconoclastic Controversy over the use of religious images.

787 Second Council of Nicaea condemns iconoclasm and restores the use of images in the Byzantine Church after much Early Byzantine art is destroyed.

843 End of Iconoclastic Controversy.

965 Cyprus regained for Byzantium from the Arabs by Emperor Nicephorus II Phocas.

965–1185 Middle Byzantine period. Cyprus flourishes. Kiti, Episkopi and Lapithos founded.

1094 Kykkos monastery, and churches with several cupolas at Geroskipou, Kiti and Peristerona, founded.

11th–12th CENTURIES Foundation of Machairas and Neofytos monasteries, and castles at Hilarion, Kantara and Buffavento.

1184 Reign of terror under Isaac Comnenos.

1191 Cyprus is taken by England's King Richard the Lionheart.

1192 Island sold to Knights Templar, who sell it to the French Crusader Guy de Lusignan.

1192–1489 Lusignan (Frankish) rule.

13th–14th CENTURIES St Sophia in Nicosia, St Nicholas in Famagusta, and abbey of Bellapais built.

1372 War with Genoa.

1374–1464 Genoese occupy Famagusta.

1426 Island overrun by Mamelukes from Egypt, and forced to pay tribute to Cairo.

1427 Peasant uprisings.

1460–1473 Reign of Lusignan King James II. In 1472, he marries the Venetian Caterina Cornaro, who becomes queen on her husband's death.

1489 Caterina Cornaro cedes Cyprus to Venice.

1517 Egypt conquered by Ottoman Turks, to whom Cyprus is forced to pay tribute.

1562 Rebellion against Venetian rule.

1570 Ottoman troops invade Cyprus and take Nicosia.

1571 Famagusta capitulates.

1571–1878 Ottoman rule. Religious and ethnic diversity tolerated. Christian and Muslim uprisings.

1660 Turkey bestows the right of independent representation upon bishops.

1774 Archbishop recognised as Ethnarch – the representative of the Christian population.

1804 Turkish population rebels against dragoman Georgakis Kornesios, who is executed in 1808.

1816 Hala Sultan Tekkesi built near Larnaka.

1821 Greece's war of liberation against Ottoman rule leads to massacre of Cyprus's leading Greek citizens.

1878 Cyprus leased to Britain.

1914 Britain annexes the island.

1930s Economic surge. Attempts to unify Cyprus with Greece (enosis) and to liberate the island from Britain.

1955 EOKA guerrilla activities led by General Grivas aim to secure union with Greece.

1959 Archbishop Makarios III becomes president.

1960 Republic of Cyprus formed. Guarantor powers are Britain, Turkey and Greece.

PRECEDING PAGES: prehistoric remains at Choirokoitia.
LEFT: the goddess Aphrodite.
RIGHT: Hala Sultan Tekkesi near Larnaka.

1963 Fighting between Greek and Turkish Cypriots.

1964 UN peacekeeping force stationed in Cyprus.

1967 Military junta takes over in Athens.

1974 Coup against President Makarios by the Cyprus National Guard, on the orders of the Greek junta.

July 1974 Turkish troops invade the north of the island and an exchange of people is conducted on ethnic lines. De facto partition.

1977 Makarios dies.

1983 North unilaterally declares the "Turkish Republic of Northern Cyprus". Only Turkey recognises it.

1999 Cyprus is accepted as a candidate for membership of the European Union – without the support of the Turkish Cypriots.

2000 Government decides to permit development in the Akamas Peninsula national park area.

2001 European Court of Human Rights finds Turkey guilty of widespread human rights violations arising from its 1974 invasion.

2002 UN-sponsored talks between President Clerides and Turkish Cypriot leader Rauf Denktash continue the search for a solution to the Cyprus problem.

2003 Northern Cyprus opens the gates of the Attila Line for the first time since 1974. Thousands of Greek and Turkish Cypriots are free to cross the line and visit parts they have not seen for 28 years.

2004 Reunification talks reach a frenzy of diplomacy but without a workable solution. The Republic of Cyprus prepares to join the EU without Northern Cyprus. ❑

MYTHICAL BEGINNINGS

Shrouded in myths and the mists of time, the earliest known settlements in Cyprus are thought to date back to the Neolithic period

A history of Cyprus usually begins with the description of the island by the Greek historian and geographer Strabo of Amasia. Although his text dates from around AD 19, he quotes several earlier sources (for example, Eratosthenes, from the 3rd century BC) and gives a detailed account of the original state of this fertile, densely-forested island.

In the following extract, he mentions its important mineral resources and agricultural products, as well as the changes brought about by civilisation: "As a fertile island, Cyprus is unsurpassed, for it produces good wine, good oil and also enough corn for its own use. In Tamassos there are, moreover, a large number of copper mines, containing copper sulphates as well as copper oxide, which is suitable for medical purposes. Eratosthenes tells us that in ancient times the plains used to be covered with dense forest and, as a result, could not be cultivated, but the mines remedied the situation, for the inhabitants chopped down trees in order to smelt copper and silver. Eratosthenes also says that shipbuilding was a further reason for deforestation, for the sea was a traffic route, sometimes for whole merchant fleets. Since the islanders were unable, in spite of this, to master the sheer extent of forest on the island, they allowed anyone who was willing and able to fell trees to adopt the land thus won as their own property, without having to pay any taxes." *(Strabo 14.6.5)*

Earliest history

Strabo's account does not go back as far as the Neolithic period (7000–3000 BC), to which the earliest known settlements of Cyprus are thought to belong. Archaeologists have discovered finds all over the island linking Cyprus with Asia Minor, Syria and Palestine, many of them in fertile river-valley regions such as Choirokoitia (Khirokitia), Petra tou Limniti,

Troulli and Kalavasos. It is evident that the people lived from hunting and fishing, but the existence of primitive forms of agriculture and animal husbandry (sheep and pigs) has also been determined. From roughly 4800 BC onwards, rough brown pottery was manufactured. The houses, made of rubble, wood and

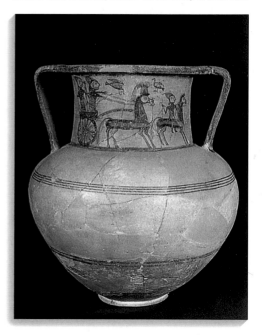

mud-brick, were elliptical in shape, and some were built underground. Religious life featured primitive forms of the Near Eastern "great mother goddess" or *magna mater*, influencing later concepts of God.

From around 3000 to 2300 BC, during the Chalcolithic (literally, "copper-stone") period, copper played an increasingly important role, as Strabo stresses, and the metal that proved so plentiful probably gave the island its name. The word "copper" cannot be traced back to Indo-Germanic or Semitic roots (the theory that the island derived its name from the Greek word for the henna-bush or cypress tree has been rejected). One of the first copper implements, a

---

LEFT: a smile from former times.
RIGHT: amphora decorated with chariots and riders, from Marion (850–700 BC).

simple chisel discovered in Erimi, is thought to have been imported by immigrants from Asia Minor or southern Palestine.

Soon, however, around 2000 BC, from the Early Bronze Age onwards, Cyprus was exporting its own copper. It was tempered by a complicated process, and then reduced to metal over a charcoal fire. Tamassos (Politiko), mentioned by Strabo, was the centre of copper production on Cyprus from the Middle Bronze Age (2000–1600 BC) onwards. Tombs provide much of the evidence of settlements from this period, a time when the island must have been densely populated and prosperous.

receiving at the hands of the Hyksos Kingdom (c. 1650–1550 BC), although current evidence suggests that Cyprus was not subjected to any large-scale raids.

In the Late Bronze Age (1600–1050 BC), Cyprus hosted a major influx of immigrants, initially merchants and craftsmen and then, by the end of the 13th century BC, refugees: the Greek Achaeans, bearing the Mycenaean culture. Integration with the indigenous population, the so-called "Eteo-Cypriots", or "True Cypriots" (traces of whose non-Greek and also non-Semitic language survived in Cypro-Minoan syllabic script until the 4th century AD,

It was in close contact with the rest of the eastern Mediterranean. The earlier advanced civilisations of Mesopotamia, for instance, were developing fast, and the pyramids were being built in Egypt. In particular, it kept in touch with the coast of Syria and Palestine, and with Minoan Crete.

Cyprus retained its political independence and its unique culture based on the production of weapons and other high-quality metal artefacts and ceramics featuring red-on-black paintings of men and animals. Various fortifications (in Krini, Agios Sozomenos and Nitovikla for example) were built during this period, a sign of the harassment the island was

especially in the kingdom of Amathus), resulted in the birth of a Near-Eastern/Aegean/Greek culture unique in the Mediterranean.

Vases portraying chariots, ships, bulls, birds and human figures, as well as high-quality ivory carvings and seals, all bear magnificent witness to this period.

Archaic cults and myths

Later records (in particular those of Herodotus) and archaeological finds give us only a vague idea of the sheer profusion of temples and cults on Cyprus, but it seems that many belief systems were ecstatic as well as mystic: Temple IV at Kition (Citium) contained an opium pipe for religious use. The cult of Aphrodite (the symbol of the island for medieval religious travellers and pilgrims) at Pafos is typical of the island's heterogeneous religious culture – a characteristic which can trace its roots back as far as the Bronze Age. In Salamis a male deity was subsequently put on an equal footing with Zeus. This Semitic god Resheph, with his two horns, then became the mighty Apollo.

According to legend, Cinyras was priest-king of Old Pafos before being driven from power

SANCTUARIES

Few places in the Mediterranean had so many religious sanctuaries in such a confined area. The goddess Aphrodite for instance was worshipped at 12 different sites on the island.

is the earliest written evidence identifying Cyprus with craftsmanship.

The legend of Agapenor and Cinyras reflects the generally peaceful colonisation by the Greek Achaeans of areas that had often already been settled.

Proof of Achaean colonisation can be found all along the "Achaean Coast" – the name given to the northern tip of the island – with evidence including the Mycenae-like fortifications at Egkomi, Palaeokastro, Maa and Kition, ceramics, and

by Agapenor, king of Tegea and leader of the Arcadian troops at Troy.

Agapenor's ship was driven off course after the city had fallen, and he ended up at Pafos. Pindar, who died in 445 BC, refers to Cinyras as "the darling of Apollo, the gentle priest of Aphrodite" *(Pythien. Ode 2.15)*, and his forefathers are said to have come from Assyria. Agapenor built a new temple of Aphrodite.

Homer's *Iliad* tells us that Agamemnon, the Greek leader at Troy, received a coat of mail from Cinyras as a present *(Iliad II, 19-23)*. This

---

LEFT: one of the many fertility symbols.
RIGHT: embossed gold plaques (700 BC).

traces of the Arcadian-Aeolic languages in Greek-Cypriot names and inscriptions.

Cyprus, which was known as *Alashiya* or *Alasia* in Ugaritic and Egyptian records (after its capital of Alashiya [Egkomi] of that time) and as *Kittim* to the Hebrews (cf. *Joshua 23.1 and 12*), retained its independence until the end of the Late Bronze Age – even when the Egyptian Pharaoh Rameses III (1192–1160 BC) claimed sovereignty over the island.

The Early Iron Age

When many Late Bronze Age settlements (such as Egkomi and Kition) were destroyed by earthquakes in around 1050 BC, and while colonisa-

Aphrodite

Aphrodite, known as Venus to the Romans, was worshipped by several cultures in the ancient world, and was also associated with Ishtar and Astarte. She arrived from the east, as the magna mater, or great mother, and was worshipped as the goddess of war as well as of the sea. Her reputation for valour did not last, however. She was disarmed by the ancient Greeks and thus reduced to the erotic functions and attributes associated with her today.

In the Iliad, Homer thus had Zeus, the father of the gods, say: "Fighting, my child, is not for you. You

are in charge of wedlock and the tender passions."

In the 12th century BC, long before Homer wrote the Iliad, the first sanctuary to Aphrodite was built at Palea (Old) Pafos. Its high priest was Pafos's founder-king, Cinyras. As Herodotus relates, the cult in Palea Pafos (Kouklia) included temple prostitution, whereby young women sacrificed their virginity, ostensibly to the goddess but in fact to whomever was visiting the temple at the time. Virgins would go to the temple, where they would loiter until chosen by a man, and then submit to a night of unbridled passion. The proceeds earned from such sacrifice were dedicated to the goddess. In spring, the temple's festival of Aphrodite and her lover Adonis drew pilgrims from all over the ancient world.

Surviving artefacts from the cult include a statue of a phallus with salt, symbolising the birth of Aphrodite from the sea-foam. This myth is famously illustrated by Botticelli's The Birth of Venus, in which the goddess rises from the waves on a vast scallop shell. According to the legend related by Hesiod, Aphrodite was born from the white foam produced from the severed genitals of Uranus (Heaven) when he was castrated by the Titans. (According to some versions of the legend, she rose from the waves off the island of Kythera in the Peloponnese but, finding the land there too rocky, sped away on her shell to Cyprus.) The claim that Aphrodite was descended from a man is usually seen as an attempt to integrate the eastern goddess of fertility into the patriarchal pantheon of Greek gods. She was worshipped as Aphroditos, a bearded man, in many Cypriot towns, particularly at Amathus.

As patroness of love and desire, and as the very embodiment of feminine beauty, Aphrodite features in numerous Greek legends. These include the myth of Atalanta, also associated with Cyprus, in which the eponymous heroine is left to perish at birth by her father and to survive has to fend for herself in the forests. She grows into a beautiful woman, and offers to marry anyone who can outrun her – but vows to spear those whom she overtakes.

Among the suitors is Hippomenes, the great-grandson of the sea-god Poseidon. Just before the contest begins, Eros, son of Aphrodite, shoots one of his famous arrows at Atalanta. Overcome with love for Hippomenes and fearful of his fate, she implores him not to enter the race. Distraught at her inability to change the rules of the contest, which she herself has devised, Atalanta thinks of a trick: she plucks three golden apples from a tree on Cyprus and tells Hippomenes to drop them as he runs. When he drops them, she stops to pick them up, and thus loses the race to Hippomenes, who consequently wins happiness for them both.

Today Aphrodite's legendary birthplace, the rock known as Petra tou Romiou to the south of Pafos, is bewitching, and especially romantic at sunset.

If you have come to Cyprus in the hope of finding something of the Aphrodite spirit, or have brought somebody who could benefit from her influence, it might once have helped to take a quick swig from the Fontana Amorosa. The waters of this spring, found near the northeastern point of the Akamas peninsula, not far from the Baths of Aphrodite, were said to enamour anyone who drank them. Sadly, however, only a marshy pool remains. ❑

LEFT: the Baths of Aphrodite in the Akamas peninsula.

tion continued elsewhere (for example in Palea Pafos, today's Kouklia), the so-called Dark Age descended on Cyprus and Greece. The island became insignificant and poverty stricken. The only archaeological evidence of this period comes from finds in family tombs.

The Early Iron Age (1050–750 BC) saw the arrival on Cyprus of Phoenicians from Tyre (in today's Lebanon). Experienced merchants and sailors, they introduced a highly sophisticated Semitic-Syrian culture to the island. At first only trading posts were founded on Cyprus, but at a later date – perhaps as early as the 10th century BC – Kition had grown into a full-

The Archaic Period

During the Archaic Period of Assyrian domination (*circa* 750–470 BC), seven Cypriot kings were overthrown, as a stele erected at Kition by the Assyrian king Sargon II (721–705 BC) makes clear. The cities were not destroyed, however, and the Assyrian influence was probably rather nominal.

It is at this stage that the seven (or possibly 10, depending on the interpretation of Assyrian documents) kings of Cyprus begin to play a more distinct role. Their city-kingdoms were hereditary, and were probably sacred in character too, especially at Pafos. In some cities, such

blown colony, independent of the rest of the country, with its own king.

After 850 BC, Phoenician temples to Astarte and Melqart were constructed above the remains of older temples that had probably been destroyed by earthquakes.

The magnificent Royal Tombs of Salamis, which date from the end of the Early Iron Age, bear witness to the prosperity of the upper social classes during this era. Ceramics dating from this period developed the ideas and designs of the Late Bronze Age, and have been traced to Eteo-Cypriot influences.

ABOVE: gold jewellery dating from 750–600 BC.

as Amathus and Kition, the dynasties were of Phoenician descent, while others, such as the Teucrid dynasty in Salamis and the Cinyras dynasty in Pafos, were Greek.

Egyptian domination

After the break-up of the Assyrian Empire, there was a brief period of Egyptian domination of Cyprus, under Pharaoh Ahmose II (569–525 BC). Politically this period was peaceful and not particularly significant, but the influence of Egyptian culture was very evident on the island. Human figures acquired a rigidity, similar to that of the Kouroi style of Ancient Greece, and scarabs were copied.

Cyprus under Persian rule

In 545 BC the Cypriot kings transferred their allegiance to the initially very relaxed rule of the mighty Achaemenid (Persian) kingdom, and deferred to a culturally superior power structure that was also open to Greek influence. This was the greatest political system of its kind to arise in the Near East before Alexander the Great. Embroiled in the tensions between Greece and Persia, in 498 BC Cyprus joined the Ionian Revolt in western Asia Minor. Herodotus does not explain what

> **THE HELLENISTIC ERA**
>
> Cyprus retained Near-Eastern characteristics, but the cultural influence on the island was predominantly Hellenistic.

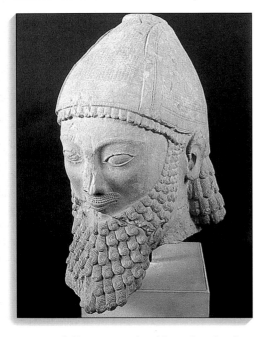

prompted Cyprus to take this action; he does not even mention the existence of any Greek nationalist sentiment on Cyprus.

Onesilos, the younger brother of the king of Salamis, persuaded all of Cyprus's major cities to join the Greek side. Only Amathus, with its strong Eteo-Cypriot and Phoenician influence, demurred. At the decisive battle against the Persians near Salamis, the king of Kourion, Stasenor, deserted his allies, and the Salaminians followed suit. Once the ignominious revolt had ended, Salamis's inhabitants impaled the head of Onesilos above their city gates. It was only in Soli that the Persians encountered tougher resistance. Rulers friendly to Persia

were installed in power there, and provided with Persian troops for protection.

At the Battle of Salamis (in Greece) in 480 BC, a Cypriot contingent of 150 ships fought with the Persians, alongside Egyptians, Cilicians and Pamphylians. "A bunch of good-for-nothings", pronounced Queen Artemisia of Caria *(Herodotus VIII, 68)*.

Greeks against Persians

During this period (470–325 BC) Cyprus continued to be affected by the political tensions between Greece and Persia. Neither Athens nor Sparta succeeded in establishing a firm foothold on Cyprus for any length of time. By now the island was being seen as a highly desirable naval base, as well as a valuable source of wood for shipbuilding, and Cyprus remained Persia's most important Mediterranean naval base; the Persian fleet which put paid to Spartan naval domination near Knidos in 394 BC set sail from Cyprus.

At this time, Cypriot art came under strong Attic influence, as discoveries in the handsome palace of Vouni reveal. Greek sculpture and vase-painting were widely imitated, but the traditional Cypriot forms held their own against the new trends and influences.

King Evagoras I of Salamis (411–374 BC) became a symbol of Attic influence. An adept politician, he had wrested control of Salamis from a Tyrian called Abdemon, under the successful pretext of being descended from the city's ancient kings. He capitalised on the tensions between Persia and Athens, and despite resistance from the Phoenician-based dynasties of Kition, Amathus, Golgoi and Soli, he succeeded, through the use of force, in uniting the island politically for the first time. According to his eulogist, Isocrates, he "assumed control of the government [of Salamis], which as a result of Phoenician domination was run by barbarians; the city despised the Greeks, showed no interest in the arts and had neither a market place nor a harbour; Evagoras remedied all these deficiencies and increased the city's territory still further, surrounding it with new walls and providing it with triremes..." ❏

LEFT: limestone head of a general or king.
RIGHT: statue of Aphrodite in the Pafos museum.

HELLENES AND ROMANS

The importance of the Hellenes and Romans in the history of Cyprus is evident

from the profusion of their cultural remains throughout the island

The history of Cyprus is in many ways quite different from the histories of other Mediterranean regions: the island had experienced a special kind of "Hellenism". There was an interplay of Greek and Near Eastern influence in its political, cultural and religious life long before the campaigns of the Macedonian gic base, and as a supplier of copper, silver, grain and wood (for use in shipbuilding), it acquired vital economic importance. Politically, however, its kingdoms were divided into two camps: Salamis, Pafos, Soli and Amathus lined up strongly on the side of the Ptolemies; Kition, Lapithos, Keryneia and Marion took the side

general Alexander the Great. So when a Cypriot fleet, with soldiers and technicians, fought alongside Alexander's army in his campaign to conquer the east, the island's integration into his enormous empire (356–323 BC), which stretched to India, was inevitable.

Power struggles

The power struggles that ensued between Alexander the Great's successors – Ptolemy, governor of Egypt; Antigonus, the governor of Phrygia, whose power base was Macedonia and Greece; and the Seleucid Empire, based in Asia Minor, Syria and Persia – proved politically disastrous for Cyprus. The island was a strate-

of Antigonus (the rulers of Kition and Lapithos were of Phoenician descent, but spoke Greek).

In 318 BC Ptolemy set out to subdue the cities. Only Nicocles of Pafos tried to oppose him. The consequences were tragic: King Nicocles fell on his sword, together with his wife and family. Inscriptions inform us that he was closely connected with the Hellenism of Argos, Delos and Delphi, and the luxury and splendour of his court were embellished into legends.

By the beginning of the 2nd century BC an astoundingly diverse assortment of peoples were living on Cyprus, including a Jewish community.

The Ptolemaic Kings

For the next two centuries (294–58 BC) Cyprus was a province of Ptolemaic Egypt, ruled by a governor general, or *strategos*. These *strategoi* resided in Nea Pafos, and were often related to the Ptolemaic royal family. The *strategos* of Cyprus was also in full command of the entire Egyptian navy. The local dialect on Cyprus was replaced by the common idiom of Hellenistic Greek, and the island's coins started to bear the heads of the ruling Ptolemies. The cities on the island were ruled by tough garrisons of foreign mercenaries under the command of Greek officers (most of whom were not Cypriots), and

rulers of the island. The cities all joined forces to form a new cultural organisation which was known as the *Koinon Kyprion.*

Egyptian cultural and religious influence, in particular that of Alexandria, the centre of Hellenistic city culture, increased on the island. Serapis, Isis, Osiris, Zeus and the Libyan god Ammon were just a few of the deities worshipped, and the market-places and gymnasia were decorated with sculptures and carvings influenced by Alexandrian craftsmen. The Tombs of the Kings at Nea Pafos (Kato Pafos) are the most important archaeological find dating from the Hellenistic period on Cyprus

by local Phoenician families (such as the Lapithos and Kitions). Greek Cypriots started filling important political posts only at the beginning of the 1st century BC.

It was in the realms of culture, arts and religion that the flourishing cities, with their magnificent market-places, gymnasia and theatres, enjoyed most independence. New towns were founded, three of which were called Arsinoë in tribute to the sister of Philadephus, one of the Ptolemaic

(by which time there were no longer any Cypriot kings) and are based on Egyptian designs. Cypriot literature was written exclusively in Greek, and the island produced a modicum of literary talent, such as Stasinos with his epic *Kypria*, and Sopatros, who wrote comedies.

The philosopher Zeno of Kition (334–262 BC) occupies a central place in the history of European thought. The son of a merchant named Mnaseas, he frequented as a young man the philosophy schools of Crates, Stilpon and Xenocrates in Athens. In 308 BC he founded his own Athens school: the Stoic School. His ideas were heavily influenced by Greek tradition.

PRECEDING PAGES: Persian fleet, with Cypriot ships, at the battle of Salamis.
LEFT: mosaic from the Cyprus Museum, Nicosia.
RIGHT: Aphrodite and Apollo, most favoured deities.

Roman rule

The Roman Senate decided to take control of Cyprus but only on a "provisional basis". Although Egypt managed to regain its rule of the island twice during the civil wars of the Republic, the Romans managed to hold on to Cyprus for good once the Empire was established. The puritanical Marcus Portius Cato tried to persuade the last of the Ptolemaic rulers to relinquish all claim to Cyprus in return for the office of high priest of the Aphrodite cult at

> ### ROMAN CONTROL
>
> The transfer of control of Cyprus to the Roman Empire in 58 BC completed Roman domination of the Mediterranean and left Egypt politically isolated.

Romani) dating from this period can still be seen in the area around Salamis, which gradually decreased in importance as Pafos grew. Two well-preserved Roman theatres can be seen at Soli and Kourion.

The splendid mosaics of the 3rd-century, 70-room House of Dionysos at Nea Pafos – as well as the fine mosaics discovered in Kourion – illustrate the smoothness of the cultural transition. An oath of allegiance to the emperor Tiberius, dating from AD 14, demonstrates Cyprus's loyalty to Rome:

Pafos. (The unfortunate ruler opted to commit suicide.) The orator Cicero was a proconsul of Cilicia, to which Cyprus was attached, but even he, a staunch critic of corruption, was noticeably passive in his attitude towards the civil servants who bled the island dry with extortionate "loans".

The Romans adopted the original strict administrative structure of the Ptolemies. Cyprus was now ruled by a proconsul and his officials from Pafos. The road network on the island was improved, but there were few changes that affected the native population. The Roman military contingent on Cyprus numbered only 2,000 men. Ruins of some of the spacious public buildings (*ager publicus populi*

"By our Aphrodite of the mountains, by our mistress, by our Apollo Hylates, by our Apollo of Kyrenia… by all the gods of Cyprus together with the council, the gods and goddesses of our fathers who belong to this island, the birthplace of Aphrodite, by Caesar Augustus who is our god, by eternal Rome and by all other gods and goddesses, we and our children do hereby solemnly swear… to remain loyal to Tiberius Caesar and to honour him… to accord holy honours to Rome and to Tiberius Caesar Augustus… and only to the sons of his blood." (*Rise and Fall of the Roman World* by T.B. Mitford.) ❑

LEFT: hedonistic pursuits.

Zeno: The original austere Stoic

Stoicism is an attitude which visitors frequently need in Cyprus, especially at those times when their wishes are not met as quickly or as efficiently as they might be elsewhere. It is fitting, therefore, that the philosophy of Stoicism – according to which virtue and happiness can be attained only by submission to destiny and the natural law – dates back to the Cypriot philosopher Zeno, born in 336 BC in Kition (Latin Citium), north of today's Larnaka. In the words of F.G. Maier, the island's famous Stoic made "a unique and inestimable contribution to the history of European thought."

Impressed from an early age by the Greek thinkers, and by Socrates in particular, Zeno left Cyprus in about 312 BC for Athens where he could devote himself to the study of philosophy. He visited a number of philosophy schools in the city, including that of the famous Cynic, Crates. In contrast to today's definition of this term, the Cynics of ancient times were not bitter and vicious fault-finders but thinkers whose philosophy stressed the benefits of returning to a more "natural" life, free of social conventions.

In about 300 BC, Zeno decided to found his own school. He did not have the capital to buy a building of his own, and possibly due to his cynical attitude to property, he gave his lectures in the agora (marketplace) in Athens, in the colonnade known as the Stoa Poikile. It was this venue that gave Stoicism its name.

The Stoic school was less formally organised than some of its rivals, such as the Epicurean or Peripatetic schools. Indeed Zeno was the only philosopher in Athens at that time to run a school of philosophy from a public building.

Zeno maintained that man's highest aim in life should be to live in harmony with nature. According to Zeno, conscious abstinence from passion and the active cultivation of apathy allowed man to develop enough insensitivity to face the good and ill fortunes of life with equanimity. In living a thoroughly austere life, Zeno certainly practised what he preached.

In the context of the laws of nature, he said, the joys and sorrows of the individual were insignificant. If man lived a life according to rationally established values, one that was in harmony with his own inner being, he would then become insensitive to the human dispositions of pain, suffering, love and even

death. This philosophy was accompanied by a belief in the divine nature of all things.

In his lifetime Zeno's teachings did not acquire many followers, though his short work, the Politea, attracted more attention and abuse than any other work by a Stoic. Indeed by the mid-2nd century Stoics were trying to minimise the importance attributed to this work. After Zeno's death, his successor, Ariston of Chios, diverged from the master's teachings and reduced Stoicism to the verge of insignificance.

It was only under Chrysippus of Soli (281–208 BC) that the school flourished again: Chrysippus adhered strictly to Zeno's original teachings, but bolstered them with tenets of his own, thereby laying the foun-

ZENO FLORVIT OLIMP. 190.
Exigua prudens arctatur zeno tabella'
Immensum cuius mentis acumen erat.

dations for Stoicism as understood today. In the words of Diogenes Laertius, in The Lives and Opinions of the Philosophers, "Without Chrysippus there would have been no Stoa."

Zeno's teachings were particularly popular in the Roman Empire, whose citizens appreciated the possibility of securing a personal happiness quite independent of external circumstances and social conditions. The Roman emperor Marcus Aurelius (AD 121–180), a supporter of Stoicism, illustrated what he called the "trivial nature of life" with the slogan "a drop of sperm today, a handful of ashes tomorrow!"

Zeno died at the age of 72 when he committed suicide. What, one wonders, could have robbed him of his equanimity? ❑

RIGHT: the philosopher Zeno.

SITES TO BEHOLD – OF HELLENES AND ROMANS

Cyprus has a wonderful profusion of Greek and Roman remains – in the ground, dotting the landscape and filling the shelves in museums

From 294 BC, when it was incorporated into the Hellenistic kingdom of Egypt, through the Roman era and up to the 7th century, when it was attacked by the Arabs, Cyprus enjoyed almost 1,000 years of peace. The Greeks and Romans put this long period of non-belligerence to good use.

Greek culture reigned supreme under the Hellenistic rulers. Cypriot cities were graced with fine marketplaces and temples, and the construction of many of today's leading historical sites began at this time. During six centuries of the *Pax Romana*, only the occasional earthquake troubled the island's prosperous cities. Pafos, the seat of the Roman governor, was endowed with magnificent villas and mosaics and is now a designated UNESCO World Cultural Heritage Site.

Pafos remains the single biggest complex of ancient ruins, even though much of the site has disappeared beneath a car park. This, and other impressive ancient sites, such as the hillside Theatre at Kourion, and the city of Salamis in northern Cyprus, bear comparison with all but the finest of the Mediterranean's Greek and Roman heritage attractions.

Ancient sites appear in unlikely places; some have been incorporated into resort hotels. It is often the least-visited sites which offer the most memorable experience. The windy tranquillity of the Greco-Persian palace at Vouni in the north and the underwater ruins of the harbour at Amathous, to cite just a couple, may offer the best opportunity for those who want time and space to hear the ghostly voices of ancient times.

▽ **WOODLAND GOD**
The Greek god Apollo was worshipped at Kourion in the guise of Apollo Hylates, god of the forests. Partially restored, his sanctuary conjures up a vivid image of the ancient scene.

▷ **PICTURE SHOW**
The Roman-era mosaics at Pafos are among the most dazzling and best-preserved in the Mediterranean. This mosaic is from the House of Theseus, probably the Roman governor's palace.

▽ **MARKET FORCES**
The agora (marketplace) of ancient Amathous stands beside the busy coast road east of Limassol. More of the ancient city, including its Phoenician-era harbour, lies in the sea just off the rocky shore.

◁ **NAKED TRUTH**
This bronze statue of the Roman Emperor Septimius Severus (ruled AD 193–211) was found at the village of Voni in northern Cyprus and is now a prized exhibit at the Cyprus Museum in Nicosia.

◁ THEATRICAL SCENE
The spectacularly sited Odeon at Kourion was built by the Greeks, used by the Romans as a blood sports arena and, today, is again a venue for classical drama.

△ TESSELLATION
Mosaics were a widespread art form in Cyprus in the classical period, and the technique was revived much later for use in Early Christian and Byzantine churches.

EMBARRASSMENT OF RICHES

It is almost impossible to plough anywhere in Cyprus without turning up evidence of the cultures which have left their imprint on the land. In the narrow Kalavasos Valley (near Limassol) alone, several hundred historic sites have been identified.

For the under-resourced and overworked Department of Antiquities, rescue archaeology is a top priority; when one of Cyprus's many development schemes hits ancient remains, researchers rush in to pick up the pieces before it is too late.

Foreign missions play an important role in excavations. Pictured above is the site at Fabrica Hill (Nea Pafos), where Australian excavators have brought to light an 8,000-seat Greek theatre. The effective international cultural boycott of northern Cyprus mitigates against excavation work there. As a result, some partially excavated sites, including Salamis and Soloi, seem to be in danger of neglect.

Periods closer to our own also demand attention. One Cypriot archaeologist reckons that much of her career will be spent among the ruins of a Venetian sugar factory at Kolossi.

△ LAST RESORT
The Tombs of the Kings are located beside the sea at Pafos. No kings were buried here but it was the last resting place of Pafos's high and mighty.

▽ ROMANCING THE STONE
An indelible air of romance wafts around the Rock of Aphrodite outside Pafos, where the Greek goddess of love was borne ashore from the sea foam.

THE RISE OF THE CHURCH

*A few Cypriots became Christians as early as AD 40 and their numbers
increased rapidly after the conversion of Emperor Constantine*

The decision of the Roman emperor Constantine (*circa* AD 247–337) to give preferential treatment to Christianity over the many other forms of religion in the Roman Empire led to far-reaching religious, cultural and political changes across the whole Mediterranean region. The Christians, who had hitherto been widely oppressed, now became the merciless persecutors of their pagan rivals. A politically and economically powerful ecclesiastical hierarchy arose, a kind of "state within a state". The effects of this on Cyprus, with its strong pagan traditions, were immense.

The spread of Christianity

From quite early on, perhaps even as early as AD 40, a number of Cypriots had been followers of St Stephen in Jerusalem. Some also became missionaries in Syrian Antioch, and on Cyprus itself (see *Apostles 11,19 f.*). A few years later, the converted Cypriot Jew Joseph Barnabas (see *Apostles 13,14 f.*) began his own missionary work, initially with the apostle Paul. Travelling from Salamis to Pafos, they came across several Jewish communities.

The conversion of the Roman proconsul Sergius Paulus (*circa* AD 46–48) is undisputed, but the story relating to the appointment of bishops in Soli and Tamassos at about the same time belongs to the realms of legend.

In contrast with Asia Minor, Cyprus bears few traces of Christianity before Constantine's time. After the conversion of Constantine, however, there was a swift increase in the number of bishoprics (which numbered 12 in AD 344 and 15 by 400), reflecting the island's Christianisation. The emperor's mother, St Helena, is said to have brought a number of reliquaries of the Cross to Cyprus on her return from Jerusalem. (Some of them still survive in the island's monasteries, for example at Stavrovouni.)

PRECEDING PAGES: Christ between the Apostles in the church of Agios Neofytos, near Pafos.
LEFT: Virgin and Child, Agios Lazaros, Larnaka.
RIGHT: St John with toothache, in Panagia Kiti.

Early Christian basilica construction reached its zenith in the 5th–6th century. Two particularly impressive examples are the remains of a three-aisled basilica with mosaic decoration at Kourion, and the extensive church complex (four basilicas with hot springs) at Cape Drepanum. Very little remains of the former seven-aisled

basilica at Salamis, which is a shame because the building broke new architectural ground.

It was in the 5th century that the Church of Cyprus succeeded in becoming autocephalous, in other words, independent of other patriarchates, particularly that of Antioch. The archbishop of Cyprus thus enjoyed a great deal of political power, which is still invested in the position today. Prompted by a vision, Archbishop Anthemius of Constantia (Salamis) found the Gospel of St Mark in the tomb of St Barnabas. In AD 488 he sent it to the emperor Zeno, who granted the archbishop of Cyprus the imperial privileges of carrying a sceptre rather than a crozier, wearing a purple cloak, and writing his signature in red ink. This special status was confirmed at a council in AD 692, the so-called Trullanum.

The Byzantine Empire

As a province belonging to the Diocese of the Orient, and governed by a consul based in Salamis (or Constantia as it became known from AD 342), Cyprus was subject to the rule of the east Roman or Byzantine Empire at Constantinople. In the 6th century the island became an independent administrative unit,

---

ROMAN RICHES

In the latter part of the 4th century, the Roman historian Festus Rufius commented that the island of Cyprus was "famed for its riches".

---

unleavened bread for the Sacrament were controversial issues that distinguished the faithful from representatives of Western Christianity – the "Latins" – in the 13th century. The tenets of Orthodoxy remained firm, however, and the faith still constitutes a fundamental influence on the people of Cyprus today.

Taking traditional Roman administration as its model, the Byzantine Empire developed its own system of bureaucracy. Officials were well known for their ruthlessness and the islanders frequently

known as *quaestura exercitus* – a sign of its growing importance. It was thus a part of the Byzantine Empire, and as such gradually dissolved its political and cultural links with the West, and with the capital city of Rome. It was to survive the decline of the western half of the empire by more than 1,000 years.

Several new church movements developed under the tough conditions of the Byzantine Empire which was now taking shape. Among them was the Orthodox Church, comprised primarily of Greek-speaking Christians and possessed its own dogma and liturgical and institutional forms. The marriage of priests, the lack of a papal primate and the utilisation of

suffered at their hands. Nevertheless, up until the Arab raids of the 7th century – a few attacks by pirates from the mainland in about AD 404, and a brief uprising led by a governor notwithstanding – the island enjoyed 300 years of peace, as it had during pagan Roman times. A period of severe drought at the beginning of the 4th century greatly reduced the island's population, and two earthquakes, in AD 332 and 342, destroyed Pafos and Salamis (Constantia). Only Salamis – the seat of the consul – was rebuilt.

The island was the first target of the Arabs in their astonishingly swift rampage through the Mediterranean in the 7th century. The first Arabian Mediterranean fleet was constructed in Syria in AD 648, and Cyprus was conquered the following year.

The next three centuries, up until the final re-capture of the island by the Byzantine emperor Nicephorus II Phocas in 965, were among the darkest in the history of Cyprus. In 688 the islanders were obliged to pay tribute to both the Byzantine Empire and the Islamic Caliphate. This state of joint-owned neutrality was unique in the Mediterranean. The arrange-ment did not deter either side from pillaging the island's cities, and taking punitive actions, for example sending large swathes of the pop-ulation into exile.

transferred to the island in the second half of the 6th century as guards and these immigrants mingled with the militarily weak Cypriots. The result was a population that, according to the Byzantine patriarch Nikolaos Mystikos at the beginning of the 10th century, would not raise its hand against either the Byzantine Empire or the Caliphate. Its faithful vassals were "more loyal to the Arabs than to the Byzantines".

Many Cypriots were forced to withdraw to remote areas in the mountains; their cities lay in ruins. Between 911 and 912 the island was pillaged for a full four months by a notorious pirate, Damianus of Tarsus.

Between 692 and 698, following a new resettlement programme instigated by the Byzantine emperor, and yet another Arab invasion, Cyprus became virtually depopulated. Its inhabitants were later allowed to return from Syria and Asia Minor (today Anatolia in Turkey). We do not know whether the popula-tion underwent Islamisation at the hands of the Arabs, nor whether any Islamic families settled on Cyprus on a permanent basis.

More than 3,000 Armenians had been

LEFT: fresco in St John's cathedral, Nicosia.
ABOVE: the legends of the saints provide endless inspiration for icon painters.

The Early Middle Ages

From 965 until 1192 the island was subject to the sole rule of the Byzantine Empire. This was a period of economic and cultural prosperity for the ecclesiastical elite, who busied themselves building monasteries and churches while the officials, despite the church's protests, drained the rural population dry. The law tied most country people to the land; even though some had the status of peasant proprietors or free tenants, they were still subject to ferocious tax-ation. In a dialogue written towards the end of the 11th century (and quoted on the following page), Nikolaos Muzalon, the archbishop of Cy-prus, uses such unflattering terms as "Prince of the Evil Spirits" and "Beelzebub" to describe his chief official, and refers to his tax-collectors as "out-and-out robbers":

Questioner: *Does the land (on Cyprus) produce anything?*

Muzalon: *All kinds of fruit grow there.*

Questioner: *Gratifying indeed!*

Muzalon: *It only results in more complaints.*

Questioner: *How do you mean?*

Muzalon: *The tax-collectors devour whatever the farmers produce.*

Questioner: *A tragedy!*

Muzalon: *And they demand even more besides.*

Questioner: *Oh dear!*

Muzalon: *They maltreat those who have no property of their own...*

A social class comprised of merchants and businessmen was responsible for the foundation of several new towns, including Kiti, Lapithos and Episkopi. As was the case elsewhere in Byzantium the new urban centres were built at a respectful distance from the coast. It was also during this period that the island's most magnificent monasteries, with their profusion of wonderful paintings and frescoes were constructed. These included Kykkos – which, under the patronage of Emperor Alexius Comnenos, incorporated the famous icon of the Virgin Mary – and later the Machairas and Neofytos monasteries.

The arrival of the Crusaders, the proximity of the Christian kingdom of Little Armenia in Asia Minor and the increasing activity of the Italian seafaring towns eventually put Cyprus back on the Mediterranean map. In 1148 Venice obtained numerous far-reaching trading privileges on the island.

There are virtually no traces of any Cypriot regional or national feeling. The short-lived and bloodily suppressed attempts at independence on behalf of individual Byzantine governors that took place in 1042 and 1092 were probably inspired by demands for tax cuts rather than nationalist feelings. Even when the brutal despot Isaac Comnenos, a relative of the imperial family in Constantinople, finally succeeded in freeing himself from central control in 1184, it was a rebellion from above rather than below that had no popular support. ❏

RIGHT: a relic containing fibres from the hemp ropes said to have bound Christ to the cross is kept in the Omodos monastery, in the Troodos Mountains.

CRUSADERS, LUSIGNANS AND VENETIANS

Between 1191 and 1571 Cyprus was first won by Richard I of England and then ruled by the Knights Templar, the Lusignans and lastly the Venetians

The 900 years of east Roman-Byzantine imperial rule came to an end almost accidentally. What ensued was nearly 500 years of Latin rule in the eastern Mediterranean – a period that outlasted the Crusader states of Palestine. The broker in this power shift was King Richard I (the Lionheart) of England.

Seized by the English

Richard the Lionheart's journey to Palestine in May 1191 was beset by misfortunes, such as the sinking of some of his ships. The vessel carrying his bride, Berengaria, limped into port near Limassol where it was received by Isaac Comnenos. The Byzantine usurper, who hated Latins, held the lady and her entourage captive, even depriving them of water.

When Richard arrived on the island several days later, he swore revenge and immediately requested reinforcements from Palestine. In the battle which followed, Comnenos underestimated Richard's strength. He subsequently suffered a quick defeat, and went down in history as the last Byzantine ruler.

For the most part the Cypriot population, most of whom were of the Greek Orthodox or Armenian persuasions, watched the collapse of Byzantine rule impassively, though some positively welcomed it. But the Cypriots were soon to realise the drawbacks of Crusader rule: the population was allowed no say in government, they were obliged to part with 50 percent of their capital, all the island's castles were occupied by Crusaders, and the men were made to shave off their beards as a sign of subjugation. In a letter written shortly after the arrival of the Crusaders, the Greek monk Neofytos said:

PRECEDING PAGES: crusaders at the siege of Antioch.
LEFT: St Hilarion (now Agios Ilarion) in northern Cyprus, seized by the crusading Richard the Lionheart.
RIGHT: the cathedral of St Nicholas (now Lala Mustafa Paşa mosque) in Famagusta, which was built by the Lusignans.

"Our country is now no better than a sea whipped up by storm winds." The population was still subject to Byzantine law, however, and for the time being, ecclesiastical and religious matters were left alone.

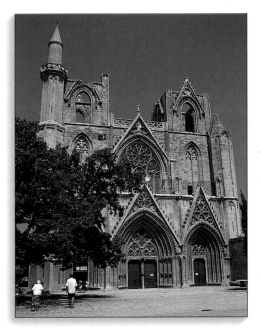

The Knights Templar

As far as Richard was concerned, the island was a bonus: Comnenos had been an exceedingly greedy despot, and had left considerable riches. Having failed to trade the island for half of Flanders, Richard sold it to the crusading order of the Knights Templar for 40,000 dinars and the pledge of a further 60,000 dinars to be drawn from its future income. In fact, the Knights Templar never managed to make a profit out of the island.

At the end of 1191 an uprising by the Armenians and the Greeks was brutally suppressed, and in the spring of 1192 the tyranny of the Knights Templar prompted the residents of

Lefkosia (which soon became known as Nicosia) to a renewed attempt at resistance. An appalling bloodbath ensued. The rebellion was one of the most important uprisings against a foreign oppressor in the history of the island. A guerrilla war flared up once again in 1194, under the leadership of a certain Kanakis, but then the Cypriot population sank into centuries of passive and gloomy resignation, broken only by sporadic and fruitless guerrilla uprisings.

ADAPTABLE CHRONICLER

Only a small number of Greek Cypriots, such as the 15th-century chronicler Leontius Machaira, were able to adapt to the rule imposed by the Crusaders.

The Knights Templar, preoccupied with their

provide them with it. Thus they came, from the Kingdom of Jerusalem, from Tripoli, from Antioch and Armenia. They were then... provided with land, and he gave the towns civil rights; many of the new arrivals were from the lower classes, and some were non-Cypriot Greeks."

The small governing class in Lusignan's feudal state was mostly comprised of Latins, from the west and the Crusader states. The Greek property-owners and nobles on the island had been largely wiped out by the Knights Templar.

battles against the Saracens, sold the island for 40,000 dinars – the sum they themselves had paid – to one of Richard's henchmen, Guy de Lusignan, the dispossessed king of Jerusalem, thus introducing the 300-year rule of the Lusignan dynasty. The measures taken by Guy during his two years as king of Cyprus reveal the dire straits into which the island had fallen.

"When he took the island as his own property, he sent out messages in order to win back the trust of the inhabitants, and he populated the cities and castles anew; and he sent forth tidings to all the surrounding countries that all the knights, nobles and citizens desirous of fiefs and land should come to him, and he would

The Greeks on the island fared particularly badly. They were hardly represented in the administration, nor in the ranks of the Italian, southern French and Catalan merchants who had settled into relatively isolated enclaves in the coastal cities. A deep gulf divided the ruling Latins from the Greek Cypriot population.

Indeed, the social status of the Cypriot population had worsened considerably since the Byzantine period: the peasant proprietors who, in addition to paying taxes, were obliged to provide their overlords with one-third of their income and two days' work a week, had lost the majority of their rights. Their fear of their rulers seems quite justified given the prevalence of mutilations and executions as contemporary forms of punishment.

Latin versus Orthodox

The conflict between the Roman Catholic and the Greek Orthodox Churches, fuelled by inflexible papal policies and fanatical monks, became more pronounced during this period. The *Constitutio Cypria* (also known as the *Bulla Cypria*) of Pope Alexander IV in 1260, which was officially meant to end the ecclesiastical controversy, reduced the number of Greek bishoprics on the island, leaving only four in remote villages. The bishops had to

of any reliquary cult. The Latin Church, its ranks swelled by Augustinians, Dominicans and Premonstratensians, maintained its dominance until the Ottoman era. Its power was symbolised by the French Gothic structure of the 13th-century cathedral of St Sophia (today the Selimiye mosque); the coronation church of the Lusignans in Nicosia; the cathedral of St Nicholas in Famagusta: and the Belapais abbey, the "white abbey" near Keryneia.

The nobility flourishes

The abject poverty of the Cypriot population stood in stark contrast to the late medieval

swear an oath of loyalty and, according to a remark made in a letter by the Latin archbishop Raphael in 1280, their presence on the island was merely "tolerated".

When 13 Greek monks were condemned to death at the stake by a Dominican padre in 1231, Greek resentment escalated. (The Inquisition became an institution of the Roman Catholic Church the following year.) The remains of the unfortunate monks were mixed with those of animals to prevent the possibility

LEFT: the coronation of Richard the Lionheart in 1189.
ABOVE: the castle of Kantara, the comfortable base of the Lusignans.

pomp at the court of the Lusignans and in the castles of the wealthy ruling class. For many, especially those benefiting from the advances made by the two great trading rivals, Genoa and Venice, it was a period of prosperity. Between 1336 and 1341, during the reign of the Lusignan king Hugo IV, the Westphalian pilgrim Ludolf von Suchen travelled through Cyprus, and was impressed by the wealth of merchants living in Nicosia. He was also taken by the cult of Aphrodite in Pafos, in particular its temple prostitution, a source of interest to many pilgrims:

"For the princes, the nobles, the barons and the knights of Cyprus are the wealthiest in the world. Anyone with an income of 3,000 florins treats it as if it were no more than an income of three marks. When it comes to hunting, however, no amount is too high to spend. I know a certain Count of Jaffa; he owns over 500 hounds, and one servant for every two of them, to protect them, bathe them and rub them with ointment; that is how well dogs are treated here. Another nobleman has 10 or 11 falconers, and gives them special wages and special rights. There are certain knights and noblemen upon Cyprus who pay less to keep and feed 200 armed men than they do their hunters and falconers… Thou shouldst know that all the princ-

es, noblemen, barons and knights on Cyprus are the wealthiest and most noble in all the world. They once lived in the land of Syria, in the wealthy city of Acre, but when that land and that city were lost to them, they fled to Cyprus and have stayed here ever since."

The history of Cyprus during this period is full of political intrigue. The intense political rivalries in the royal household of the Lusignans and among the island's powerful barons were positively Shakespearen. Peter I (1359–69) was the last of the fanatical Crusaders. He even succeeded in conquering Alexandria in 1365, albeit only briefly and with appalling loss of life. He was brutally murdered in his mistress's bedchamber by the mightiest barons on the island, after taking revenge for the alleged infidelity of his wife Eleonore.

It was not only the barons on Cyprus who kept the power of the Lusignan kings in check: Genoa and Venice, the increasingly powerful Italian trading powers, formed independent, rival states within the Lusignan kingdom. An unscheduled event marred Peter II's coronation in the cathedral in Nicosia in 1372: a fleet of seven Genoese warships arrived on the coast. A year of bitter warfare followed, during which the island was duly pillaged.

As a result, Famagusta and the surrounding area was subjected to 90 years of occupation and exploitation by the Genoese. The extortionate sum of 40,000 florins had to be paid annually to secure the return of the other areas that had been taken.

Life under the Venetians

Venice wanted Cyprus for its trade connections and as an advanced base against the Ottoman Turks. It prepared the ground by helping King James II to send the Genoese packing and got its reward when he married a Venetian noblewoman, Caterina Cornaro. James did not long survive the nuptials, dying in 1473. When his son and successor, James III, the last of the Lusignan line, died the following year it began to look as if the fates were favouring Venice. Caterina Cornaro tried to hold onto the throne, but she was leaned on by the Most Serene Republic and handed Cyprus over to the Venetians, a situation that was made "legal" in 1489.

For all its strategic importance, Cyprus was difficult to defend. In 1507 only a quarter of Nicosia was inhabited, and the city walls were weak. Sixty years later, a team of master builders spent 10 months trying to reinforce the walls. Smaller fortified sites, such as the castles at St Hilarion (Agios Ilarion), Pafos and Kantara, were dismantled.

All the island's defences were concentrated at Nicosia and Famagusta, where the city's four bastions, and the walls and towers connecting them, had undergone regular inspection and renovation since 1492. Its force of 800 soldiers was far too small and, not surprisingly, there was not a Greek among them; this force, whose task was to guard the city and its various nationalities, was changed every few years.

The social stratification remained just as it

had under the Lusignans. In order to obtain money and soldiers, the *signori* tried to persuade the peasant proprietors to buy their freedom. The Venetians also had to recover enough money from the population of the island (estimated to be less than 200,000) to pay tribute to the Turks.

The island's natural wealth was mined extensively as Venice sought to increase its trading profits through the production of traditional products such as wine, flax, hemp, cotton, wax, honey, sugar, indigo, oil and saffron. The saltworks at Larnaka, too, were important, and grain exports were strictly controlled.

The Ottoman invasion

In July 1570, after several warnings went unheeded, a flotilla of 350 Ottoman ships landed at Larnaka and the island quickly fell to the Turks. The battle for Nicosia was a catastrophe for the Venetians and their Cypriot subjects: they waited fruitlessly for the arrival of reinforcements, and their defences were completely uncoordinated. When the Turks, who brought in their own reinforcements unhindered from the mainland, sent in an attack force of 16,000 men, the city's resistance crumbled. In the bloodbath that ensued, the Greeks fought bravely on the side of their Latin rulers and

The biggest uprising on Cyprus since the beginning of Lusignan rule broke out in 1562. Significantly, the head of a Greek cavalry unit, the *Megadukas*, was involved, thereby justifying the Venetians' distrust of Greek Cypriot soldiers. Frankish noblemen, led by Jacobus (aka Didaskalus), a teacher in Nicosia, also joined the uprising. The Venetians executed the ringleaders and thousands of peasants, gathered in readiness in Nicosia, dispersed.

LEFT: ruins of the castle of St Hilarion (Agios Ilarion), built on the site of a Byzantine monastery.
RIGHT: St Neofytos, a hermit and stern critic of Richard the Lionheart.

incidents of open siding with the Turks among the rural population were rare.

The 10-month-long battle for Famagusta raged from 23 September 1570 until 1 August 1571. In the course of seven major offensives, all of which were repelled, the Turks allegedly lost 80,000 soldiers out of some 200,000–250,000. By contrast, the defenders had only 3,000–4,000 infantrymen, 200–300 cavalrymen and 4,000 Greeks. When the gunpowder finally ran out, the white flag of surrender was hoisted. In flagrant defiance of the terms of capitulation, the Venetian commander-in-chief Marco Antonio Bragadino was taken prisoner. His nose and ears were cut off, and he was flayed alive. ❑

بِسْمِ اللَّهِ الرَّحْمَٰنِ الرَّحِيمِ

الم ۝ ذَٰلِكَ الْكِتَابُ لَا رَيْبَ ۛ فِيهِ ۛ هُدًى
لِّلْمُتَّقِينَ ۝ الَّذِينَ يُؤْمِنُونَ بِالْغَيْبِ وَيُقِيمُونَ
الصَّلَاةَ وَمِمَّا رَزَقْنَاهُمْ يُنفِقُونَ ۝ وَالَّذِينَ يُؤْمِنُونَ
بِمَا أُنزِلَ إِلَيْكَ وَمَا أُنزِلَ مِن قَبْلِكَ وَبِالْآخِرَةِ هُمْ يُوقِنُونَ

سورة فاتحة الكتاب

بسم الله الرحمن الرحيم
الحمد لله رب العالمين ۝ الرحمن الرحيم ۝
مالك يوم الدين ۝ إياك نعبد وإياك نستعين ۝
اهدنا الصراط المستقيم ۝ صراط الذين أنعمت
عليهم غير المغضوب عليهم ولا الضالين ۝

THE OTTOMANS

During the rule of the Ottomans, the Christian population of Cyprus
mingled remarkably little with their conquerors

The violent battles and subsequent emigration of the Latin-Frankish inhabitants resulted in a catastrophic reduction in the population's numbers. (Those who survived, and stayed, were forced to convert to Islam.) Whereas a census recorded a population of 200,000 in 1570, the number fell to 120,000 by 1600, and continued to plummet. In 1740, after waves of further emigration, and a series of natural disasters, there were only 95,000 people on the island. Cyprus had become a poverty-stricken province of the Ottoman Empire.

In the early days of Ottoman rule, relatively few Turks occupied the large and soon-to-be-rebuilt fortresses at Nicosia, Famagusta, Pafos, Limassol and Keryneia: there were only 1,500 to 2,000 cavalrymen *(sipahi)* and the same number of infantrymen *(janissaries)*. In 1590 a contemporary observer by the name of Memmo estimated the number of Turkish troops on Cyprus to be around 4,800. Six *firmans* (sultan's decrees) ordered the forcible immigration of workers from Anatolia, Greeks included. "Islamising" or "Turkifying" the island was not the intention of these *firmans*.

By 1600 the Turkish sector of the population had increased to 22,000, though this growth stagnated in the following two centuries. According to a census taken in 1841, the Turks formed only 31 percent of the island's population. At the beginning of the British Protectorate, there were 45,458 Turks on the island out of a total of 185,630 people.

Christians and Muslims

The Muslims occupied a higher administrative and social stratum than that of the "infidels" *(rayas)* who, in addition to their lowly status, were subject to a three-tiered tax *(kharadsh)*, and who had to sacrifice their most promising sons for the elite troops of the *janissaries*. Yet the

Christians did enjoy a certain degree of self-government. In the mid-19th century the traveller-historian Mas Latrie counted 705 Christian and mixed villages, and 130 villages with a Turkish majority. He estimated the population of Nicosia at 11,950, of whom 8,000 were Turks, 3,700 Greeks and 250 Armenians

CHANGE FOR THE BETTER

Archbishop Kyprianos, who wrote an extensive, if very one-sided, chronicle of Cypriot history in 1788, was forced to admit that the Greeks were quite happy with the change from Venetian to Ottoman rule. The Orthodox Church had regained the status it enjoyed at the end of the Byzantine period. The serflike status of the peasant proprietors was abolished, and the taxes they had to pay were much reduced. The islanders' working week was cut from two days to one, and market duties were abolished. Towns and villages were home to both Christian and Muslim communities, though they tended to reside in separate neigbourhoods.

PRECEDING PAGES: Cypriot culture opens up to Islam.
LEFT: Ottoman-style salon, House of the Dragoman Georgakis Kornesios, Nicosia.
RIGHT: Gothic cathedrals were turned into mosques.

or Maronites (the latter being a Christian community that had emigrated to Cyprus, predominantly from Lebanon). Larnaka, the island's main port, was an important European colony. On the other hand, according to Latrie, Famagusta, much of which was ruined, was inhabited only by Turks; the Greeks were confined to the suburbs. The Turks wanted to keep the infidels away from the cities and their fortifications.

The administrative system

In theory, it was the declared duty of the Sublime Porte to avoid tyranny and suppression, to achieve peaceful coexistence between population groups and secure a just system of administration in order to revive the island's natural riches. At least, this was the substance of the various *firmans* that were issued, and of the various administrative reforms.

In reality the island was suffering from the same old disease it had inherited from Byzantium: its officials could not be controlled and corruption was rife. As the English captain Savile noted at the beginning of British rule: "What needs to be reformed is not so much the law itself as the application of the law. The Ottoman government is famous for its numerous *firmans*, laws and regulations, which can hardly be bettered for their comprehensiveness or their jus-

tice: all the problems of this land have been caused either by a failure to observe these laws, or by their improper application."

Christians and Muslims suffered equally from the pressure of high taxation, and its arbitrary nature. Famine, droughts, swarms of locusts, attacks by pirates, and the plague (1641) all contributed to the serious reduction in the number of inhabitants, which reached its lowest point at the end of the 17th century. Thus it was that the uprisings, which had been occurring on a regular basis since 1572, were directed at overly high taxation rather than against population groups with different reli-

gious beliefs. Both the Greeks and the Turks complained about the *dragoman* Markoulles (1669–73). Turks and Christians also showed solidarity in their rebellions against the unscrupulous governor Chil Osman Agha in 1764 as well as against the illegal rule of the adventurer Hadj Baki (1771–83). Nonetheless it was during this period that the incipient tensions which were later to split the two peoples asunder developed.

The Greek clergy

The power of the Orthodox Church was at its height during this period, exerting a crucial influence on both the economy and administration: as early as 1660, the sultan had recognised the Orthodox archbishop and the three other bishops as spokesmen of the Orthodox population, and they were granted the right to send their petitions directly to the Porte in Constantinople, and even to go there in person. In 1754 a *firman* bestowed the title of "ethnarch" – head of the autocephalous Church of Cyprus and leader of the Greek Cypriot nation – on the archbishop of Cyprus.

The Church was thus drawn into the corrupt Turkish administration, and as an English diplomat noted in 1792, it was soon practically running the island. The unpleasant task of col-

is allowed to employ every method of exploitation. The Turks would thus be subjected to the same wretched conditions as the Christians, had the latter – in addition to the demands made on them by the government – not been forced to lend their support to a number of lazy and greedy monks. Every matter concerning the Greeks is presided over by the archbishop and the dragoman of Cyprus (one of the officials appointed by the Porte), who is responsible to the non-Orthodox community for levies, taxes, and the like."

The most fertile and also the most pleasant areas of the island were the regions of Cerina

lecting taxes remained the responsibility of the *dragoman*, or "interpreter" to the Porte, who was very influential and often of Greek descent. In 1814, John Macdonald Kinneir, a "captain in the service of the East India Company", described the wretched conditions on the island, and the role of the Church in perpetuating them:

"The drastic effects of the Turkish system of government are nowhere more evident than on Cyprus, where the governor, appointed annually by the island's official owner, Capudan Paşa,

LEFT: the minarets of Nicosia.
ABOVE: wood-block engraving illustrating the weaving industry during the Ottoman period.

(Keryneia) and Baffo (Old Paphos) where, according to Tacitus, Aphrodite rose from the waves. Here, there were forests of oak, beech and pine, as well as olive and sycamore trees. Cyprus was justly famed for the quality of its fruit, wine, oil and silk; its oranges tasted as sweet as those from Tripoli, and its wines – both red and white – were shipped to the Levant, where they were adapted to suit the tastes of the English market. The island produced two different kinds of silk, yellow and white, but the former was preferred. The corn grown on the island was of excellent quality, and rice was grown in regions where the producers could amass enough capital to prepare the soil. However, the Greek rural population, who constituted the only labouring class on the island, had been under the thumb of Turks, monks and bishops for too long and were now reduced to extreme poverty; many emigrated at the first opportunity.

Growing dissatisfaction

The governor and the archbishop traded more grain than the rest of the population put together; they frequently decided to confiscate the entire year's grain harvest for export, or they would withhold it until they could sell it for a higher price. Tensions began to mount

between the island's Christians and Turks, who, as a French observer, L. Lacroix, put it, "were reluctant simply to stand by and watch those whom they had vanquished lord it over them now." In 1804 the Turks in Nicosia and in the surrounding villages rose up against their governor, who had been a willing tool of the Greek clergy. The fact that two paşas with Ottoman troops from Asia Minor had to quell a revolt by their own people only served to increase the tensions between the two sectors of the population.

As Lacroix makes clear, 1804 was a dress-rehearsal for the bloody events of 1821 when the Greek nationalist revolution against

Ottoman rule on mainland Greece erupted. The strong-willed and highly educated Archbishop Kyprianos, who founded the famous *Pankyprian Gymnasium* in Nicosia, kept himself aloof from the solicitations of the *Philike Hetaireia* (Greek Revolutionary Union). As Lacroix observed, the Greek population wanted only to be left in peace.

For all the passivity of the Greeks, Governor Kucuk Mehmed had Kyprianos, the high clergy and every educated Greek person on the island arrested on conspiracy charges. In Nicosia alone 470 people, including Archbishop Kyprianos, were put to death. Elsewhere the Greeks were systematically massacred, their houses were looted, their property confiscated. For six months the Greek population lived in terror. Greek notables who succeeded in escaping the pogroms fled to European consulates.

It was in this murderous climate that the so-called rule of the bishops came to an end in 1821. Yet still the Ottomans were not content. Contemporary observers remarked on the comparatively poor level of education among the Turkish community. The education gap between the Turks and the Greeks widened further by the establishment of new Greek schools. Moreover, the island's educated classes were increasingly influenced by the intellectual trends, particularly the advent of nationalism, that were developing elsewhere in Europe. The Turks also envied the Greeks' prosperity.

But it was neither nationalist ideals nor internal tensions that ended Ottoman domination of the island: it was rather the greatest power in the eastern Mediterranean – Great Britain. Her Majesty's diplomats were becoming increasingly interested in the internal affairs of Cyprus, and the Levant Company had become the leading trader in the region.

The political weakness of Turkey in relation to Russia, tension with the second great power in the Mediterranean, France, and the secure passage afforded by the opening of the Suez Canal in 1869 finally led the Porte to present Cyprus to Britain. The Porte did not ask for any payment for the island, and the sultan was allowed to remain as the island's sovereign. On 12 July 1878, British troops arrived on Cyprus.   ❑

LEFT: worshippers in the Turkish quarter of Nicosia look towards Mecca.
RIGHT: dawn beckons the faithful to prayer.

WANTED MEN
IN CYPRUS

This booklet must be looked after. It was expensive to produce and will not be replaced. It should be issued ..... on signature. A few bl..... have been left f..... be pasted in.

..... Nov. 1956.

CHIVAS GEORGE THEODOROU, ... NICOSIA, 5'6½".

..ATSIS KYRIAKOS CHRISTOFOROU .... ..LEKHORI, FORMERLY MITSERO,

GEORGHADJI POLYKARPOS COSTA .... PHLEKHORI,

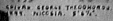

LEMAS STYLIANOS CHRISTOFI, ... NICOSIA, 5'5".

..AVLOU PAVLOS GEORGHIOU @ ..AVLAKIS 1931 VAROSHA 5..

SFANGOS NICOS SAVVA 1934, ..., 5'5".

SYMEONIDES PHIDIAS MIKHAEL, LASOUDERA, FETA AY. OMOLOTITADA.

SOFOCLEOUS, NEOPHYTOS 1936, PEYIA, 5'6".

GEORGHIOU NIKOS 1939, ...KHORI, ... NICOSIA, 5'7".

MIKHAELIDES ALEXANDROS NICOLA @ KOUNERAS 1937 AMIANDOS, 5..

GEORGHIOU ANDREAS @ KARAGENA,

ΜΕΛΗ ΤΗΣ Ε.

ΡALLIKARIDES, EVAGORA, MYLTIADHOUS
1938 T. KIANA S.S.

PAPACHRISTOFOROU CHRISTOFOROU KYRIAKOS
KIPEROUNDA

CHRISTODOULOU, DEMETRAKIS
1936 OHEKTRIA S.S.

...DOPOULOS ...TONIS CONSTANTINOU
VAROSHA

CHRISTOFOROU KYRIAKOS
KIPEROUNDA

ARISTIDOU YIANNAKIS, 2 "DROUSHIOT
IOANNIS" 1932, DROUSHA S.S.

...DRIDES ANDREAS CHRISTOU, 1934
...KTIMA S.S.

EPAMINONDA YIANNAKIS 1932
PEDHOULAS, ...NICOSIA S.10"

PAPAVERKIS GEORGIS
PANO ARMENES

FIOULLAS MIKIS KYRIAKOU, 1936

A BRITISH COLONY

With the British occupation, the centuries-long isolation of Cyprus
from the rest of Europe came to an end

The Roman ruins of Curium (Kourion) lie on the road that leads from the harbour city of Limassol to Pafos in western Cyprus. The view from the rectangular stadium, stretching all the way to the Troodos Mountains, is marred by several tall radio masts. A few miles further on, a series of British-looking terraced houses are grouped together not far from the roadside; barbed wire separates them from the main road. To the left, in the distance, you can sometimes make out a military aircraft taking off or landing. Down in the valley, there is a well-tended football pitch, its grass every bit as green as the playing fields of London. Welcome to the British Sovereign Base of Akrotiri.

Akrotiri, along with Dekelia and a military radar station at the highest point of the Troodos Mountains, Mount Olympus, is just one of the remnants of British rule in Cyprus. Inside these autonomous enclaves, British law is observed. The Union Jack, lowered for the last time in Nicosia in 1960, continues to flutter here. When Cyprus became independent, Britain secured 260 sq. km (99 sq. miles) of the island for military purposes, and these bases have remained, the final vestiges of the former Crown Colony.

British rule on Cyprus began on Saturday, 13 July 1878. "In the name of Her Majesty Queen Victoria, I hereby take possession of this island," proclaimed Admiral Lord John Hay before a gathering of the island's notables in Nicosia. "Long live the Queen!" shouted the crowd. British troops had landed near Larnaka on the previous day.

Sir Garnet Wolseley was appointed High Commissioner, but at this stage Cyprus had only been leased to Britain by the Ottoman Empire, in payment for British help in wars against the tsars of Russia, and wasn't officially British at all. Britain collected the annual "ground rent" it had to pay Istanbul from its Cypriot subjects.

Schools and hospitals

The British began modernising the administration and accurate statistics for the island were

obtained for the first time. A total of 186,173 people were living in Cyprus in the year 1881, including 140,793 Greek and 42,638 Turkish Cypriots. A modern education system was introduced, with separate schools for Christians and Muslims. The island's first ever hospitals were also built, and the malaria-infected swamps near Larnaka were drained.

Administratively, the British introduced a legislative council, a committee composed equally of native Cypriots and the new rulers for making joint decisions. Compared with conditions under Ottoman rule this was a strikingly liberal system of government. Political clubs were founded, and the island's first newspapers

PRECEDING PAGES: heroes of Cypriot resistance, Omodos Museum in the Troodos Mountains.
LEFT: newspapers first appeared in Cyprus when the British took over.
RIGHT: hoisting the British flag in 1878.

were published. Trade with Europe increased, and a Cypriot upper class of craftsmen and merchants evolved. A programme of modernisation had a marked influence in the cities, but in the villages, where the great majority of Cypriots lived, conditions barely changed.

However, even in the cities disenchantment with the British soon set in. The hoped-for economic and technological developments were much slower than many had at first assumed, and people continued to labour under heavy taxation. (Many had hoped, rather naively, that all taxation would be abolished under British rule.) Britain invested very little in the island: a

British had Alexandria at their disposal. The Egyptian port enjoyed an even better strategic position than that of Cyprus, as a result of which the military importance of Cyprus declined. At times the island was garrisoned by a single company of 200 to 300 troops.

Even World War I did little to change things. In fact, the only thing that did alter as far as the Cypriots were concerned was a legal technicality: when Turkey joined the war on the side of Germany in 1914, Britain formally annexed the island. In 1923, under the terms of the Treaty of Lausanne, Turkey officially confirmed Cyprus as a British possession. In 1925,

few roads were rebuilt, a small railway was constructed and the harbour at Famagusta was dredged. The only jobs to be found were in the asbestos and copper mines, where workers slogged away for 10–12 hours a day under hideous conditions, receiving very little pay. Most smallholders were hopelessly in debt, and living on the verge of starvation.

This lack of investment in the island was simply a reflection of British interests: Cyprus was important to the empire only from a strategic point of view. It was from here that sea traffic to India via the Suez Canal could be controlled, and any Russian intervention in the Mediterranean checked. But from 1882 the

the island was elevated to the status of a Crown Colony – a mere formality which did nothing to improve conditions there.

It was only during the 1930s that the Cypriots began to see benefits in their economy. The introduction of farmers' cooperatives meant that agricultural production could be stepped up. Craft and trade flourished. With the onset of World War II the island's military importance grew rapidly. More and more Allied troops were dispatched to Cyprus, and the war gave the island's economy a huge boost. When Crete fell under German occupation and Rommel landed in Africa, the entire Near East seemed vulnerable to the Nazis. Cyprus was now an important military outpost along with Egypt, Palestine and Lebanon. Around 25,000 Cypriots volunteered to fight, many of them hoping to liberate the Greek motherland from the Germans. They comprised an entire contingent in the British army. Fortunately, no fighting took place on Cyprus itself during the war. Indeed, British soldiers stationed on the island were thoroughly bored.

In 1945, after the war had ended, a second edition of the tourist guide *Romantic Cyprus* was published. Hotels, in particular those in the Troodos Mountains that benefited. At the time beach holidays were unfashionable.

In the realm of politics, increased efforts were made by Greek Cypriots for enosis – union with Greece. Britain's reaction to this new manifestation of nationalism was distinctly cool: "It has always been clear that certain parts of the Commonwealth, because of special conditions, can never expect to be granted full independence," was the message sent to Cyprus by the British secretary of state for colonial affairs in 1954.

COLD WAR

The military importance of the island increased dramatically with the onset of the Cold War in 1945.

The Quay, Lanarca, Cyprus

mountains, advertised in the hope of drawing tourists. The guide's publisher, Kevork Keshishian, wrote: "The precise nature of post-war transport routes cannot be predicted, but one thing is fairly certain: Cyprus, because of its geographical situation and the excellent opportunities it offers, will play an important role in the forthcoming age of the aeroplane."

Sure enough, there was a slight increase in tourism in the following years. Unlike today, though, it was largely the summer spas in the

LEFT: British ships in Larnaka harbour saluting the Duke of Edinburgh's birthday.
RIGHT: the quay at Larnaka during the British heyday.

Struggle for Greek union

Initially the British used military force to suppress the guerrilla struggle for enosis, which began in 1955. But Britain was no longer in a position to quell local insurgencies and a civil war between the island's Greeks and Turks soon broke out. This endangered the nascent NATO alliance, and Britain was compelled to negotiate. The military planners in London were satisfied with the result: Cyprus was given its independence in return for allowing two British sovereign bases to remain. On 16 August 1960 British colonial rule ended, and the last governor handed over his official duties to the government of the Republic of Cyprus. ❑

THE CIVIL WAR

*In 1958, after a bomb exploded in Nicosia's Turkish press office,
the island of Aphrodite became a battlefield*

E ven during the very first year of the British occupation of Cyprus the islanders tried to persuade their new rulers to leave. Kyprianos, bishop of Kition, begged the first crown governor in 1878 to allow Cyprus to be "reunited with the Greek motherland".

The island's leading clergymen felt a deep affinity for Greece and it was not long before Greek Orthodox craftsmen and merchants joined the movement. The few educated Greek-speaking Cypriots saw Greece as the source of their culture. They were tied to the motherland by language and religion and, furthermore, they invested in Greece their long-standing hopes for an economic upswing. While Britain invested little in the island, the impoverished Cypriots were starving. The call for union with Greece (enosis) was also a social protest.

The island's Muslim community was highly sceptical of enosis. A significant minority, the Muslims feared being marginalised by the mooted union with Greece. Indeed, due to the disproportionately large number of Turkish-speakers working for the administration (compared with a much smaller representation in trade and crafts), the island's Muslims wanted to either prolong the island's colonial status or return to rule by Istanbul.

The conflict had no effect on daily life. Christian and Muslim Cypriots still lived in harmony with one another. In the mixed villages they sold agricultural produce side by side, and all Cypriots participated in the island's festivals, regardless of their ethnic background.

Emergent Greek Cypriots

As a result of economic developments and the growth of nationalism, the island's Greek Orthodox inhabitants suddenly became Greek Cypriots. Turkish Cypriots emerged only after

PRECEDING PAGES: Turkish and Greek Cypriot unity, late 19th century.
LEFT: Odos Lidras, dubbed "murder mile", in Nicosia.
RIGHT: EOKA men crowned by laurel wreaths in Rhodes.

the modern state of Turkey was established, in 1920. Turkey relinquished all claims on the island in 1923 but this did little to further the aspirations of the Greek Cypriots, which remained frustrated. Instead of enosis, Cyprus was developing closer ties with Britain. These created a swelling core of ill-feeling that was

only fuelled by the British failure to develop significant institutions of self-government.

In 1931 underlying social tensions erupted into a full-scale rebellion. Originally planned merely as a protest against increased taxes and customs duties, it grew into an all-out nationalist demonstration against Britain. A prominent Greek Orthodox priest hoisted the Greek flag, and declared that the revolution had begun. The governor's house was set on fire and, although most of the rebels were unarmed, the British were forced to send troops to Cyprus.

More than 2,000 Greek Cypriots were arrested, all political parties were outlawed and censorship of the press was introduced.

After World War II the calls for enosis grew louder. In 1950 the young bishop of Kition, Makarios, soon to become archbishop, organised a constitutional plebiscite: 96 percent voted for enosis. But Britain had no intention of ceding Cyprus, its "unsinkable aircraft-carrier" in the Mediterranean, to Greece. It had become far too important militarily. From 1954, Greece adopted a more robust position in support of its union with Cyprus. Two years later Turkey maintained that the island was an extension of the Turkish mainland. Tensions thus developed into an international conflict, and the notorious "Cyprus question" was born.

ENOSIS BY FORCE

A crucial factor in the development of events was the decision of Archbishop Makarios III and General Georgios Grivas to use violence to achieve enosis. On 1 April 1955, Nicosia was rocked by a series of bomb explosions perpetrated by the National Organisation of Cypriot Struggle (EOKA). This conservative guerrilla movement wanted to achieve enosis by force, by executing British army officers and murdering any of their own fellow Greeks suspected of leftist sympathies. The British could not gain the upper hand over the partisan movement. The only effect of the mass arrests was increased interest in EOKA by the Greek Cypriots.

The British formed a local anti-terror unit, recruiting members from the ranks of Turkish Cypriots. Helped by Ankara, Turkish Cypriot nationalists formed their own terror unit to fight for Turkish interests – against enosis and in favour of *taksim*, or partition of the island. The bloodshed was a foregone conclusion, and military confrontations between partisans and the British army led to conflicts between the island's ethnic groups.

Civil war

On 7 June 1958, a bomb exploded in the Turkish press office in Nicosia. It sparked a civil war in which Cypriot fought against Cypriot, churches were set ablaze, and houses and apartments looted. Members of racially mixed communities were forced to leave their homes, a migration that turned several city neighbourhoods into ethnic enclaves.

At an international level, NATO partners Greece and Turkey were threatening to go to war over Cyprus, and fearful states sought a compromise. The US put pressure on Athens and Ankara to abandon their main claims and find a diplomatic solution.

Makarios climbed down on enosis, and after meetings between Greece, Turkey and Britain the London and Zurich treaties were signed: Cyprus was to become an independent state, but the Cypriots would not have any say in the drawing-up of their own constitution.

The treaties set the official seal on the division of the two ethnic groups: the island's Greeks and Turks were each given their own presidents, vice-presidents and ministers, as well as separate representation in parliament. Votes were taken separately. To prevent any discrimination of the minority population, the Turkish Cypriots were granted the right of veto as well as over-proportional representation in the administration, the police and the army. The development of a single Cypriot nationality was effectively blocked. The island was populated by Greeks and by Turks.

Greece, Turkey and Britain declared themselves "guarantor powers", with the right to intervene should the Cypriots decide to change their constitution. On 16 August 1960, Cyprus was granted its independence. ❏

LEFT: General Grivas, leader of EOKA.
RIGHT: statue of Archbishop Makarios.

INDEPENDENCE – AND PARTITION

Only 14 years elapsed between Independence and the division of the island into two autonomous communities separated by an impenetrable barrier

On 16 August 1960 the last governor of Her Majesty's Crown Colony, Sir Hugh Foot, handed over his official duties to Makarios III, who was henceforth president of the Republic of Cyprus. An archbishop was now head of state. The tradition of a religious leader exercising both spiritual and secular

power, which had originated in Ottoman times, was thus continued in the new state. Makarios was the ethnarch and the undisputed leader of the Greek Cypriots.

At Makarios's side stood the vice-president, Fazil Küçük, who was elected by the Turkish Cypriot minority. After a bloody civil war, during which one side had fought for union with Greece and the other for partition of the island, the leaders' task was to build a combined republic. In theory, political activity would no longer centre on the separate interests of the island's Greeks and Turks, but on the concept of a unified state and one people – Cyprus and the Cypriots.

Relations between the two ethnic groups returned to normal in daily life, and in most cases good neighbourliness was re-established. Inhabitants who had fled returned to their homeland, and the murders and lootings seemed to be ills of the past. On the political level however, relations between the two communities were severely tried by the constitution. The republic's ministers, MPs and bureaucrats were all elected and recognised by only one of the two ethnic groups, and they saw themselves as representing either Greeks or Turks, never the island itself. The two sides disagreed over taxation, development programmes and infrastructure, both communities trying to keep the larger slice of the cake for itself.

The government and the executive were preoccupied by endless quarrels over resources. Political representatives of both ethnic groups showed little if any interest in genuine cooperation. Indeed, many of them saw the collective state as only a temporary solution. Greek nationalists continued to demand enosis, while more and more Turks called for *taksim* (partition).

A return to violence

An uneasy peace lasted for three years. In spite of difficulties, the economy managed to recover, and in foreign affairs Cyprus became a committed member of the non-aligned states. But at the end of 1963, President Makarios called for a far-reaching revision of the constitution which would have deprived the Turkish Cypriots of many of their guaranteed rights. He insisted that the minority's right of veto, and the ethnic quota system in the police, army and administration be scrapped. The Turkish Cypriot side refused to support his proposals, and the Turkish government threatened to intervene if they were introduced unilaterally. The situation finally came to a head at Christmas 1963: fighting broke out in Nicosia, and soon spread to the rest of the island. Former partisans of EOKA and the Turkish Cypriot terror unit TMT were reactivated.

Members of the police and the army split into their constituent ethnic groups and Turkish

Cypriot ministers and MPs staged a walkout of the parliament. Widespread civil violence was initiated by many of the nationalists responsible for the bloodshed of the 1950s. Ever since, the island's Greek and Turkish communities have been blaming each other for triggering the hostilities. According to the Greek Cypriots, the Turkish Cypriots had attempted to achieve partition by starting a rebellion. In the opinion of the Turkish Cypriots, the Greek Cypriots had wanted to exterminate the Turkish minority and introduce enosis.

More than 500 people were killed during the summer of 1964. It was only when a United

not endear him to the US, which saw him as not only insecure and unreliable but, more seriously, as a Castro in priest's clothing. The US disapproved of his dealings with communist states and feared that he would turn Cyprus into the Cuba of the Mediterranean.

The conflict ended the hopes of peaceful coexistence between the ethnic groups. Many Turkish Cypriots found shelter in rural enclaves and urban ghettos while their pro-partition leaders ensured that there could be no further contact with their former neighbours.

The Greek Cypriots, with all the state power to themselves, began a trade embargo. Soldiers

Nations peacekeeping force arrived that the violence was brought to a halt. When the fighting was at its peak, the Turkish air force attacked Greek Cypriot positions and for a while it looked as if Turkey was threatening to invade. War between NATO partners Greece and Turkey looked increasingly likely. The US, searching desperately for a diplomatic solution, suggested that the island be divided between rule from Athens and Ankara with both zones belonging to NATO. President Makarios rejected this proposal out of hand. His intransigence did

LEFT: Sir Hugh Foot, the last British governor.
ABOVE: march for independence.

patrolled the borders separating the rival ethnic groups: Greek Cypriots were forbidden to enter Turkish Cypriot ghettos, while Turkish Cypriots suffered harassment if they entered Greek-controlled areas. Closed off and isolated in this way, the minority became dependent on relief packages, and their standard of living steadily worsened.

In the junta's shadow

Makarios lifted the embargo in 1968. Turkish Cypriots were once again allowed to work and live wherever they wanted. The Greek Cypriots' desire for enosis began to fade due to the greater prosperity created by a burgeoning economy and, no less importantly, the advent, in 1967, of a military junta in Athens. Only the most extreme nationalists supported union with Greece's military dictatorship. Talks between the two ethnic groups began, under the auspices of the United Nations. The Turkish Cypriots wanted a bizonal federation with a weakened central government, but the Greek Cypriots would not comply, fearing that it might help to pave the way towards partition. Negotiations took place nonetheless.

As the situation on Cyprus calmed down, tensions rose between the governments in Athens and Nicosia. The Greek dictatorship

was unhappy with Makarios, whom it accused of trying to provoke friction by offering asylum to persecuted democrats and by refraining from the press censorship that applied in Greece. Criticism of the Cypriot president also grew more vocal in the US. With the support of the 950-strong force of Greek soldiers and officers stationed on Cyprus and a nationalist terror group known as EOKA-B, the Greek junta decided to rid itself of Makarios. But its attempts to assassinate the archbishop failed.

Police units loyal to the government imprisoned numerous EOKA-B terrorists, and for a while it seemed as if Makarios had gained the upper hand.

Greek military attack

On 15 July 1974 the island's capital of Nicosia was rocked by gunfire. The presidential palace went up in flames. Terrorists and soldiers supporting the Greek junta embarked on attacks all over the island. The republic was helpless. Troops interned thousands of democrats and members of left-wing parties, and murdered their wounded rivals, even those in hospital beds. The "news" of Makarios's death was broadcast on the radio. Only the Turkish Cypriots were left unscathed by the junta, which did not want to provide Ankara with an excuse for intervening. The longed-for enosis with the motherland had happened overnight but, as an imposed union, it was a far cry from the natural association fondly imagined by Greek Cypriots. The majority supported their elected government, and could only watch helplessly as the Greek military took control.

One part of the Greeks' plan went hopelessly wrong: President Makarios had managed to escape from the burning presidential palace and find his way to the British base of Akrotiri, where he was kept out of the junta's reach. Nikos Sampson, a right-wing radical who had been involved in the mass murder of Turkish Cypriots during the civil war of 1963–64, was proclaimed president in his place. The coup was announced as an internal affair of the Greek Cypriots. Athens was convinced that Turkey wouldn't intervene. How such a grave misjudgement could have been made has never been satisfactorily explained. The relevant documents are still lying in a safe in Athens.

At daybreak on 20 July, five days after the coup, Turkish motor torpedo boats landed on the north coast. The Turkish air force dropped bombs on the island's capital. In contrast with the events of 1964, the US did nothing to prevent Turkey from carrying out its plans. This "peace operation", as the propaganda termed it, seemed to be quite justified under international law because the Cypriot constitution condoned intervention by the guarantor powers should it be necessary. The troops quickly succeeded in occupying an area to the north of Nicosia where many Turkish Cypriots lived. Meanwhile Muslims rejoiced at their liberation from Greece's military dictatorship.

LEFT: Canadian and UN flags fly over Nicosia.
RIGHT: a British gunner digs in.

The mini-junta in Nicosia and the real junta in Athens were equally surprised by the invasion. Two days later, the Greek military dictatorship fell as a direct result of the Cyprus fiasco. The leader of the mainland's junta, Dhimitrios Ioannides, had tried to force his country into a war with Turkey, but his military officers refused to comply with his orders. In Makarios's absence, the post of president in Nicosia was taken by Glavcos Clerides, the head of parliament. In Athens, Konstantin Karamanlis took over the premiership. Democracy was thus restored in Cyprus and Greece, but the island's tragedy had just begun.

In defiance of a United Nations Security Council resolution, the invading Turkish army refused to withdraw, and on 14 August, despite intensive peace talks held in Geneva, the Turkish soldiers advanced across the island.

Tens of thousands of Greek Cypriots ran for their lives, leaving all their possessions behind. Thousands were taken prisoner. Any who returned home for any reason were shot. Turkish tanks rolled across the island, encountering almost no resistance. Two days later the Turks had achieved the objective of their operation: 37 percent of the island was occupied and partition was a reality. ❏

THE TRAGEDY OF WAR

Following the Turkish invasion, nearly 165,000 Greek Cypriots fled from the north to the south. For years thereafter they had little choice but to live in refugee settlements. After the Turkish invasion, unemployment in the south reached 39 percent. For their part, at least 55,000 Turkish Cypriots moved in the opposite direction to the safe haven now provided by the occupied north.

In retaliation, terrorists and junta soldiers inflicted bloody reprisals on the Muslim communities in the south. The island's legal government could only watch helplessly. Paramilitary units massacred the entire male populations, from babies to the elderly, of Turkish Cypriot villages.

On the other side, more than 1,600 Greek Cypriots, soldiers and civilians alike, disappeared. Many were named on International Red Cross lists of prisoners-of-war being held in internment camps in Turkey. Nearly every Cypriot family lost at least one member in the civil war: some 6,000 people died in the bloody summer of 1974. The effects of the devastating conflict still linger on, though hope is now in sight. While the heavily guarded "border" still exists Turkish, and Greek Cypriots alike may now visit each other without fear of retribution. It remains to be seen whether future generations who never knew war will cast its spectre aside for ever.

THE SEARCH FOR UNITY

*For a quarter of a century, UN-sponsored negotiations have repeatedly
foundered on the incompatible demands of the Greek and Turkish communities*

In the immediate aftermath of the 1974 catastrophe, southern Cyprus was confronted with an enormous task: refugees needed housing, farmers needed land, workers needed jobs and the self-employed needed new opportunities. Unemployment in the Republic of Cyprus for the second half of 1974 was 59,000.

By the following year almost all of the 55,000 Turkish Cypriots living in the south had been resettled in the Turkish-occupied zone. They, like their Greek compatriots in the north, left their homes and possessions behind. The better dwellings and valuable land were snapped up by Greek Cypriot refugee families, sometimes after rental agreements had been negotiated with their rightful owners. All Turkish Cypriot-owned housing and land was officially registered; even today Turkish houses in southern Cyprus can be identified by the registration number painted on their outside walls.

Legally, the Turkish houses on the island are still the property of their former owners. Unsurprisingly, the refugees have shown little inclination to invest in renovations, and the properties are dilapidating fast.

Despite numerous hardships, many refugees have managed to do quite well in southern Cyprus's newly affluent society; they have built their own houses, and they have progressed to good jobs. If you ask anyone if they would like to return to their former home the instinctive answer is a resounding "yes", the reality is that such a prospect may not really be so desirable. Quite a few of them would find their former homes in ruins, for many of the buildings left behind in the north have not been occupied since 1974.

Reunification intent

The Cyprus government's declared intention is to effect the island's reunification. In the years since 1974 Greek Cypriot politicians have proposed some far-reaching compromise solutions, but ongoing negotiations have yet to produce a meaningful breakthrough.

UN Security Council resolutions and resolutions by the UN General Assembly have called for the withdrawal of Turkish troops. "The Security Council requires that all states acknowledge the sovereignty and territorial integrity of Cyprus... [and] demands that foreign military intervention in Cyprus cease immediately", ran the text of the United Nations resolution of 20 July 1974, the day the Turkish invasion commenced. The United Nations Security Council also condemned the self-proclaimed "Turkish Republic of Northern Cyprus" on 18 November 1983. These resolutions have made no difference to the situation.

Plan for peace

Some potential areas of agreement have been identified. One basic outline of a solution was prepared in 1977, when the Cypriot president, Archbishop Makarios, held meetings with Rauf Denktash, leader of the Turkish Cypriots, in Vienna. The talks resulted in the following four guidelines, which were agreed by both sides:

"**1.** We shall strive towards the foundation of an independent, non-aligned, bizonal federation. **2.** The size of the territory administered by the respective communities shall be discussed in the light of economic viability and ownership of land. **3.** Fundamental issues such as freedom of movement, freedom to settle, property rights and other specific matters are open to discussion, whereby the fundamental basis of a bi-zonal federative system and certain practical difficulties that may arise

No Solution

All the talks, both direct and indirect, between the Greek Cypriot and Turkish Cypriot sides have so far failed, even though UN leaders have tried everything in their power to find a solution.

hopes for eventual reunification. Indeed the document signed by Makarios and Denktash lays the foundations of a future federation. In contrast with the stipulations of the 1960 constitution, the first guideline of this historic document suggests a federation composed of two federal states: a Greek Cypriot entity to the south and a Turkish Cypriot one in the north.

The second paragraph, relating to the size of the respective federal states, implies a reduction in the size of the region at

with respect to the Turkish Cypriot population should be taken into account. **4.** The competence and function of the central government will guarantee the unity of the country while taking the bi-zonal character of the federation into consideration."

A new federation

Although a whole generation has grown up since the guidelines were formulated, these four principles remain the most important basis of

Left: guarding the Green Line.
Above: as refugees from northern Cyprus flooded into the south, emergency housing mushroomed.

present occupied by Turkey. As a result of the Turkish invasion of northern Cyprus, 18 percent of the population occupies 37 percent of the island. This imbalance constitutes the basis of the Greek Cypriots' territorial claim.

The third point addresses the provision of basic liberties for all citizens of the republic. Although this detail would be taken for granted in most liberal democracies, the circumstances in Cyprus are hardly amenable to the universal application of civil rights so it remains a bone of contention between the conflicting sides.

The final point makes it clear that the aim of these endeavours is not a loose union between two states but a single, joint federation, with a central governing authority representing the whole of the country.

The distribution of power between the central government and the island's various districts remained unclear. The Greek Cypriots expressed their desire for a powerful central authority, while the Turkish Cypriots were in favour of strong district authorities.

The four guidelines contained two fundamental flaws. Firstly, they did not address the issue of international guarantors for the new federation. Secondly, the issues of individual liberties and territorial rights in general were left unresolved.

ment, the right to settle and property rights should be guaranteed to all citizens in every part of the federation, pointing out that such freedoms are an accepted feature of any democratic state. It was the intention that all Greek Cypriot refugees be given the right to return to their homes. The Turkish Cypriot side, however, rejects this right. It argues that if all the refugees were allowed to return, the Turkish Cypriots would become a minority in their own land.

The property issue is also controversial for most of the fields and houses presently farmed and inhabited by Turkish Cypriots are actually Greek Cypriot property.

Maps on the table

Of all the problems, the easiest to resolve is probably that of the two federal states' size. Even the Turkish Cypriot leader, Rauf Denktash, realised that the sector occupied by Turkish Cypriots was disproportionately large. Maps showing proposed new borders have often been circulated among diplomats in Nicosia. One version suggested a 10 percent reduction in the size of the Turkish Cypriot territory. This would allow some 90,000 Greek Cypriot refugees the chance to return to their old homes.

The question of individual liberties is more complicated. Here, the Greek Cypriot side insisted until recently that freedom of move-

Turkish immigrants

The four guidelines omit to mention those settlers, largely from Anatolia, who immigrated to the northern sector from Turkey. Their presence has transformed the island's demography. They have filled the formerly underpopulated occupied sector, drastically increasing the number of Muslim inhabitants on the island. Some 70,000–80,000 Turkish settlers now live in the occupied sector. Their fate is likely to be an essential issue of any peace negotiations.

This wave of Turkish immigrants has called Cyprus home for nearly three decades, and a new generation of ethnic Turks have been born on the island. But the Cypriot government maintains that the Turks are foreigners, and advocates their immediate expulsion. Naturally members of the Turkish Cypriot leadership think otherwise and want to grant them Turkish Cypriot citizenship.

Also disputed is the presence of Turkish troops in the north, and the question of international guarantors for such a federation. The Greek Cypriots demand the total withdrawal of all Turkish occupying forces, and stoutly reject Ankara's guarantor status. On the other side the Turkish Cypriots – be they in government or members of the opposition – insist on protection from Ankara, and the continued presence of the Turkish army. Those prepared to compromise have offered to reduce the size of Turkey's military commitment on the island. Another sign of optimism is the willingness of the republic's government to discuss the possibility of the UN assuming guarantor status over the new federation and its constitution.

In an effort to speed up negotiations, UN mediators have introduced a number of confidence-building measures. Reductions in military forces, youth exchange programmes, a more liberal approach to "cross-border traffic" and a project involving economic cooperation between the Greek and Turkish communities have all been proposed. It was hoped that improvements in the Turkish Cypriots' economic prospects would increase their willingness to compromise. Wages in the republic are four times higher than in the north. But none of the confidence-building measures have actually seen the light of day as agreements between the two sides remain elusive. In 1994 the North Cypriot parliament declared that, rather than create a federation with the Greek Cypriots, it would seek closer ties with Turkey.

Gloomy prospects

Developments in the 1990s intensified both the military and diplomatic pressures surrounding the search for a solution, at the same time as creating new opportunities for a settlement. The end of the Cold War removed the threat of a Soviet thrust into the eastern Mediterranean; it also ended the always uncertain cooperation between those ostensible NATO allies, Greece and Turkey. Several times the two states

appeared to be on the brink of war over disputed territorial claims in the Aegean Sea. Both sides built up their military forces. Opposing warplanes routinely buzzed each other in disputed areas. Cyprus could easily have become an explosive ingredient in this incendiary mix, especially after Greece and Cyprus signed a defence agreement providing for joint military exercises and for Greek air and naval units to use bases at Pafos in western Cyprus.

Southern Cyprus's economic progress enabled it to acquire modern weaponry, ranging from tanks and artillery to rocket launchers and surface-to-air missiles. Such military hardware

did not give the 15,000-strong Cyprus National Guard parity with the 35,000 Turkish troops in the north but it showed that the Greek Cypriots were prepared to defend their interests. The weapons were almost put to the test in 1999, when the Greek Cypriots planned to deploy Russian-made S300 long-range surface-to-air missiles. Turkey vowed to attack the missiles, Greece said such an escalation would mean war. Eventually the Cypriot government backed down and the missiles were deployed on Crete. While sabres were rattling noisily in the background, Cyprus's journey towards membership of the European Union was progressing, and new settlement initiatives from the EU,

LEFT: barbed-wire blight from a divisive war.
RIGHT: Turkish Cypriot leader, Rauf Denktash.

the United Nations and the United States were making their tortuous way through diplomatic channels. In 1997 Cyprus was accepted into the group of future EU members while Turkey was sent to the back of the queue. The Turkish Cypriots wanted a presence at the accession talks, but in the guise of representing the Turkish Republic of Northern Cyprus, and only if Turkey was included in the list of EU members in the same wave. The EU would have accommodated the Turkish Cypriots if they had joined the Cypriot delegation but in the event the EU would not accept the preconditions.

Under UN auspices, Clerides and Denktash

quake. Such mutual assistance showed that the countries' mutual hostility was not eternal, and led to improved prospects for defusing tensions over Cyprus. The EU decided that Turkey's membership application would finally be acted upon, and the Greek Cypriot and Turkish Cypriot leaders met again under UN auspices.

April 2003 saw a dramatic shift in the stalemate over cross-border movement. In that month Denktash opened the Attila Line dividing the north from the south and allowed citizens of both sides almost unconditional access. A flood of anxious and nostalgic Greek and Turkish Cypriots poured across the border to

met in Vienna. As usual, the talks were fruitless, with Denktash taking most of the international heat for his intransigence. Having seen Turkey rebuffed over EU membership, and having failed to secure representation at the accession talks, the northern Cyprus authorities announced that they would pursue integration of their zone with Turkey.

Hope at last

The end of 1999 saw a marked improvement in Greek-Turkish relations. Greece provided generous assistance to the victims of Turkey's devastating earthquakes that year. Turkey returned the favour when Athens was hit by a

visit places most had not seen for 29 years.

Turkish-Cypriot elections in December 2003, while not exactly decisive for reform-minded pro-unity groups, nonetheless paved the way for a further relaxing of the relationship. But additional UN talks held in early 2004 faltered just weeks ahead of the date set for the accession of Cyprus – at least the Greek-dominated Republic of Cyprus – to the EU. All observers of the Cyprus conundrum wait with baited breath for the prospect of lasting peace and unity on the long-troubled island. ❑

LEFT: the north–south border crosses a street in the divided city of Nicosia.

Along the Dividing Line

A white jeep, flying the blue and white flag of the United Nations, rumbles its way across the broken tarmac of what used to be the city centre of Nicosia. The area is now a wasteland of overgrown buildings and wrecked cars sprouting flowers in their torn upholstery.

Ruined houses are home to whole colonies of feral cats. Barriers of sandbags protect the Greek Cypriot and Turkish soldiers' trenches. Here, only a few metres from the hustle and bustle of the city, the silence is frightening. No Cypriot is allowed to cross this closely guarded no-man's-land. The burned-out houses lining Odos Ermou and melted neon signs are a reminder that this was once the heart of the city.

Occupying a narrow, lifeless strip of territory, the Green Line – which is only 20 metres (60 ft) wide in places – bisects the old part of Nicosia. It crosses the city's ancient fortifications, divides its districts, and then extends to the old airport, today the operational headquarters of the UN's military presence. The demilitarised buffer zone dividing the island is 180 km (112 miles) long, and extends from Kokkina in the northwest to Famagusta in the southeast.

The United Nations Force in Cyprus (UNFICYP) has been a familiar feature of life on Cyprus since 1964, when its mission, to act as a peacekeeping force, was established. Its most urgent task was to separate the Turkish Cypriots and their paramilitary units from the National Guard of the Republic of Cyprus.

Since the Turkish army's invasion of northern Cyprus in 1974, the UN force has ensured that the Cyprus National Guard and the Turkish soldiers have kept to their respective sides of the demarcation line.

About 1,200 soldiers are stationed in Cyprus, with Britain, Austria and Argentina providing the largest contingents. The Republic of Cyprus now contributes a portion of the $50 million required to meet the costs of the troops' presence. On the far east of the island a dirt track leads to an inspection post, from which the respective armies' ceasefire lines can be easily observed. Here, Turks and Greek Cypriots have dug primitive-looking shelters.

The beach, distant and inaccessible to the UN troops, can be seen through binoculars. As a squad of peacekeepers sitting in a corrugated-iron shelter on a small rise verify, one of the worst aspects of their job

---

RIGHT: UN peacekeepers on patrol.

is boredom. The blue-helmeted soldiers are on duty 24 hours a day for two weeks at a time, and invariably nothing happens. Elsewhere, though, the buffer zone is not as lifeless as it is in Nicosia. In many areas farmers are still allowed to cultivate their fields. And the UN soldiers have an entire village to supervise in their zone: in Pyla, a village between the two battle-lines guarded by military police, Greek and Turkish Cypriots still live in relative harmony, disrupted occasionally by minor disputes.

The UN peacekeeping force has the situation mostly under control. The only danger of military escalation has been in Nicosia, where soldiers on both sides occasionally start sparring. But it is seldom

that shots are exchanged and lives lost. "Keep the peace and make the peace" is the UN troops' motto.

For genuine peace, Cyprus still has a way to go, yet the chances of reunion are looking better than at any time during the 29 years of the conflict. Despite the military posturing along the closed sections of the dividing line, citizens of both sides calmly cross back and forth at the open crossing points while minding their own business. In the year following the opening of the border there have been few incidents of note and most Cypriots seem relieved that a tangible solution is in sight. What has become apparent once more is that it is not culture, character, religion or language which hitherto divided the population. The greatest divisive force has been politics. ❑

CONTEMPORARY CYPRUS

In recent years the Greek Cypriot south has attained a higher standard of living than that found in the north, in Turkey, or in Greece

The most striking feature of modern Cyprus is the jagged line that cuts across the island, dividing it into two armed camps and making movement between the two sectors subject to checks and possible delays. But how much of that reality does the visitor actually notice on the ground? Much of the time, surprisingly little. Most tourists are too busy trying to find a little free space at the beach, or filling up on *meze* and island wine at their local taverna to worry overmuch about a situation that has been set in political concrete since 1974. Which is just as well, or the Cypriot economy would collapse. So you will hear few complaints on either side of the line if you leave the geopolitics to others.

An economic success story

Southern Cyprus has rebounded from the economic disaster of the Turkish invasion to such an extent that it is now four times richer, per capita, than Turkey and the north, and also wealthier than Greece and most of the rest of non-EU Europe. Given the cataclysmic events of 1974, this is an incredible achievement. The republic was burdened with 165,000 refugees and, moreover, had suffered the loss of the island's best agricultural land as well as its main tourist centres, Keryneia and Famagusta. The international airport was occupied by the UN and consequently closed to civilian traffic.

Since those dark days, the construction and tourism industries have boomed side by side, as new hotels, apartment blocks and leisure facilities have been built to meet the needs of a steadily growing number of visitors. The refugees from the north contributed to growth in two mutually-dependent sectors: they provided a ready supply of labour and presented a massive demand for urgently needed housing. Agriculture, shipping, trade and manufacturing

have also underpinned the economic expansion. More recently, these sectors have been joined by a fast-developing financial and services sector as Cyprus capitalises on its role as an offshore business centre and a bridge between Europe and the Middle East and Gulf regions.

Even without the civil strife and invasion,

this would have been a notable feat. In the last decade of British colonial rule, the island was hugely underdeveloped. Most Cypriots worked in agriculture or in the copper, iron and asbestos mines. Independence gave an immediate boost to the economy, as long overdue irrigation schemes made agriculture more productive and a consumer manufacturing base was established. Between 1960 and 1974, Cyprus achieved a higher standard of living than any of its neighbours, with the exception of Israel.

Recreating and surpassing that level of prosperity since 1974 has put the Republic of Cyprus in the front line for membership of the European Union – a step set to be realised on 1 May 2004.

PRECEDING PAGES: a Turkish memorial.
LEFT: keeping up with developments.
RIGHT: Glafkos Clerides, elected president of the Republic of Cyprus in 1993 and again in 1998.

The social scene

The social benefits of the new prosperity have been immense. Where there used to be unemployment, today there is a labour shortage, despite the fact that many Cypriots work at two jobs. (Some people have both a regular job and a family farm or shop to maintain.) Guest workers, as foreign labourers – some of whom are miserably exploited – are known, have therefore been imported in large numbers, mostly from eastern Europe, south Asia and the

HARD CASH

Most analysts ascribe the economic upswing to the sharp rise in tourism, an industry which now draws in more than 2 million visitors a year and is a vital source of hard currency.

much practical necessities as status symbols, though the same cannot be said for many of those used by urban office workers.

The face of most towns and villages has changed forever. Traditional old homes have been demolished in favour of brash villas and apartment blocks which, despite their sometimes dubious standards of construction, are indelible signs of the modernity and affluence craved by their owners. There are Cypriots who fear that their drive to be Western, wealthy and

Philippines. Cyprus's powerful trade unions regularly manage to negotiate generous wage rises for their members. The quality of social care – measured by the average life expectancy, the infant mortality rate, the number of doctors per thousand inhabitants, and the standard of education – demonstrates that southern Cyprus stands comparison with any of the wealthy industrialised Western nations.

Greek Cypriots now demand, and many can apparently afford, the good life. Rare is the farmer who does not have an expensive imported pick-up to transport him to and from his orchards or vineyards. In the countryside, with its rough and ready dirt-tracks, these are as

cosmopolitan is changing them in ways they may regret. But generally they are too preoccupied to reach such negative conclusions.

Big spending

The income from tourism has made it possible to finance today's high expenditure on expensive imported consumer goods, such as cars. Military purchases to upgrade the republic's defences consume a significant sector of the new prosperity. This is hardly surprising given that Cyprus is effectively in a state of emergency, with a large and well-equipped foreign military force occupying much of its territory.

The Greek Cypriots have resisted the temptation to put all their eggs in the tourist basket. Tourism is a notoriously capricious industry, and the Mediterranean is particularly prone to sudden debilitating shocks, such as the Gulf War of the early 1990s and, more recently, the conflicts in Afghanistan and Iraq. The republic invested in the modern infrastructure needed to provide a bedrock for further economic development and to compensate, at least in some measure, for the amenities which had been lost as a result of the invasion. The government built new airports at Larnaka and Pafos, new harbour facilities at Limassol and Larnaka, a well-developed road network, including a

products such as shoes, clothing, paper and synthetic goods. In recent years exports have also been targeted at EU member states to good effect.

A good image

The authorities in southern Cyprus have had great success in promoting the island as an ideal location for doing business with the Middle East and the Persian Gulf. At the same time the number of offshore companies registered in southern Cyprus is continuing to rise. Among these are banks, insurance companies, architectural firms, property concerns and consultancies. The offshore sector, benefiting from

motorway from Nicosia to Agia Napa, Limassol and Pafos, and modern also telecommunications facilities.

Perhaps the greatest achievement of the south Cyprus economy has been its increasingly successful industrialisation. In the 1970s refugees from the north provided a cheap source of labour, but of greater long-term significance was the potential presented by the prosperous Gulf states.

Cyprus moved quickly to take advantage of the Arab countries' need to import industrial

LEFT: Cyprus offers classic attractions to visitors.
ABOVE: Larnaka's airport, a hub for many tourists.

favourable tax and ownership regulations, has supported the growth of service industries and, through a knock-on effect, boosted employment in such white-collar jobs as financial services, commercial and tax law, and consultancy.

As a result of its non-aligned status during the Cold War, and the strength of AKEL, its Communist party, Cyprus used to enjoy close links with the USSR and Eastern Europe. Since the collapse of communism, these associations have taken on a more commercial nature and guest workers from these countries now play a major role in filling Cyprus's labour shortage. In the 1990s newly wealthy Russians formed a conspicuous presence on the island. For a while in the middle of the decade, 100,000 Russian tourists made annual visits. Many of them indulged in free-spending splurges, from villas to designer sunglasses, often paying cash in US dollars. They filled offshore bank accounts with billions of dollars, much of it the ill-gotten proceeds of organised crime. Russian wealth – and cash siphoned out of Yugoslavia during the Milošević regime – helped Cyprus's economy, in particular its tourism industry, to survive a few lean years, though it hardly gilded the nation's reputation for financial probity. Much of that money vanished in Russia's subsequent economic downturn.

The southern part of Cyprus can no longer be considered to be underdeveloped, but progress is a double-edged sword. The construction boom, ongoing industrialisation and intensive farming methods are taking a heavy toll on the environment, and the level of foreign debt has grown to dangerous proportions.

By the turn of the millennium, there were increasing signs that the economic model that had proved so successful for 25 years was under strain. The tourist industry professed itself to be in a more or less permanent state of crisis, due not to a fall in demand but rather a surfeit of supply. Too many hotel rooms were competing for a limited number of tourists, leaving accommodation facilities operating at a fraction of their capacity, and car-hire firms charging ruinously low off-peak rates. While there were too few big-spending, upmarket tourists, at the other end of the scale competition from lower-cost destinations, such as Turkey, took a significant toll. To holiday-makers, the resultant profusion of bargain deals was good news.

Meanwhile the manufacturing sector suffered from a failure to invest in new products and processes, and the future of local agriculture was threatened by several years of near-drought which had left the island's freshwater reservoirs all but empty. The reputation of the country's big merchant fleet was also at a low ebb: Cypriot-flagged ships were regularly seen as prime suspects whenever safety violations in European ports were reported.

Cyprus's own ports were in a state of crisis, largely due to the corruption of local officials, and Cyprus Airways, the national carrier, suffered from high cost structures and inflexibility. As the island pursued its application to join the EU, its leaders were left in no doubt as to the scale of its economic problems.

In recent years organised crime has become something of a growth industry, especially in Limassol. The Russian mafia has played a role in the spread of often violent lawlessness but most of it originates with home-grown gangs with links to shady nightclubs. Bombings, gun battles and contract killings have become staples of local news broadcasts and the level of corruption in the police force prompted President Clerides to issue a sharply worded condemnation. In the north, too, Turkish gangster bosses imported their operations and feuds.

Political brands

Politics permeates all levels of Greek Cypriot life. Goods made by the co-operative movement (linked with the PEO trade union) are associated with the left wing of the party spectrum so consumers can drink the co-operatives' "leftist" brandy or the "rightist" brandy produced by private firms. Even his choice of local *kafeneion* reflects a villager's political affiliation.

In the decades since independence was granted in 1960, Greek Cypriot politics has been split between communists and conservatives. The left is represented by the progressive party of the working people, AKEL, formed in 1941, and the KKK, the successor of the

Communist party, which was banned under British rule. AKEL and its affiliated trade union federation, the PEO, have traditionally represented the interests of farmers and blue-collar workers, and have long been a powerful force in the local political firmament.

The right wing was initially represented not by an actual party, but by Archbishop Makarios and his followers, the clergy and the business establishment. After independence, the Democratic Front was founded as a conservative collective movement. Only since 1968, when the Democratic Front disbanded, has Cyprus had a modern party political system resembling that of

from all government bodies, since when their posts have remained vacant, and the 24 seats reserved for them in the 80-seat House of Representatives have been left empty.

Executive powers reside in the office of the president of the Republic of Cyprus. In addition to formulating government policies, the president can appoint and dismiss ministers. The voting procedure allows for the best-placed candidates in a presidential election's first ballot to compete again in a second ballot. The legislature takes the form of a House of Representatives, whose members are elected by a system of proportional representation. ❑

Western democracies. By that time the communists were firmly entrenched in government.

The republic's political system is derived from the London and Zurich accords, which formed the basis of the island's independence. Greek and Turkish Cypriots were given separate municipal administrations and separate representation in the government and the law courts. The president was a Greek Cypriot, the vice-president a Turkish Cypriot.

But in 1964 the Turkish Cypriots withdrew

LEFT: visitors to Cyprus have been quick to discover that bargains are there for the taking.
ABOVE: turning a back on political messages.

PATTERNS OF ALLEGIANCE

Even today, a politician's place of origin and his family's reputation can be far more decisive than his ideological position when it comes to the ballot box. The close connection between individuals, families and politics is particularly apparent in rural villages. Here the communists have been overwhelmingly successful for decades, even though very few villagers give the impression of being radical left-wingers. Similarly, those villages that vote for the far right are not exactly bastions of fascism. To some extent, as the island's modernisation catches up with the remote areas, this old-fashioned pattern of local allegiances is changing.

ENVIRONMENTAL PROTECTION

*Progress comes at a price. The environment is paying the cost
of economic growth in southern Cyprus*

Salt used to be extracted commercially from Larnaka Salt Lake, but pollution from the nearby international airport has left the salt unfit for consumption. In winter pink flamingoes still feed in the lake's shallow waters, where they must now swallow a garnish of hydrocarbons along with the brackish

water's pink crustaceans. The recent decline in their numbers reflects the scale of local environmental damage.

The coastal regions have been the hardest hit by the effects of economic development. In some places frenzied building has irreparably destroyed the once beautiful scenery. The resulting mess threatens to drive away the very tourists whose demand encouraged the construction boom in the first instance. The Agia Napa-Protaras-Pernera corridor south of Famagusta has been heavily developed, as has the coast along Larnaka Bay and Limassol Bay. The modernisation of Pafos started later but the opening of the Pafos airport served to has-

ten the process. To the despair of environmentalists there seems little to stop the development juggernaut. Zoning rules and regulations exist, but where one form of construction, hotels for example, is discouraged, other forms – villas and apartment complexes – move in. Planning rules are routinely relaxed, to the extent that a giant hotel complex was built on the edge of the wild and scenic Akamas Peninsula, an area that has been a candidate for national park status since 1986.

The case of the Akamas

The drive to create an Akamas Peninsula National Park has become a *cause célèbre* for environmentalists. It is not only starry-eyed greens who advocate the establishment of a national park to preserve the area's flora and fauna (including the Mediterranean monk seal, which is on the verge of extinction), scenic attractions and historic sites. A 1995 World Bank report makes the same case, and the European Union is keeping a close eye on Cyprus's handling of this sensitive issue.

The cause was dealt a blow in 2000 by the government's decision to allow "mild and controlled" development in the Akamas. The plan reduced the size of the reserve from a proposed 230 sq. km (90 sq. miles), covering the entire peninsula, to 70 sq. km (27 sq. miles) in the interior. Legal protection was given to a few beaches where turtles breed. The ecologists' main fear concerned the elasticity of the term "mild and controlled" development, and how it could be stretched by property moguls and their government backers. To many the death knell of a unique environment had been sounded.

The north coast around Polis and Latsi, and eastwards to the demarcation line has, as yet, escaped the fate of resort areas developed in recent decades. But the locals are fighting the few restrictions that have been applied to them. They resent being told by outsiders what they can and can't do with their own land and don't see why they should be denied the chance to raise their standard of living.

Lara Bay, north of Pafos, has become a stark symbol of the seriousness of local wildlife's plight. This is the last resort for green and loggerhead turtles, the former officially categorised as "vulnerable", the latter as "endangered". Turtle nests are protected here and pregnant females happily come ashore to lay their eggs. Unfortunately other beaches once used by the turtles are now given over to sunbathers.

There are several ironies in the argument between development and preservation. For instance, Agia Napa hoteliers don't want the Akamas developed. This is not so much because they are unenthusiastic about the arrival of more competition (which they are, in fact), but because they want attractive destinations that they can offer guests as excursions.

Another irony is that many of the coast's most protected areas lie within the grounds of Britain's two Sovereign Base Areas, where only small-scale commercial development is permitted. Here priority is given to military development, which has been responsible for eyesores such as the forest of radio antennae on the Akrotiri Peninsula. The British forces used to conduct occasional live-fire exercises in the Akamas, but in 1999 the firing ranges were moved to Cyprus National Guard properties.

The tree campaign

To witness the most spectacular environmental success story, head inland, particularly to the Troodos Mountains, where the forests that once blanketed the island are being restored.

In the ancient world, Cyprus was known as the Green Island, undoubtedly on account of its forests. The apostle Paul is said to have navigated his way through thick forests when travelling from Famagusta to Pafos, even on the plains. This wealth of trees, together with a favourable geographical location, was instrumental in Cyprus becoming both an important exporter of wood and a shipbuilding centre.

When an inspection was made of the island's forests in the early years of British colonial rule, officials claimed that the Ottoman Empire was to blame for destroying this wonderful natural resource. The Mesaoria Plain was left a barren steppe after virtually the entire population of fruit trees had been axed. The only

remaining forests were in the mountains. As a result of the arboreal depredations suffered at the hands of the Ottomans, Britain established a forestry commission in Cyprus – the first such organisation in the British Empire. The island's first forestry laws were passed in 1879.

In stark contrast to other aspects of colonial governance, Britain's priority in this area was the maintenance and regeneration of the forests rather than their economic exploitation. As a result of this enlightened policy, the British bequeathed nearly 1,750 sq. km (670 sq. miles) of forests, constituting 19 percent of the whole island. Moreover, the method, initiated by

Britain, of reporting forest fires through a network of "forest telephones" remains a model system to this day. Since 1951 the Cyprus Forestry College in Prodromos has promoted the regeneration of Mediterranean forests.

The Cypriot Forestry Commission has continued the work of the British, but large tracts of forest went up in flames in the wars of 1964 and 1974. The Turkish invasion led to the destruction of about 16 percent of state-owned forests. These areas were reforested by 1982.

Today barren terraces are being replanted across Cyprus, and conservation is taken seriously, to the extent that the work is done without recourse to bulldozers. ❏

LEFT: more beautiful than concrete.
ABOVE: the Forestry College, set up by the British.

THE FACE OF CYPRUS

The island's diverse topography, featuring peninsulas, mountains and steppes,

owes much to the azure waters of the Mediterranean

Like Aphrodite emerging from the sea foam, Cyprus rose dripping out of the primeval Tethys Sea, which lay between what are now Eurasia and Africa during the later Palaeozoic Era and into the Mesozoic.

By the Cretaceous Period, some 90 million years ago, two chains of islets had formed from the tips of mountains and volcanoes forced up from the sea floor by the slow-moving collision of the African continental plate with the European plate. These were the basis of the Troodos and Keryneia mountains. Erosion and the emergence of subterranean land created the Mesaoria Plain and the coastal lowlands. These broadly defined geological formations are the main features of Cyprus's topography.

The Mesaoria ("Between the Mountains") Plain occupies the middle of the island, along with a rolling westward extension known as the Morfou Plain. The plains merge along their southern fringes with the foothills of the Troodos massif – which dominates the west and rises in waves to the 1,950-metre (6,340-ft) summit of Mount Olympus (Khionistra) – constituting the island's highest point.

South and west of the Troodos lies rugged, hilly country fringed by a narrow coastal plain. The sharp-edged Keryneia range lines the northern coast from about Cape Kormakitis in the west to Cape Apostolos Andreas in the east, fading out at either end.

The peninsulas

Distinctive appendages to the main body are a quintet of major peninsulas, whose configuration led commentators in ancient times to compare Cyprus to a spread-out sheepskin. The Karpas Peninsula in the northeast forms the tail, with the Cape Kormakitis and Cape Gkreko peninsulas the hind legs, and the Akamas and Akrotiri peninsulas the forelegs. Nowadays, a frying pan, albeit a misshapen one, is a more

PRECEDING PAGES: the wild shores of Pafos; Cyprus is renowned for its abundance of fruit and flowers.
LEFT AND RIGHT: Troodos trees and landscape.

popular and, given the summer heat, perhaps appropriate image of the island's shape.

Troodos Mountains

The Troodos Mountains, the island's most conspicuous geographical feature, are visible from all over the centre and west. Their central core,

roughly 30 km (18 miles) long, consists of igneous rock. Mount Olympus itself is composed of dunite. Over the course of millions of years the dunite was gradually transformed into serpentine, leading to the mining of asbestos in the upper Troodos. The process has left massive scarring of the mountainside around Amiantos and the practice has now been stopped. The undulating, spacious landscape is awash with light and dark browns and various shades of grey.

To the east lies the Pitsylia district. This rugged, hilly and sparsely populated region, which gradually fades away towards Nicosia and the Mesaoria, is dotted with villages. To the northwest lies Tilliria, a wild and scenic landscape that makes Pitsylia seem tame and densely populated by comparison.

North of the mountains are the gentler landscapes of the Marathasa and Solea valleys. This rich agricultural country is thick with orchards. A lack of dense natural forest cover opens up some spectacular views, as far as the sea in one direction and up towards the mountains in the other. Just off the southern periphery of the Troodos is the Commandaria wine region, while off to the

> **BEST FOOT FORWARD**
>
> There is almost nothing to see in Tilliria apart from some of the island's most testing settings for hill and forest hiking.

west and the long, slow descent towards Pafos, are more vineyards and wine villages.

The Keryneia Massif

In stark contrast to the Troodos is the other mountainous region of the island, the Keryneia Massif. This is also known as the Pentadaktylos ("five-fingered") range because one of its mountains has five separate peaks. Turks refer to the massif as the Besparmak Mountains. Characterised by rough rock walls and steep precipices, it is largely formed of hard, compact masses of whitish-grey limestone.

To the north and south the range is divided into numerous small valleys and ravines. On the northern slopes, the hard limestone is covered by much softer clay, resulting in a varied coastline. The mountains crowd the northern coast, rising up steeply a short way inland from the sea and looming over the coastal settlements.

Deep river valleys, swollen in spring with mountain torrents, lead from the Keryneia range to the coast. The isolated villages on the slopes are linked by narrow roads, some of which climb up to the mountain ridges.

Beyond the settlements, the forest tracks that lead across the entire length of the massif provide magnificent views of the steep limestone walls, fabulous rock formations and forests. Clear paths pick their way through dry pine forests, which rarely become either dense or dark: some have been diminished by forest fires. Up here you can move easily between views of the north coast on one side, and down into the plains on the other.

The Mesaoria Plain

The Mesaoria Plain between the Keryneia and Troodos mountains extends from Morfou in the west to Famagusta in the east. The plain used to be covered by forest but the trees have long since been chopped down, leaving a steppe in their place. In a number of areas, erosion of the alluvial soil has exposed the underlying sandstone and other rock. Rivers have carved up the landscape and water and sand have shaped it. Although the Mesaoria has been dubbed "the breadbasket of Cyprus", large parts frequently lie fallow. This is due not to any shortcomings in the land's fertility but rather because the region suffered severe depopulation after 1974.

The coastline

In the Troodos region and up in the Keryneia range, the land tends to drop down quite steeply before it reaches sea level. In spite of this incline, most of Cyprus is distinctive for its relatively flat coastline. And it is here that, apart from Nicosia, the main towns are located. Larnaka, Limassol, Pafos, Morfou (a short way inland), Keryneia and Famagusta are neatly spaced out around the coast. The areas around the towns of Morfou and Famagusta contain broad expanses of flat coastline. To the southwest of the island, too, near Pafos, and also in

Akrotiri Bay and around Larnaka, the coastline is broad, with smooth flat beaches.

Although steep sea-cliffs are a rarity, some can be found at the points where the Troodos massif runs steeply towards the coast on its north and south sides: between Pomos and Kokkina in the north, and to the west of Cape Aspro in the south. In the extreme northwest of the island, northeast of the Akamas Forest, there are further stretches of rocky coastline, but the wide-open expanses of sand unprotected by cliffs are equally attractive. Visually stunning and varied stretches of coastline can be found wherever the chalk of the hill country meets the sea. The hilly landscape near Kourion, for example, drops sharply to the narrow strip of intensively farmed land beside the sea; the few trees here have been bent towards the land by the prevailing onshore wind.

The coastline of the Keryneia range is even more varied. It tends to be low and steep with slabs of limestone jutting out above the clay below. It is worth visiting this coastal zone, which extends from Cape Kormakitis in the northwest to Cape Plakoti in the northeast, if only to see the fine rock formations and characteristic coastal flora. Included among the best beaches are those along the broad sweep of Famagusta Bay and along the coastline of the Karpasia Peninsula, where they are extensive and almost entirely deserted.

Akamas and Karpasia

The Akamas and the Karpasia peninsulas, separated by the entire width of the island (as well as by the transient man-made scar of the demarcation line), though quite different in character, are equally notable places. The Akamas is short, squat and rugged; the Karpasia is long, thin and rolling. Each may eventually become a national park, although the authorities on either side of the great divide seem to be in no hurry to establish them.

Rivers, springs and lakes

The map of Cyprus shows a large number of quite small rivers flowing straight into the sea from the hills and mountains. Most carry water only in the winter and spring, and dry up with the onset of summer. Yet during sudden sum-

mer thunderstorms, a dried-up riverbed can turn into a torrent in little more than half an hour. Much of the island's distinctive appearance comes from the deep valleys created by these rivers, with their broad gravel beds.

The longest river in Cyprus is the Pedieios, which rises near Machairas monastery in the hills southwest of Nicosia, and flows into the sea near Famagusta. Together with the River Gialias, with which it flows parallel, it irrigates the Mesaoria plain. The Gialias has been dammed in two places to form reservoirs.

Two springs in the Keryneia range are both called Kefalovryso. One is near Kythrea and

the other near Lapithos. Several more springs, shaded by plane trees, can be found in the Troodos Mountains below an altitude of some 1,600 metres (5,250 ft). Some of them, such as the spring near Kalopanagiotis, are rich in minerals and for centuries have been used for therapeutic purposes. The only major natural lakes in Cyprus are the saltwater lakes near Larnaka and Limassol, which were originally lagoons. Over the millennia they became separated from the sea. They are rich in bird life, particularly during the December and April migrations between Europe and Africa. They have been joined by a number of artificial lakes, to preserve as much fresh water as possible. ❑

LEFT: coastline on the road to Vouni.
RIGHT: Avgas Gorge on the Akamas Peninsula.

ISLAND OF FLOWERS – A BOTANIST'S DREAM

Cyprus is one of the most rewarding places in Europe to see wild flowers, thanks to the island's position in the Mediterranean Sea.

Spring arrives early in Cyprus, making it heaven for botanists and hell for gardeners. March and April present a magnificent cornucopia of flowers and fragrances: hillsides resemble giant rock gardens and brilliant patches of untended waste ground outdo northern Europe's carefully tended herbaceous borders with ease. The flowers are at their best in the inland parts of the Akamas Peninsula, the high Troodos Mountains, and the limestone Keryneia hills in the north.

The richness and diversity of the flora are due in part to the proximity of three continents (Europe, Asia and Africa), partly to the favourable climate, and partly to the variety of habitats. Winter rains followed by a warm, frost-free spring, produce a season's flowers compressed into just a few weeks before the summer's heat becomes too much. By May or June the flowers have gone, the seeds for next year's show are ripening, and greens are fading to brown to match the tourists on the beach.

Except in the cooler, higher Troodos Mountains, most plants go into semi-dormancy to survive the arid summer. The first rains of autumn, which could be in early September but may not be until late November, tempt a few autumn bulbs into flower but also initiate the germination of seeds – plants that will grow and build up strength during the winter in preparation for the following spring.

▽ **CYTINUS HYPOCISTIS**
Often overlooked, this remarkable plant is a parasite living on the roots of the *Cistus* (below). It emerges only to produce its own white or yellow flowers.

◁ **CISTUS CRETICUS**
Flowers of the *Cistus* family come in pink, purple and white. This resilient plant rarely shows signs of suffering from the presence of the *Cytinus*.

△ **CYCLAMEN**
Several types of cyclamen are found in Cyprus. The commonest is *Cyclamen Persicum*, the ancestor of the cultivated cyclamen.

△ **NARCISSUS TAZETTA**
Fragrant *Narcissus* adds November colour to rocky hillsides and marshes.

◁ **CISTUS SALVIIFOLIUS**
Cistus species smother the hillsides in May. They thrive after fires and can swiftly re-colonise burned areas. In turn, they give way to regenerating trees.

△ **SPIRANTHES SPIRALIS**
Most orchids flower in the spring, but the unusual spiralling flowers of "autumn ladies' tresses" appear, as is suggested by its common name, in the autumn.

CALLING ALL ORCHID FANS

Orchis simia, the monkey orchid (above), and the naked man orchid, *Orchis italica* (below left) are among more than 50 orchid species found in Cyprus.

Orchids thrive in undisturbed sites, particularly on the Akamas Peninsula where the displays in March can be spectacular; however, different species require different soil types, so those that are abundant on limestone will be absent from nearby serpentine, and vice versa. Often they grow near the protection of a spiny bush that discourages grazing goats.

Some are easy to identify while others, such as the brown-lipped bee- and spider-orchids, are subject to much taxonomic debate and you will need a comprehensive, up-to-date identification guide to tackle these. (Common names derive from real or fancied resemblances in the individual flowers.)

Orchids, and other wild flowers, should not be picked, but should be left for other people to enjoy in their natural habitat. When photographing them be careful not to trample on other plants nearby.

▽ **SCILLA CILICICA**
This blue squill is found in limestone crevices in Cyprus and Asia Minor, flowering in the early part of the year.

▽ **ARABIS PURPUREA**
One of approximately 110 endemics (plants native to Cyprus), purple rock-cress grows by shady rocks in the Troodos Mountains.

△ **RANUNCULUS ASIATICUS**
A spectacular and elegant buttercup with poppy-sized flowers is found in white, pink, red and shades of bright yellow.

THE CYPRIOTS

"In neither speech nor genius, has the Cypriot any resemblance to either Turk or Greek." The people of Cyprus are something else altogether

In 1879, a publication called *British Cyprus*, which was published in London, contained the following words by W. Hepworth Dixon: "What are the Cypriots? The Cypriots are neither Turks nor Greeks, neither are they an amalgam of these two races. From Larnaca to Keryneia, from Paphos to Famagusta, you will seek in vain for any sample of these types. In neither face nor figure, in neither speech nor genius, has the Cypriot any resemblance to either Turk or Greek. Nowhere have I seen a Turkish figure, nowhere a Grecian profile. It is safe, I think, to say that not a single Turk exists in Cyprus."

Cypriots are never described simply as Cypriots. The word is always prefaced by the qualification Greek or Turkish, in recognition of the two very different ethnic groups that inhabit the island: the Greek-speaking Greek Orthodox community and the Turkish-speaking Sunni Muslims. The question of their identity ought to be settled by the islanders themselves, and cannot be satisfactorily answered by sociological studies.

With two thirds of the population looking to Athens and Europe and the other third towards Ankara and Turkey, the gulf between the communities continues to widen. The slogan "Proud to be a Turk" is written in white stones high on the slopes of the Keryneia Mountains, and is visible for miles around. Turkish and Turkish Republic of Northern Cyprus flags flutter all over the northern part of the island, just as Greek and Republic of Cyprus flags adorn almost every church and town hall in the southern part.

Peaceful coexistence

In the years that followed the island's colonisation by the Ottomans, there were few incidents of social conflict between the Muslim settlers and the indigenous Orthodox Christian population. On the contrary, the two groups

---

PRECEDING PAGES: tying the knot in a courtship dance.
LEFT: the Orthodox face of Cyprus.
RIGHT: many women still play a traditional role.

joined forces several times to fight their oppressors in Istanbul (known to Greeks as Constantinople). Marriages between members of the Muslim and Christian communities were unusual, on religious grounds, but in everyday life it was quite difficult to tell the two ethnic groups apart. It was only the growth of nation-

alism during the 19th century that produced the social and political conflicts that were later to erupt so violently.

In 1960, when the British Crown Colony of Cyprus was finally given its independence, the new republic's constitution defined the Greek and Turkish Cypriots as two separate ethnic groups. At that time the members of both groups still lived in ethnically mixed villages and cities. Purely "Greek" or "Turkish" areas were few. In most cases, neighbours lived together in peace and celebrated their festivals together. Many villages operated communal cooperatives. Agricultural products were marketed on a mutual basis.

Before the border opening the majority of each community had not lain eyes on each other since that fateful August in 1974. For almost 29 years the only knowledge of each others activities was generally gained via television or furtive meeting in neutral countries. The north and south, Greek Cypriots and Turkish Cypriots, had more in common than they would care to admit. In their daily lives, the food they eat and the drink they imbibe, the gestures and the temperaments can only be described as Cypriot – not Turkish or Greek. For all the propaganda issued by both communities, 400-year-old traditions often prove more influential than a few decades of politics.

fate of their 1,600 missing from the 1974 conflict (a figure that equates to 640,000 Americans if relative population sizes are compared).

Relaxed pace

Anyone who is familiar with Athens and Istanbul will be amazed at the relaxed pace of life in Nicosia. Despite congested traffic jams, car horns are used less frequently than in the capital cities of the respective motherlands. It's fair to say that Cypriots tend to be calmer in their reactions to life's daily trials and tribulations than either the Greeks or the Turks. They follow political developments at home and abroad with

One of the saddest aspects of that division was the widespread inability on both sides, on the part of politicians and ordinary people alike, to understand the other side's pain. Greek Cypriots too lightly dismissed the trauma that Turkish Cypriots went through in the 1960s in their isolated enclaves, where they were subjected to harassment, armed attack and murder by terrorists and Greek Cypriot regular forces, and cannot appreciate that Turkish Cypriots might genuinely have welcomed the protection of the Turkish army. Turkish Cypriots, in their turn, have no real appreciation of the anguish felt by Greek Cypriots that their homes, their churches and their farms have been invaded, nor for the

less passion, even though they have more than enough reason to get aggravated. Greek Cypriot society, in particular, is more markedly cosmopolitan than it may first appear. Almost everyone has travelled abroad, not least to visit friends and relatives. Until the 1950s Cyprus was still a poor country and thousands emigrated to improve their prospects.

Today, there are large colonies of Greek Cypriots in New York and Australia, and there is a 100,000-strong community in London. Those who remained in Cyprus have retained a strong link with their diaspora relatives and friends.

Before 1992, when the University of Cyprus opened, the island had no such institute of further education so students hoping to pursue academic qualifications had no choice but to go abroad. Most went to Athens, but many studied in Britain or the US. As a result, islanders have a keen awareness of events in the outside world and visitors very rarely have problems communicating with the locals, most of whom have a good command of English.

A male society

Cypriot society is still very traditional in its outlook; the women tend to be particularly con-

a shade less virtuous, the history of Cyprus would be less eventful and much happier."

The *kafeneia* (cafés), still the domain of the menfolk, are forums of political discussion. In the villages the café is the chamber for political decision-making too. As a rule, Cypriot women are unwelcome in such cafés, and there are still few female members of parliament. Although the overall attitude persists that a woman's main role is to look after the household and the children, more and more women

servative. For centuries fanciful male travellers have looked for characteristics of the goddess Aphrodite in the island's female population, but with little success.

In the opinion of one Charles Lewis Meryon, writing in 1846, "They were not in general beautiful, nor was their dress graceful... Seen from behind they resembled nothing so much as a horse in a mantua-maker's showroom, with a dress appended to it." A more recent visitor, the humorist George Mikes, said: "I cannot suppress my feelings that had the Cypriot girls been just

LEFT: a break on the hilltop, western Cyprus.
ABOVE: a male-dominated society persists in Cyprus.

are finding employment after marriage. In the villages women have always shared the hard farming work with their menfolk.

The Turkish Cypriots' attitude to life is more Near Eastern than that of their Greek Cypriot counterparts. The influx of tens of thousands of Turkish settlers may have had the desired effect of creating a stronger relationship with Turkey, but it has also caused protests against "Anatolisation" among indigenous Turkish Cypriots. Immigrants from mainland Turkey are certainly more deeply rooted in Islam, and their adherence to observances such as those applied during Ramadan is more strictly enforced than among Turkish Cypriots. ❏

THE RURAL EXODUS

For generations, farmers in the island's mountain areas

have waged a constant struggle with the forces of nature

Drive into the pretty conservation village of Lazanias in the eastern Troodos Mountains and you might think that all the inhabitants have run away and hidden indoors at your approach. The streets are deserted, seemingly permanently. When someone finally does put in an appearance it is an old lady

dressed entirely in black, and she soon vanishes back inside her house. Lazanias may be an extreme example, but it is indicative of a problem that has struck almost all of Cyprus's villages, especially the remoter ones. Most of their inhabitants have departed, and those who remain are old. An average age of 60 is common in the mountain villages. Like the head of Janus, rural Cyprus has two faces: here decline, there (usually near the coast) the victim of rampant building activity, as holiday homes and apartments spring up like mushrooms.

The steep character of the countryside and the prevailing stony ground make the farmer's life one of unadulterated hard work. An anti-quated system of land rights, retaining elements from the Ottoman era, provides an additional difficulty: a farmer's tiny parcels of land often lie far apart from each other, for example, and over 100 different farmers sometimes have legal claims to the yield of a single olive tree. What's more, droughts can strike at any time.

Of course, 20th-century progress brought some improvements for Cypriot farmers as new agricultural techniques were introduced. The feudal system of tributes, under whose yoke generations of farmers had laboured, was abolished in the 1920s. The British were responsible for both getting rid of the exploitative moneylending system and the introduction of a close network of rural cooperatives.

Changing aspirations

Even today, agricultural life in the mountain areas, where irrigation is impossible, would support only a limited number of the local residents. However, people's demands have changed. In former years farmers were content with bread, olives, and wine, and they dressed themselves in a single *vraka* (baggy trousers). Any surplus money was invested in the future of their children, in particular the compulsory dowry *(prika)* for their daughters.

Today people can find a husband for their daughters without a dowry, but expectations concerning their own living standards have risen sharply: the material wealth of employees in the cities is demanded in the country too – television brings news of the latest products and fashions to even the remotest home.

In the 1950s, when Cyprus was still under British rule, large building projects demanded workers from beyond the agricultural sector. Since the 1960s industrial and trading companies in the large Cypriot cities have also needed workers, as have extensive hotel developments. The result was a huge migration from remote mountain areas to the towns and suburbs.

Villages within a radius of 20 km (12 miles) from Nicosia, Limassol and Famagusta experienced rapid growth. People worked in the cities but lived in their home village, where land prices were still affordable. They tended their vineyard or olive grove at weekends, and contracted a fellow villager to cultivate the land.

In the Pafos district, things were more problematic. Until the end of the 1970s there was neither industry nor tourism to any significant extent. In contrast to Limassol or Nicosia, Pafos was just a large village without any supraregional significance. Income supplements were only available to a limited number of seasonal workers in the plantations of the southern coastal areas or in the mines on the edge of the Troodos Mountains (most of which are now exhausted). The only possible option for many, especially the young and well-educated, was migration to another region. Between 1960 and 1973 the Pafos district was the only one in Cyprus to experience a reduction in the number of its inhabitants – not even the high birth rate amongst the resident population could make up for the loss through migration.

The crisis of 1974 and the division of the island brought the Pafos district further population losses. During the course of 1975 all the Turkish Cypriot inhabitants had to leave their homes to be resettled in the Turkish-occupied north of the island. In the space of one year the district lost some 15,000 inhabitants, a quarter of its total population. Only a few of the Greek Cypriot refugees took the opportunity of settling in the abandoned Turkish villages or areas. The prospects of making a reasonable livelihood from farming were simply too poor to persuade people to start a new life here.

The threat to village unity

Since the 1980s, with the rapid growth of tourism and the opening of Pafos airport, the economic conditions in the district have changed fundamentally. The coastal area of Pafos has experienced its first boom since the heyday of the ancient cult of Aphrodite, and its tourist industry is suffering from a shortage of workers. There is hardly a single *Pafitis* (as the inhabitants of the district are known) who has to leave his home village to find work. Yet whilst these newly-created jobs are of huge significance for the region, the old farmers in the *kafeneion* of Lyso or Fiti are left pondering an uneasy question: will the young people, who are today working in the hotels as receptionists, bar staff and cooks, be able to maintain their relationship with the rural world of their parents, or will they become irrevocably alienated from their roots? This relationship can only survive by continuing the business of farming, even if it is only as a sideline. The old farmer knows the situation better than anyone else: Cyprus's rural communities thrive on village unity. What's more, to many visitors, the appeal of Cyprus is its traditional lifestyle and values.

Seen from this point of view, all those projects aimed at bringing about fundamental

improvements in agricultural life and the rural infrastructure (such as schools and water supplies) are of enormous importance.

Until now the beneficiaries of the Pafos irrigation project have been mainly the landowners on the coastal plain. But other locations on the island are also benefiting from such schemes, in particular the Pitsilia Integrated Rural Development Project on the southern edge of the Troodos Mountains.

The achievements of such projects should not be measured in terms of costs incurred versus productivity. Rescuing rural Cyprus from the vicious circle of resignation, apathy and decline is what matters. ❑

LEFT: the way out.
RIGHT: priest and farmer.

CELEBRATIONS

In keeping with their love of worldly pleasures, the Greek Cypriots adore celebrations and festivals, most of which are accompanied by a feast

Witnessing a wedding in Cyprus is a real experience for the visitor, even though only a few of the original customs and rituals are still observed. For example, the length of the celebrations has been reduced from a whole week to half a day, and the stipulation that weddings may take place only on Sundays has been relaxed.

Most couples marry in the summer months; leap years are avoided because they are considered unlucky. The festivities begin with the dressing of the bride and groom in wedding finery, usually to a musical accompaniment. Then it's off to church, the time of the ceremony depending on the number of other weddings taking place that day. The guests attending the hour-long ceremony – during which the lucky couple are crowned with pearls – are usually too numerous to fit inside the church.

Afterwards, the festivities begin with the "making of the bed", the symbolic setting up and decoration of a mattress: married women carrying the future couple's bedclothes (an important part of the dowry) dance around the mattress and make the bed. Guests then decorate the finished bed with coins and banknotes.

By around 8pm, most of the guests have arrived. Each guest is offered a drink and a plate piled high with the wedding supper – traditionally a range of set dishes: fried slices of potato, cucumber, tomatoes, *kleftiko* (lamb roasted in a sealed oven or sealed earthenware pot) and *pastitsio*. Women carrying large bowls distribute *resi* (crushed wheat porridge, a speciality that no self-respecting wedding omits) and *kourabiedes* (baked almond pastries).

At this point the dancing starts, and it continues until about midnight: there's the *tsifteteli*, a simplified form of belly dance, which men and women perform separately in pairs, or the *zeimbekkikos*, a dance dating from the war of Asia Minor during the 1920s, in

which a single individual performs to the syncopated clapping of a circle of friends. Once the evening is quite far advanced, it's time for the *choros tou androjinou*, danced only by the bridal couple. This is the time for guests to shower money on the bride and groom. The couple literally disappear under long chains of

banknotes, all pinned together. The song has a number of optional choruses – depending on how long the bombardment lasts. Finally, towards midnight, the guests disperse.

Christenings

Festivities celebrating engagements and christenings are similar, but on a more modest scale and without any dancing.

Greek Orthodox christenings differ in many important respects from the common northern European version. The main difference is that the child is naked and completely immersed in water. He or she is then oiled and dressed in fine clothing. The godfather (only one is

PRECEDING PAGES: festival in Agios Neofytos.
LEFT: wedding donations gratefully received.
RIGHT: a Turkish festival in Belapais.

allowed) provides each guest with a baptismal gift, usually a small doll or animal decorated with sweets, and sometimes even a photograph of the baby. The ceremony is followed by a grand party for at least 100 guests.

Name-day celebrations are also very popular with the people of Cyprus. They are held on particular days each year by numerous monasteries, and are similar to country fairs (without the carousels). A large area in front of the monastery fills up with stalls and booths selling everything from household goods and clothing to souvenirs, cassettes, toys, nuts and honey. Sweets are particularly popular, especially *louk-*

four-year period by the domestic conflict. The entry fee entitles you to sample the various types of wine on display and to attend all the theatrical and musical activities. An estimated 100,000 visitors manage to consume an impressive 30,000 litres (6,600 gallons) of wine every year.

Excuses for a festival in Cyprus are not hard to find. Limassol – and recently Pafos, too – holds its own carnival celebrations in March every year, complete with parades, parties, music and masked balls, and in the summer the Keo company hosts a beer festival, similar to the one organised by Carlsberg in Nicosia. There are several cultural festivals in summer,

oumia (a kind of Turkish delight), chewing gum, *daktyla* (almond cakes with syrup), *lokmades* (small round cream puff pastries fried in oil) and the ever-popular *soutsoukos* (strings of almonds dipped in a thick layer of dried grape-juice).

Interested visitors might try their hand at one of the numerous games played at such events, where canaries are given away as prizes.

City festivals

The biggest city festival is the Limassol wine festival, held for 12 days every September. The tradition, started by the wine producers, began in 1961 and was only briefly interrupted for a

including the ancient Greek Drama Festival. In May, every town hosts a flower festival, with a procession through the streets and children's competitions for the best flower arrangements. Before partition, two of the most spectacular festivals were the Orange Festival in Morphou and the Carnation Festival in Varosha; both have fallen victim to the political situation.

There are also the numerous small harvest festivals and fairs *(panegyri)* in all the larger villages of the island, as well as the Dionysos Festival in Stroumpi and the Cherry Festival in Pedoulas. On these occasions, old and young celebrate in the village square, with music, dancing, feasting and drama.

celebrate in the village square, with music, dancing, feasting and drama.

The Cypriots are a deeply religious people, so a great number of church festivals are celebrated. The traditions and significance of these occasions is not what might be expected – they feature a fascinating blend of pagan superstition and Christian rites.

Families attribute little importance to Christmas, for example, but New Year's Day is celebrated with at least one *vasilopitta*, a cake made of baked semolina. A coin is hidden inside the cake, and whoever is fortunate enough to find it is assured of good luck in the coming year. An-

is a water festival of pagan origin in honour of Aphrodite, but it has developed into a Christian festival to mark the Flood. The celebrations culminate in an enormous fair, with music and dancing and readings by local poets.

Every year, on 18 April, Larnaka's citizens hold a procession headed by the icon of St Lazarus, patron saint of the city. In May, the towns along the coast celebrate Christ's baptism by lowering crucifixes into the water. The Assumption of the Virgin on 15 August and the Day of the Holy Cross on 14 September are also important church holidays, when fairs are held at many of the monasteries.

other custom is to throw olive leaves onto hot ashes, and watch the way they curl; from this, it is maintained, one can predict whether wishes will be fulfilled. *Lokmades* (doughnuts) are an integral part of the island's Epiphany celebrations; it is customary to throw the first doughnut out of the frying pan and on to the roof of your house, in order to pacify any lurking evil spirits.

Pentecost is not generally marked. An exception is the popular religious festival unique to Cyprus known as Kataklysmos, which coincides with Pentecost and is held in Larnaka. It

LEFT: a bouzouki player.
ABOVE: motherly embrace for a new bride.

NORTHERN CELEBRATIONS

In the North the festivals correspond to the main Turkish ones. As in the south, the holiday calendar is a mix of religious occasions and official commemorations. The two largest religious festivals are the Id-ul-Fitr at the end of the fasting month of Ramadan, and the Id-ul Adha later in the year. These are usually celebrated with family get-togethers and the giving of sweets and presents to children. Unlike the south, they don't go in for big bashes, but there are occasional folkloric performances at Famagusta and Keryneia castles and unpredictably timed harvest festivals on the Mesaoria plain that give thanks for the orange, strawberry and watermelon crops.

Easter

Without doubt, the most important church festival is Easter. Preparations begin a full 50 days in advance of the holiday with the onset of fasting, and a strictly vegetarian diet. During Holy Week this diet becomes even stricter – only pulses and vegetables can be eaten. On Orthodox Good Friday (which falls after the Catholic one) the Epitafios procession, led by a coffin containing a figure of Christ, is held in the villages, and every icon is draped in black cloth. Then on Easter Saturday preparations get under way for baking *flaounes*, pastries filled with a mixture of egg, cheese and raisins.

In the evening, villagers gather in church for the service celebrating the Resurrection. Everyone holds a candle, and children are given sparklers. At midnight the priest announces Christ's Resurrection with the words "*Christos anesti*" (Christ is risen), to which the answer resounds: "*Alithos anesti!*" (He is truly risen!). Then the candles are lit, and the square in front of the church blazes with light. After the service, *mayiritsa* (Easter soup) is served, and many people stay out even later. On Easter Sunday, families, all sporting new clothes, travel to the countryside for a picnic of grilled *souvla* (skewered lamb) and hard-boiled eggs that have been painted red.

Greek national holidays are also observed in the southern part of the island. Greece's Independence Day, for example, is celebrated on 25 March, and "Ochi" Day (commemorating Greece's defiant "no" to the Italians in 1940) is on 28 October. Cyprus also celebrates its own Independence Day, on 1 October.

Making music

Music in Cyprus takes a number of diverse forms. The melodies most frequently heard at festivals are those of *tsifteteli* and *rembetika* songs. *Rembetika* are songs of the Greek underworld, originally performed by refugees from Asia Minor. Other types of music range from disco and Greek pop to classical music and traditional songs. The latter have various functions and performance contexts: love songs, work songs, children's rhymes, humorous songs, wedding songs, dirges and laments, as well as epic songs traditionally performed by *poiiterides* (itinerant poets).

Musical instruments are equally varied. As well as the common instruments of pop music – the bouzouki, drums, accordion, violin and synthesiser – there are a number of old instruments, some dating back to Byzantine times. Of the instruments largely confined to the Turkish community, the *oud* is a short-necked lute, the *zorná* a kind of oboe, the *davul* a two-headed cylindrical drum, and the *kását* are small finger cymbals. Those found generally in Greek music include the *laouto* (a long-necked lute), the mandolin, the *pidkiavali* (reed pipe) and the *tamboutsiá* (a large frame drum). Other instruments include the kettledrum, trumpet and cymbals used in parades. These traditional instruments are gradually dying out due to the increasingly ubiquitous appetite for pop music. Turkish Cypriot music today is similar to the music of mainland Turkey, with the main instrument being the *saz* (a long-necked lute).

Attempts have been made by modern musicians to rescue at least some of the island's old melodies. The Trio Giorgalletto, a male-voice group belonging to a musical family that has been famous on the island for decades, frequently travels abroad on international tours. The group also performs on big festive occasions and for radio and television. ❑

LEFT: a member of the musical Giorgalletto family.
RIGHT: celebrations in the streets of Limassol.

FOOD AND DRINK

Scarcely a conversation takes place without the offer
of coffee, beer or brandy, and invariably a small snack too

Food and drink in Cyprus are an integral part of any and every social occasion. The Cypriots love food. So it is no surprise that the country's cuisine is so broad. The island's geographical position and its history have produced an interesting mix of Greek, Turkish, Arab and British culinary influences.

It is at the weekend, above all, that fathers take their families out to eat, and groups of up to 15 diners are not uncommon. These kinds of gatherings are informal, and the table is literally strained to breaking point under the sheer number of different dishes. Plates are piled high, and everyone tries a little bit of everything, washing the food down with local wines.

A little of what you fancy

This style of dining stems from the Cypriot preference for *meze*, usually a little of everything that's available that day in that taverna or restaurant and, on occasion, augmented by ingredients introduced by the customer – for example, snails they have found at the local market. There's no better way of getting a general idea of the cuisine than the *meze*, because it offers the widest range of Cypriot food in one sitting. A *meze* always includes a few Cypriot specialities, in particular *halloumi* cheese (produced by thyme-fed goats). The dishes are well seasoned but not over-spicy, and oil and fats tend to be used moderately.

Although Cyprus is an island, the price of seafood here is high: this part of the Mediterranean is not rich in fish, and many species have to be imported deep-frozen. Typical Cypriot seafood dishes include small, deep-fried fish and rings of cuttlefish.

The traditional Cypriot dishes that can be found are often modified, doubtless as a result of Britain's influence which is still so evident throughout the island. Unfortunately it's no simple matter to find genuine, unadulterated

local food, especially in the more touristy areas. Restaurants in the main resorts tend to offer steaks, cutlets and other international dishes, all of which arrive with the compulsory helping of oversized chips. The really simple and delicious local food (pumpkin slices fried in butter, wheatmeal pilau, broad bean stew, and the like) remains unobtainable for the majority of visitors, because such dishes are not generally considered to be a "full" or "proper" meal.

Nor, when sitting down to dine, should one expect the food to be emphatically Greek: the salads rarely contain sliced onion, and the *talattouri* (similar to the Greek *tsatsiki*) contains only a dash of garlic. And, unlike in Greece, the food does arrive hot.

Game dishes are particularly popular with Cypriots. Ducks, game birds, rabbits and also, unfortunately, the *ambelopoulia* – a species of small songbird – are the usual targets of the island's enthusiastic hunters.

The culinary traditions of northern Cyprus

PRECEDING PAGES: traditional *meze*.
LEFT: making no bones.
RIGHT: *souvlakia*, always a favourite.

are closely related to those of mainland Turkey: both place much emphasis on heavy meat and vegetable dishes.

A drop to drink

Unlike the Greeks (and indeed many tourists), the Cypriots do not drink large quantities of either ouzo or retsina wine. Beer, however, is extremely popular, with two brands, Keo and Carlsberg, produced locally. Brandy is also a local favourite, and the quality of the various types is excellent. Brandy

ANCIENT REPUTATION

The island has been famous for its wines since antiquity (they are even mentioned in the *Song of Solomon*) and was one of the first countries to cultivate the vine.

sour, a long drink consisting of brandy, lime juice, angostura bitters and soda, is a wonderful pick-me-up after a hard day on the beach.

Cyprus sherry (Emva Cream being the most popular brand) is known throughout the world. Less familiar to visitors are the various liqueurs made from the island's fruits. Especially delicious is *Filfar*, made from oranges and reminiscent of Grand Marnier. To quench the thirst of those not keen on alcohol, the island stocks the full range of internationally known soft drinks – the empty cans that litter the roadside give a good idea of the range.

The wines of Cyprus are worthy of particular note. Much written evidence, as early as

that of Pliny the Elder, attests to the quality of the grapes, and especially their size. Mark Antony gave Cyprus to Cleopatra, as a token of his love for her, with the words: "Your sweetness, my darling, is like the Nama wine of Cyprus." In the mid-14th century the German pilgrim Ludolf von Suchen wrote: "In all the world there are no greater or better drinkers than in Cyprus." And legend has it that Sultan Selim II ordered the invasion of Cyprus after tasting one of the island's wines.

Another important event in the history of Cypriot wine was the invasion of Cyprus by Richard the Lionheart, and his sale of the island to the Knights Templar; the latter were concentrated around Limassol, notably in Kolossi, where they had their "Grand Commandery" (later taken over by the Knights Hospitaller), which gave the island's famous Commandaria wine its name. Richard is reputed to have later said: "I must go back to Cyprus, if only to taste its wine once again." It was around that time that the Nama wine was rechristened Commandaria.

Even today, Commandaria, probably the most famous of Cypriot wines, is produced using the same age-old methods, including fermentation in open jars. The grapes are grown in a restricted area of the southern Troodos Mountains but the wine's special merit lies in the way it is blended and aged. It is sweet and heavy, tastes rather like Madeira, and should really be classed as a fortified wine. There are several different types available.

Today, winemaking remains one of the country's most important sources of income. The sunny, mild climate and the fertile soil make it a natural industry. The main wine areas can be found in the Limassol and Pafos regions, and on the slopes of the Troodos Mountains. The large wine factories of the four main producers, Sodap, Keo, Loel and Etko, are all based in Limassol and Pafos. Together with the government, these producers have encouraged the import of several European grape varieties, particularly from France. Britain has long been the biggest importer of Cyprus wine. ❏

LEFT: Cyprus wines, little known abroad, can be very palatable. **RIGHT:** Cypriot sherry, a major export.

CRAFTS

Unable to compete with imported goods, local cottage industries
are struggling to keep the old traditions alive

The twin village of Lefkara (population: 1,300) nestles in a picturesque setting at the foot of the Troodos Mountains. This attractive collection of buildings, with unusual red roofs, is said to have been a popular summer resort with ladies in the Venetian period. Kato Lefkara, the lower part of the village, is tiny, with narrow, winding streets. It has a shop that provides basic necessities, two *kafeneia*, where the male population of the village meet, and a small church.

Pano Lefkara, the upper part, is the larger. Here, restaurants and shops have sprung up around the marketplace that forms a focal point for tourist buses, and side streets are flanked by souvenir shops selling a range of silver and gold jewellery and tablecloths.

Magnificently embroidered wares hang outside nearly every shop. In good weather, village women sit outside their homes, embroidering motifs on to cotton and linen. The store owners are only too happy to invite any passing strangers to take a look around.

Da Vinci's choice

Lefkara is the island's centre of lacemaking, a local industry that has gained a global reputation for intricacy and beauty. Leonardo da Vinci is said to have purchased some *lefkaritiki* lace for the altar of Milan Cathedral (a sample hangs in Lefkara in his memory). At the turn of the 20th century, Lefkara men travelled halfway round the world selling embroidery, not least in North America, while their wives stayed sewing at home. Records show that in 1910, some £1,720 worth of Lefkara lace was exported, a handsome sum at the time.

The base material for the lace is Irish linen. Creating, say, a tablecloth can frequently mean several weeks' hard work, and so prices can be high – though not prohibitively so. Every

product is unique: no piece of Lefkara embroidery is the same as any other.

Four main companies, each employing approximately 150 workers, dominate the manufacture and marketing of lace in Lefkara. The village also contains several fine stone houses – one of which, the House of Patasalos, fea-

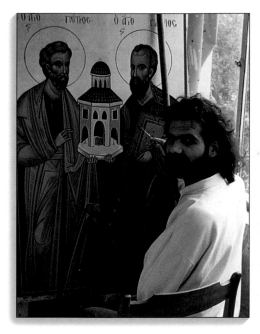

tures a museum of folk art – devoted to the history of lace and silverwork of the area.

Thanks to its buoyant lacemaking industry, Lefkara has prospered, and there is no danger that the village will decline. Other cottage industries are not faring so well and an official Cyprus Handicraft Service has been set up in Nicosia with the aim of keeping the island's handicraft traditions alive. Its workshop still uses time-honoured methods, thereby maintaining old techniques that would otherwise be forgotten. Handicrafts made on a private basis are also sold at the workshop. Anyone buying goods here or at any of the Cyprus Handicraft Service (CHS) shops in Limassol,

---

PRECEDING PAGES: modernisation has brought sweeping changes to traditional crafts.
LEFT: pottery in Kornos.
RIGHT: a young practitioner of an ancient art.

Larnaka, Pafos and Nicosia can be sure that their purchase has been handmade.

The manufacture of embroidery and lace is not confined to Lefkara. Colourful cotton embroidery is a speciality of several remote villages, such cloth being the traditional cover for dowry chests. In the wine village of Omodos, elderly ladies embroider quilts and tablecloths.

Crafts under threat

Without the CHS, production of handsomely carved wooden bride's chests *(sendoukia)*, made of pine, cedar or walnut, would have died out. In the old days these chests used to contain

can sometimes still be seen hanging outside restaurants, often in the guise of lamps.

Wickerwork and basketry are still pursued. Indeed colourful wickerwork baskets and platters are a very common sight. Decorative wicker plates with perforated rims are often used as bowls. The craftsmen tend to be elderly refugees who want to earn extra money to supplement their pensions.

Weaving mills were once widespread on the island, but the ancient looms that can be found in the remote mountain villages are rarely used these days. In CHS workshops, on the other hand, they are in use daily. Silkworms are bred

the daughter's dowry and jewellery. These days the Cypriots use ordinary wardrobes, but the old chests – the fronts of which are usually decorated with flower and tree motifs – are still used for ornamental purposes. The town of Lapithos on the north coast of the island, the former centre of chest-making, has been under Turkish occupation since 1974.

Another craft that has almost disappeared is the manufacture of gourd flasks, an industry which used to be found wherever bottle gourds grew. Unfortunately, artistically decorated gourd flasks created from the inedible bottle gourd are no longer needed by a world used to canned drinks and glass bottles. Gourd flasks

here, too, and their threads are spun into fine cloth for dresses and skirts.

All that glisters

Gold and silver jewellery is still produced today, albeit on a much smaller scale than in years gone by. Most of the island's goldsmiths and silversmiths, who would frequently share premises on the streets of Nicosia, have long since disappeared.

Copper artefacts are usually antiques, and have a correspondingly high price tag. Small-scale metalworking, however, is still undertaken in the traditional way; here, the piece to be duplicated is placed in a metal frame, which is then filled with a particular type of sand on two sides. After the mould is opened, the original is carefully removed, and liquid metal is poured into the sand mould.

Ceramics for storage

Pottery items, created from the local red clay, is still widespread. Here it's possible to differentiate between larger, simply-constructed pieces and smaller, finer work. The largest specimens – round storage jars that frequently measure up to a metre (3 ft) in diameter – are

WATER COOLERS

Even in the broiling heat of summer, water stays pleasantly cool in large unglazed clay pitchers. They often stand on metal tripods and can also be used as flower pots.

ers, however, are still made, and look much like they did a thousand years ago.

Small pottery ware is a speciality of the Pafos region. Clay figurines, glazed vases, candlesticks, bowls and complete coffee services are all available. Some are colourfully decorated with flower patterns, others are more simple, with geometrical designs. The latter, with their line patterns, are strikingly reminiscent of their ancient counterparts. Indeed some of the decorative forms date back to the Early Neolithic

commonly found lying in gardens and outside houses. Known as *pitharia*, these jars were formerly used for storing oil, olives, water or wine. The potters who made them used to travel from village to village and were held in the highest regard. They could create *pitharia* on the spot, without even using a wheel.

Unfortunately the production of *pitharia* has pretty much gone the way of so many old-time crafts. Their enormous size and incredible weight make them unsuitable for modern-day living. Large, simply constructed clay pitch-

period. The pots are formed using simple wheels, and are then hand-painted. Beware, however, of pottery depicting Greek gods, especially those with inscriptions in English – these are usually cheap, mass-produced imports.

Craftsmen are struggling to compete with the cheap, factory-produced equivalents that saturate the market: the chairmakers, for instance, who used to make the old wooden chairs with wickerwork seats and arms, are a vanishing breed. For all the hard-wearing sturdiness of their chairs, plastic ones are cheaper.

Everywhere the competition from industry is gaining ground. With refrigerators so readily available, who needs *pitharia*? ❑

LEFT: coppersmith at work.
ABOVE: Lefkara, renowned for its lace-making.

PLACES

*A detailed guide to the entire island, with principal sites
clearly cross-referenced by number to the maps*

Cyprus is characterised by the striking differences between ancient traditions and new, fast-moving, Western-influenced developments. On the one hand, archetypal Mediterranean landscapes with mountain villages and isolated forest areas; on the other, brand new farms employing modern methods of agriculture, and cosmopolitan cities with seemingly endless suburbs. Sometimes tradition and modernity coexist: not far from the hypermodern blocks of flats in the city of Nicosia, for example, are the tranquil labyrinths of the old city, full of mysterious alleys.

Some of the island's most famous sites have been victims of earth-quakes and art thieves, and their extant remains are thus modest. Yet there are still many spectacular sights, in particular the Byzantine churches and monasteries in the Troodos Mountains, with their wealth of frescoes and icons, the splendid Roman mosaics in Kato Pafos and, in the North, the ruins of the Hellenistic-Roman city of Salamis, and the Gothic abbey of Bellapais, captured so memorably in Lawrence Durrell's *Bitter Lemons*.

The Places section of this guide begins with Limassol, a popular tourist destination and convenient springboard for visiting Kolossi and Kourion, proceeds to Larnaka (ancient Kition) and moves on to the burgeoning resort of Agia Napa at Cape Gkreko. It then crosses to the southwest of the island, where Pafos offers the best of archae-ological Cyprus, and thence to the island's wilder fringes, such as Polis, and into the Troodos Mountains. Lastly, from the divided cap-ital of Nicosia, it hops into northern Cyprus.

Those who want to travel to the North may now do so with some restrictions. Firstly you may visit the North daily between the hours of 8am and midnight. The procedures for crossing to the North are informal – all that is required is your passport. Visitors on foot should use the Ledra Palace crossing in Nicosia where the only formality is the completion of a short form for the Turkish Cypriot authorities. Visitors with a vehicle must cross at either Agios Dometios, a sub-urb on the west side of Nicosia, at the Pergamos crossing in the Dekelia Sovereign Base Area (SBA), or at Agios Nikolaos also in the SBA close to the outskirts of Famagusta. You may cross in a hire car, though the companies will invalidate your insurance if you have an accident in the North.

If you entered Cyprus from the North you still may not officially enter the South. You will not of course be allowed to exit the South without a valid Republic of Cyprus entry stamp. Be aware that these regulations will be in flux for the foreseeable future so it is always best to check current rules locally. ❏

PRECEDING PAGES: Pano Lefkara, in the Troodos Mountains; Petra tou Romiou, mythical birthplace of Aphrodite; on the road in southwest Cyprus; Kourion's Early Christian basilica.
LEFT: fishing boats in the harbour at Pafos.

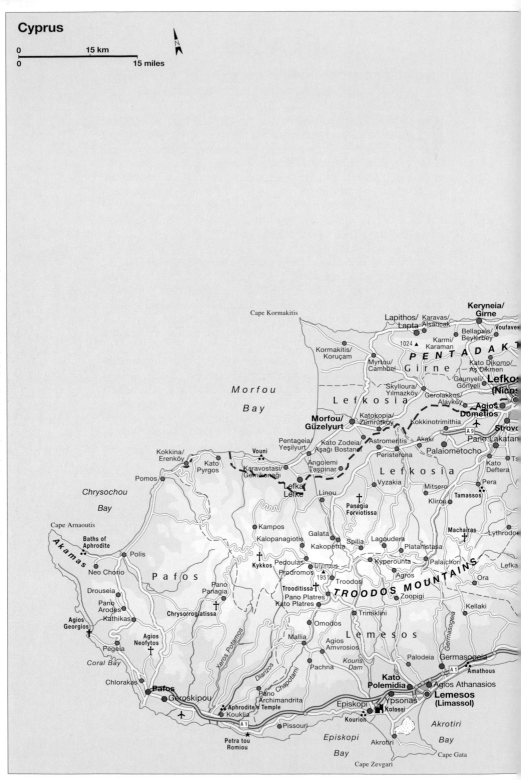

Cyprus

0   15 km
0   15 miles

Cape Kormakitis

Kormakitis/
Koruçam

Morfou
Bay

Morfou/
Güzelyurt

Pentageia/
Yeşilyurt

Vouni

Kokkina/
Erenköy

Kato
Pyrgos

Pomos

Karavostasi/
Gemikonağı

Angolemi
Taşpınar

Lefka/
Lefke

Kato Zodeia/
Aşağı Bostancı

Chrysochou
Bay

Cape Arnaoutis

Baths of
Aphrodite

Polis

Neo Chorio

Drouseia

Pano
Arodes

Kathikas

Agios
Georgios

Pegela

Coral Bay

Chlorakas

Agios
Neofytos

Pafos

Geroskipou

Pafos

Pano
Panagia

Kykkos

Chrysorrogiatissa

Kampos

Kalopanagiotis

Pedoulas

Prodromos

Trooditissa

Pano Platres

Kato Platres

Omodos

Mallia

Pano
Archimandrita

Kouklia

Petra tou
Romiou

Pissouri

Galata

Kakopetria

Olympus
1951

Troodos

TROODOS MOUNTAINS

Zoopigi

Trimiklini

Agios
Amvrosios

Pachna

Kouris
Dam

Episkopi

Kourion

Kolossi

Episkopi
Bay

Akrotiri

Panagia
Forviotissa

Linou

Vyzakia

Spilia

Lagoudera

Kyperounta

Agros

Palaichori

Mitsero

Klirou

Pera

Kato
Deftera

Lemesos

Palodeia

Germasogeia

Kato
Polemidia

Ypsonas

Agios Athanasios

Lemesos
(Limassol)

Amathous

Akrotiri

Bay

Cape Gata

Cape Zevgari

Lapithos/
Lapta

Karavas/
Alsancak

Keryneia/
Girne

Karmi/
Karaman

Bellapais/
Beylerbey

Voufave

1024

P E N T A D A K

Myrtou/
Camlıbel

G i r n e

Kato Dikomo/
Aş Dikmen

Skylloura/
Yılmazköy

Geunyeli/
Gönyeli

Lefkos
(Nicos

Katokopia/
Zümrütköy

Gerolakkos/
Alayköy

Agios
Dometios

L e f k o s i a

Kokkinotrimithia

Strovo

Astromeritis

Akaki

A 9

Pano Lakatan

Peristerona

Palaiometocho

L e f k o s i a

Tamassos

Machairas

Lythrodo

Lefka

Ora

Kellaki

Pafos

Lemesos

Cape Kormakitis

Agios

Pano

Kato

Dianzos

Chapotami

Xeros Potamos

Aphrodite's Temple

A 1

Akamas

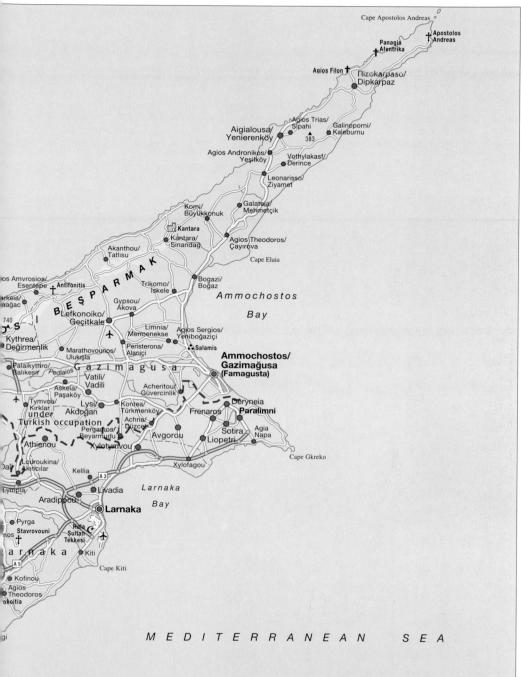

Cape Apostolos Andreas

Apostolos
Andreas

Panagia
Afentrika

Agios Filon

Rizokarpaso/
Dipkarpaz

Agios Trias/
Sipahi

Aigialousa/
Yenierenköy

Galinoporni/
Kaleburnu

383

Agios Andronikos/
Yeşilköy

Vothylakasf/
Derince

Leonarisso/
Ziyamet

Komi/
Büyükkonuk

Galateia/
Mehmetçik

Kantara

Kantara/
Sinandağ

Agios Theodoros/
Çayırova

Akanthou/
Tatlısu

Cape Elaia

os Amvrosios/
Esentepe

Antifonitis

B E Ş P A R M A K

Trikomo/
İskele

Bogazi/
Boğaz

arkeia/
ağaç

Ammochostos

Bay

740

Gypsou/
Akova

Lefkonoiko/
Geçitkale

S

Kythrea/
Değirmenlik

Limnia/
Mermeneke

Agios Sergios/
Yeniboğaziçi

Marathovounos/
Ulukışla

Peristerona/
Alaniçi

Salamis

**Ammochostos/
Gazimağusa
(Famagusta)**

G a z i m a ğ u s a

Palaikythro/
Balıkesir

Pediaios

Vatili/
Vadili

Acheritou/
Güvercinlik

Tymvou/
Kırklar

Askeia/
Paşaköy

Lysi/
Akdoğan

Kontea/
Türkmenköy

Deryneia

Paralimni

under

Frenaros

Turkish occupation

Achna/
Düzce

Pergamos/
Beyarmudu

Agia
Napa

Athienou

Xylotymvou

Avgorou

Sotira

Liopetri

Cape Gkreko

Dali

Louroukina/
Akıncılar

Kellia

Xylofagou

Lympia/

A 3

Aradippou

Livadia

Larnaka

Bay

⊚ **Larnaka**

Pyrga

Stavrovouni

Hala
Sultan
Tekkesi

nos

a r n a k a

Kiti

A 5

Cape Kiti

Kofinou

Agios
Theodoros

okoitia

gi

M E D I T E R R A N E A N   S E A

LIMASSOL AND THE SOUTHWEST

Map on page 144–5

Limassol may not quite live up to its billing as the "Paris of Cyprus" but it does have a certain appeal. One in three visitors to the island heads for the Bay of Amathous, Limassol's own riviera

L ying on Cyprus's south coast, **Limassol ❶** is big, brash and bustling. With 163,900 inhabitants, it has grown at breakneck speed since 1974, just about tripling its population thanks to an influx of Greek Cypriot refugees from the north and a subsequent boom in industry, services and tourism. With Cyprus's main port, Famagusta (Ammochostos) in Turkish-occupied territory, Limassol took over as the Greek Cypriots' shipping hub.

Not all the effects of this enforced growth have been pleasant. Little thought, care or imagination has been devoted to the process of expansion. Limassol (Lemesos to Greek Cypriots) has swallowed up hapless villages along its rim and its outer suburbs are edging up into the foothills of the Troodos Mountains, while at the same time big resort hotels have sprouted all along the bay to the east. In compensation, Limassol has a scenic setting, is cosmopolitan in the way port cities tend to be, and has nightlife, shopping, dining and drinking venues in abundance.

LEFT: alms-seeker outside a Limassol mosque.
BELOW: musician in medieval garb performing at Limassol Castle.

Soldiers' haunt

The British soldiers stationed at the military base on the Akrotiri Peninsula west of Limassol, who spend much of their free time in the nearby city, have become as characteristic a feature of Limassol as the locals who have made their living from trading since time immemorial. Nowadays, after tourism and shipping, the export of fruit and vegetables is the most significant branch of the local economy.

In the area around Limassol are extensive citrus fruit plantations of lemon, orange and grapefruit trees. Moreover, Keo, in the west of the city between Odos Fragklinou Rousvelt and the coast, has established itself as Cyprus's largest manufacturer of alcoholic drinks. The firm's complex comprises a brewery, winery and a distillery for schnapps; it is possible to tour the facility during normal working hours.

Wine-growing has a long tradition in the region. The most important vineyards stretch along the southern slopes of the Troodos Mountains, interspersed with nut bushes and plantations of cherry, apple, pear and peach trees. Every year, in September, Limassol is the scene of a wine festival, and the celebrations outdo even the local spring carnival. The arts festival in July completes the varied cultural calendar, which is increasingly orientated towards the tourist trade.

The approach road from Larnaka is lined solidly with hotels, broken only by restaurants and nightclubs. Limassol has not only taken over Famagusta's role as

Visitors to Limassol castle.

the main port on the island but also its position as the leading tourist destination. Business centres and industrial estates have sprung up, actively helped by the government of Cyprus with tax concessions and ongoing improvements in the infrastructure. Among the ventures are numerous banks – not the usual massive skyscrapers found elsewhere in the world, but buildings which blend discreetly with the surrounding cityscape. Considerable numbers of Russians also live in Limassol and many of them brought money to the town.

Ancient history

Archaeologists are not able to give a definitive account of the origins of Limassol, not least because numerous modern structures have been built over the ancient remains. Tombs from the Early and Middle Bronze Ages, whose burial gifts – mainly ceramics – can be dated to the end of the 3rd or 2nd century BC, are proof that there were settlements in the city around this time. The discoveries are displayed in the local Archaeological Museum.

In the suburb of Agia Fyla, which lies to the northwest of Limassol, a cemetery from the Late Bronze Age (around 1300 BC) was discovered. It has been proved that the ancient coastal settlement of Nemesos, or Lemesos, which gave its name to the modern city, was situated here. At that time, however, the settlement was in the shadow of the more important nearby coastal cities of Amathus (today Amathous, to the east of Limassol) and Kourion (further west on the other side of the Akrotiri Peninsula), and so played only a very minor role.

After a number of severe earthquakes in the Byzantine era, the rebuilding of the area under Emperor Theodosius II (AD 408–50) was concentrated on the area of present-day Limassol, to the detriment of the previously more significant

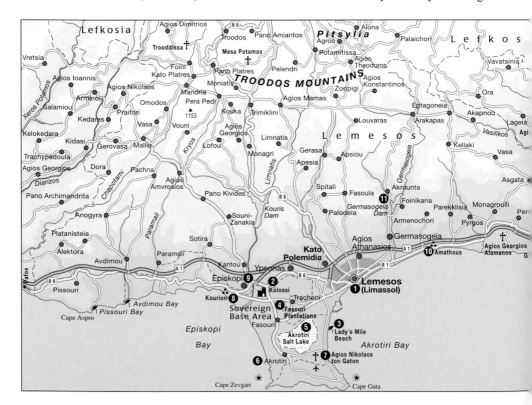

settlement at Amathous. The port of Theodosias, named after its builder, was founded anew in the wide bay. In the following period Theodosias was also the see of the bishops, the most significant of whom was Leontius (AD 590–668).

During the Third Crusade, King Richard the Lionheart, on his way to the Holy Land, chose Limassol as a landing place for his army and as a base from which to conquer the island. The marriage of Richard and Berengaria of Navarre took place in the citadel of Limassol, and the Spanish noblewoman was thereby crowned queen of England. Before the bridegroom continued his journey to the Holy Land he sold the island of Cyprus to the crusading Order of the Knights Templar, who subsequently sold it to Guy de Lusignan.

In the following period the city was fortified, and continued to serve the Crusaders as an important base from which they could fend off attacks from the Saracens. It also provided accommodation for the Hohenstaufen emperor Frederick II, both on his way to the Holy Land in 1228 and on his return the following year. The Lusignans and the Knights Templar contributed to the economic upturn in the city, as did the Order of the Knights of St John of Jerusalem (the Hospitallers). In 1303 the last Grand Master of the Templars, Jacques de Molay, took his leave from the city, having been ordered by Pope Clement V to return to France, where he was burned at the stake six years later.

Having suffered many severe earthquakes, Limassol was set on fire by the Genoese in 1371 and plundered by Egyptian raiders in the first half of the 15th century. What was left was then destroyed by the Ottomans in 1539. As early as 1480 the traveller Felix Faber complained about the deplorable state of the city. The only building of any consequence left standing was a single church, and that was virtually ruined. Even here the church's bells had been stolen. The

Blacksmith at work in the backstreets of Limassol.

BELOW: tombs of Limassol Castle's past occupants.

Southwestern Cyprus

continuing decline of the city was vividly described by a succession of European visitors who followed in Faber's footsteps.

There were already tensions between the established Greek population and the Turkish-Ottoman newcomers. One traveller who visited Limassol soon after the devastating earthquake of 1584 reported that the entrances to the modest dwellings of the Greeks were so low that you had to bend down to enter them. The entrances were built in this style to prevent Turkish knights from using them as stables for their horses. As late as 1815 an English traveller described Limassol as a rundown settlement of 150 mud houses, in which the proportion of Greeks to Turks was two to one.

The city's only importance at that time was based on the shipping of wine. In 1881 Limassol had over 6,000 inhabitants. When the export of wine was increased considerably towards the end of the 19th century, and the rebuilding of the harbour had been finished, the city quickly recovered its former prosperity. The capacity of the old harbour was soon no longer sufficient, and a new complex was built to the southwest of the city, complete with firefighting equipment and ship-repair yards.

Around the town

The busy coastal road, with its four lanes and grassy central reservation, starts from the old harbour and runs to the north. The first section is Odos Spyrou Araouzou (the Tourist Information Office can be found at the corner of Spyrou Araouzou and Nikolaidi). After that the street is officially known as Odos Oktovriou 28, after the Greek national holiday. Hotels and restaurants serving fresh fish are sprinkled between shops and residential buildings, along with bars and English-style pubs.

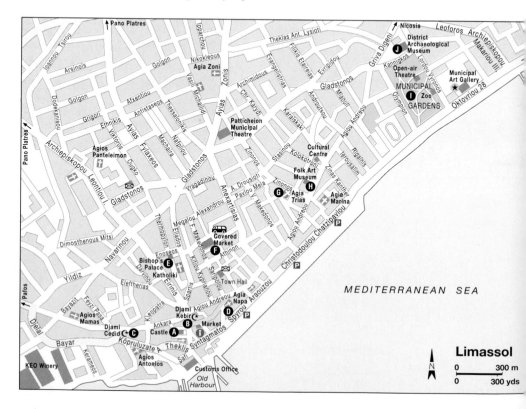

Limassol

Just a little way from the road to the north of the old harbour (but hidden from the road itself) is **Limassol Castle** (open daily; entrance fee; tel: 25-305419). This, the only authentic historic site in the old town, is situated in the middle of a small fenced-off area surrounded by a labyrinth of narrow streets and old buildings. The castle now serves as a museum. On the way there from the coast, you pass a small roundabout, not far from which is an interesting **Reptile Museum**.

The castle

At the beginning of the 14th century the Crusader citadel was built on top of the ruins of the Byzantine castle. Part of the eastern wall of the castle was still standing and was integrated into the western wall of the citadel. The marriage of Richard the Lionheart and Berengaria took place in the chapel of the Byzantine castle, followed by the coronation of Berengaria as queen of England by the bishop of Evreux.

King Janus (1389–1432) handed Limassol Castle to the Knights of St John of Jerusalem, who had made their headquarters in the castle of Kolossi. They also carried out further renovations to the castle of Limassol. After 1570 the Turks moved into the castle and totally rearranged the internal layout. (The Great Hall had already fallen apart after one of the supporting pillars collapsed in 1525.) Prior to 1940, the castle served as a prison for the British administration, and for a while as an army headquarters. Extensive restoration work in 1950 included reinforcement of the vaults.

With the division of the island, the Medieval Museum in Nicosia lay right on the border between the Greek and Turkish halves of the city. As a result the exhibits were moved, with the financial support of the Amathus Ltd shipping

Map on page 146

TIP

Those of squeamish disposition should avoid visiting the snake terrarium at the Reptile Museum shortly before the close (7pm), when the animals are fed with small rodents.

BELOW: sturdy walls of Limassol Castle.

company, to Limassol Castle, and since then they have been housed there in the new **Cyprus Medieval Museum**.

The entrance to the castle leads into a small anteroom. From here you can enter the lower-lying, almost quadrangular Gothic Great Hall to the right. On the left-hand side, spread over two floors, there is a group of smaller rooms, which can be reached via a central corridor. These rooms house objects from the Byzantine and medieval periods.

The most spectacular exhibits are the three silver plates discovered among the famous Lambousa Treasure in 1902. Unfortunately a further six silver plates from the same collection were smuggled abroad and can now be found in the Metropolitan Museum in New York. The plates, which date back to AD 620, show scenes from the youth of King David. They were discovered in the ancient town of Lapithos, on the north coast of Cyprus, in the part of the island now under Turkish occupation.

From both the Great Hall, and from the smaller rooms on the left, steps lead up to the roof of the castle. From here there is a wonderful view over the port and, above all, over the old city. The two mosques' minarets, which tower over the city, provide a lasting reminder that a significant Turkish population once lived in Limassol.

Heading north

BELOW: fresh fruit and vegetables and lots more on sale at the Covered Market.

The Episcopal church and its neighbouring **Bishop's Palace ⒺE** can be reached via Odos Eirinis, which begins at the citadel, crosses Odos Ankara and then continues further north. Two turnings further to the east lead to the **Covered Market ⒻF**, where fruit, vegetables, meat and poultry are on sale.

Map on page 146

If you follow Odos Agiou Andreou to the north, away from the coastline, you can make a short detour to the right, to visit the **Holy Trinity** church (Agia Triada) **G**, which can be easily seen from the road. Going back to the turn-off, and continuing along Odos Agiou Andreou, leads to a corner house (No. 253) standing alone on the left-hand side at the junction of Odos Othonos and Odos Amalias. Since 1985 this has housed the **Folk Art Museum H** (open Mon–Fri; entrance fee; tel: 25-362303), where agricultural implements and traditional furnishings, ceramics and textiles are on display.

A little further along, on the same side of the street, is the **Cultural Centre**, with rooms for art exhibitions and a library. If you turn into Odos Kannigkos at the top end of Odos Agiou Andreou, you reach the northern edge of the **Municipal Gardens I**, which contain an open-air theatre and a raggedy little zoo, and which form the setting for the Limassol Wine Festival in September. A little further along the coast road, at 103 Odos Oktovriou 28, is the **Municipal Art Gallery** (open Mon–Fri; entrance fee; tel: 25-586212).

The garden area to the north houses the **District Archaeological Museum J** (open daily; entrance fee; tel: 25-305157), which was set up in the 1970s. The majority of the exhibits here are from the discoveries at Kourion and Amathous, along with a number from other sites in the region around Limassol. The exhibitions are organised both thematically and chronologically: the first display case documents the history of Cypriot ceramics. Other interesting artefacts include terracotta figures. The larger sculptures nearby reveal both Greek and Egyptian influences, the latter being most obvious in the monumental and ornately decorated capital from Amathous, which bears the unmistakable cow's head of the Egyptian goddess Hathor.   ❑

The remains of the castle gate.

BELOW: reminder of a once-substantial Turkish population.

THE TURKISH DISTRICT

A fter visiting the castle you can walk between the two mosques, the *Djami Kebir* **B** ("the large mosque") in the east and the *Djami Cedid* **C** (also known as the Köprülü Haci Ibrahim Aga Mosque) in the west, and appreciate the typical Turkish architecture of the area, which was once the Turkish commercial district. Particularly notable are the pronounced oriels on the first floors which lean over the street. On some of the houses you can still see Turkish inscriptions, and the further west you go, the more often you come across Turkish street names: Odos Agiou Andreou joins Odos Ankara, which at its western end fans out into a mass of small Emirs and Paşas. Here the Djami Cedid (Köprülü Haci Ibrahim Aga Mosque) towers above the river bed of the Garyllis – invariably bone dry.

In the immediate neighbourhood of the Djami Kebir there is a *Turkish bath*, and, just a little further east, the *Agia Napa* **D** church, consecrated with St Veronica's veil (offered to Christ on his way to the Crucifixion), rises up between the promenade and Odos Agiou Andreou. The present church, built in 1903, houses a series of icons preserved from its early-18th century predecessor. Further on, Agios Andronikos church hides in a cul-de-sac that is accessible only from the waterfront.

KOLOSSI AND KOURION

*Take the scenic route to the knights' castle of Kolossi
and to Kourion, perched on a bluff over the sea – the most
spectacular archaeological site in the South*

Map
on page
144–5

Lefkosia/
Nicosia

L imassol itself wasn't always the island's centre of power: during certain periods this role was enjoyed by the fortress of **Kolossi** ❷ (open daily; entrance fee; tel: 25-934907), which dominated the Episkopi Plain in the western hinterland of the city. King Hugo I, a member of the Lusignan nobility, handed the fortress over to the Knights Hospitaller in the 13th century.

This area was economically important for a long time as a result of its sugar cane plantations. *Zucchari de Cipro* appeared on European trading documents as long ago as the beginning of the 14th century. Nowadays it is the vast citrus fruit plantations, known as *Fasouri*, which shape the appearance of the landscape and form the economic backbone of the region.

About 15 km (9 miles) west of Limassol, the castle of Kolossi of the Order of St John rises up above the fertile landscape of the plain of Episkopi. Its walls contain a fortified tower with living quarters and also a sugar-processing factory for the cane sugar which was grown in the area at the time.

The Knights of St John

The countryside surrounding Limassol was given to the Order of St John by Hugo I (1205–18); in return he received their support in battles against the Muslims. When the Christians lost Syria to the Arabs in 1291, the Order of St John chose Cyprus as their headquarters. They stayed here until 1310, at which point they founded their own state on the island of Rhodes, where they remained until driven out by the Turks in 1522, after which they fled to Malta.

In Cyprus the Order of St John had to compete with the Knights Templar for possession of the castle of Kolossi. It was only after the Templars were proscribed by the Pope in 1308 that the Knights of St John could take proper possession of the castle. In fact they received not only the castle itself but also the property and serfs of 60 neighbouring villages.

Along with oil, wheat and cotton, the main products were wine and sugar cane. The **Hall of the Sugar Factory** – situated near the aqueduct that was used for transporting the water needed for sugar production – has survived into modern times. A millstone with a diameter of over 3 metres (11 ft) that was used to press out the juice from the cane, also still exists.

The Knight von Gumppenberg mentioned the place in his *Pilgrim's Travels*: "We rode to a house, that of the Knights of St John, and sugar grows there and the house is called Koloss."

Kolossi was not the only sugar-producing area. There was competition from nearby Episkopi, in the form of the Venetian noble family, the Cornaro. As various historical documents prove, there were con-

LEFT: Kourion's spectacular theatre.
BELOW: the castle of Kolossi.

The royal coat of arms on the tower of Kolossi castle.

tinual disputes between this family and the knights over the rights to use the water in the region. In the end, Catarina Cornaro, widow of the last king of Cyprus before the island was taken over by the Venetians in 1489, dispossessed the Knights of St John and took possession of the castle and its factory. Moreover her nephew, Cardinal Marco Cornaro, was then appointed Commander of the Order of St John. An inscription from 1591, which Murad, paşa of Cyprus at the time, had carved in the south wall, is evidence that the Ottomans, who had conquered the island some 20 years before, carried on this lucrative industry.

Near the sugar factory is the **fortified tower** with its three floors. It rises from a quadrangular ground plan whose sides measure 16 metres (52 ft). Its present structure was built in 1454 on the remains of a previous building dating from the time of the Crusades. The semicircular foundations of the original building and a well on the east side of the fortified tower have survived.

A group of coats of arms has been chiselled into the east wall within a cross-shaped frame. In the middle, directly under a crown, the royal coat of arms is divided into four parts, comprising the emblems of the kingdom of Jerusalem, the Lusignans, the kingdom of Cyprus and Armenia. This royal coat of arms is flanked by that of the Grand Masters of the Order, Jean de Lastic (left) and Jacques de Milli (right). In the lower arm of the cross is the emblem of Louis de Magnac, one-time grand commander of Cyprus, who is believed to have commissioned the building of the new fortified tower.

At that time, this *donjon* could only be entered via a drawbridge leading to the first floor. After proceeding through a further entrance gate, at one time protected with a machicolation, visitors move on to a kitchen with an open fire, and a day room with paintings of scenes from the Crusades. These paintings can be

BELOW: the Hall of the Sugar Factory.

dated from the coat of arms of Louis de Magnac. A spiral staircase leads up to the second floor and two living rooms, one of which has a fireplace. (The same coat of arms can be seen on the chimney.) The staircase leads up to the roof. Going down instead of up, visitors proceed to three vaulted chambers in the basement, two of which have wells.

Map
on page
144–5

Lady's Mile and Fasouri

On the way from Limassol to Kolossi, on the southwestern edge of the city, is **Lady's Mile Beach ❸**. It lies inside the territory of the British Sovereign Base and is mostly used by British service personnel and their families (actually it's mostly deserted). A long stretch of fine golden sand, it has a less than scenic view across to the Limassol harbour installations. Lady's Mile apparently got its name because it was the place the colonel's wife walked her horse, or had it walked for her, back in the rose-tinted days of empire. Inland from here are the **Fasouri Plantations ❹**, whose air is heady with the tang of citrus fruits.

The roads in the area are lined with cypress trees that serve as windbreaks protecting the orchards. Sadly the prettiest such road, where overhanging cypresses once formed a tunnel of trees, must have been hit by one wind too many, and most of the trees were deemed a hazard to traffic and chopped down.

Simple gardens visible below Kolossi castle.

Flamingos and cats

Kolossi lies at the northern end of the Akrotiri Peninsula. Crossing the peninsula in the direction of the coast to the south, you come to the basin of the large **Akrotiri Salt Lake ❺**, which is usually dry. Whole colonies of flamingos can be seen here when the lake bed fills up in winter, though their number has been

BELOW: luscious citrus fruits are abundant in the region.

declining in recent years, and migrating birds also use the area as a stopover en route to and from Africa. As is the case with the salt lake near Larnaka, however, no salt is extracted here any longer. In the immediate neighbourhood is a British military air base – photography is strictly forbidden – and the small village of **Akrotiri ⑥**, which gave its name to the peninsula.

On the edge of the village is a modern monastery which has replaced the abandoned monastery of **Agios Nikolaos ton Gaton ⑦** (St Nicholas of the Cats), to the eastern edge of the military airport. The eastern tip of the Akrotiri Peninsula, Cape Gata, also takes its name from the felines which the monks in the old monastery employed as a defence against snakes. Today the nuns who have replaced the monks in residence at Agios Nikolaos maintain the tradition of being kind to cats. Masses of lazy felines lounge in the garden and in the shade of the cloister, and not one of them looks as if it would know how to tackle a snake if it suddenly came fang to whisker with one.

Kourion

To travel from Limassol to the impressive ruins of **Kourion ⑧** (open daily; entrance fee; tel: 25-997048), which stand in solitary splendour on a massive rock ledge 70 metres (230 ft) above the sea, take one of the public buses which leave from Limassol Castle throughout the day. What you see on arrival, however, dates only from the Hellenistic, Roman and Early Christian times: the relics of the pre-Hellenistic capital of the local kingdom of Kourion have yet to be discovered.

BELOW: enjoying the acoustics and the views at Kourion.

Most of what we know about this period comes from the writings of Herodotus. According to the great historian, the victory of the Persian invaders during the Persian Wars in 497 BC, following their suppression of the Ionian

rebellion, was made possible only by the cowardly retreat of Stasanor, the king of Kourion. Pasicrates, the last king of Kourion, supported Alexander the Great as naval leader in the fight against the Persians during the siege and storming of Tyre from a position off the Lebanese coast.

During the period of the Roman Empire, the city flourished both economically and as a centre for the worship of Apollo, a cult which soon gave way to Christianity. The basilica, built in the 5th century, eloquently testifies to the early importance of Christianity, but when Arab invastions in the 7th century prompted the relocating of the bishop's residence to neighbouring Episkopi, Kourion lost its status and fell into decline.

Map on page 144–5

Sites to see

Today the ruins of Kourion *(Curium* in Latin) extend across three areas. Coming from Limassol, you reach the most imposing of the sites first. A gravel path leads off the asphalt road to the left and gives an impressive view over the sea. Following the road up the mountain in the direction of Pafos, you reach the **stadium** on the right-hand side after about a kilometre (half a mile). Unfortunately all that remains is an elongated, oval-shaped wall. Near the stadium is a small basilica. Far more impressive are the ruins of the **Sanctuary of Apollo** (open daily; entrance fee; tel: 25-997049), which are slightly off the asphalt road. A signpost indicates the way. Excavations have revealed the pilgrim halls and a holy precinct. You have to pay an entrance fee to visit each of the sites, with the exception of the stadium ruins. This means that, although you will already have passed the first of the villa ground plans (with its mosaic-decorated floor) on the left-hand side at the junction of the aforementioned gravel road,

A young theatregoer.

BELOW: Christian influence is evident in many of the mosaics at Kourion.

Looking east from the Temple of Apollo.

you have to drive or walk to the little ticket house before gaining access.

Once inside the fenced-off compound, if you stay on the inner side of the fencing, parallel to the approach road, you come to the **House with Wells**, whose water has now run dry, and then to the **House of the Gladiators**, named after its mosaics of armed warriors in action (the names of the villas are inlaid in mosaic). Finally, near the asphalt road, you reach a villa with a 4th-century mosaic scene depicting the legend of Achille. To prevent Achilles from entering the Trojan War, his mother, Thetis, dressed him in women's clothes and hid him among the daughters of King Lykomedes. Odysseus blew his cover by displaying a range of weapons alongside a selection of jewellery and watching Achilles's reaction. Another mosaic in the same villa, showing how Zeus, disguised as an eagle, kidnapped the young Ganymede, has been badly damaged.

In the area next to these villas is a sector where excavations, begun in 1975, are in progress. So far, a longitudinal **stoa** from Roman times has been uncovered, with accompanying rows of columns. The stoa measures 65 metres (213 ft) long and 4.5 metres (15 ft) wide and was built over part of an extensive Hellenistic house of unknown purpose. Parts of a **Roman forum** (meeting place) have also been dug out. This area can be easily recognised from the columns, whose shafts are not grooved vertically but fluted with winding threads.

Directly to the northwest of this area, archaeologists stumbled across an enormous **cistern**, which once fed a nymphaeum measuring 45 metres (148 ft) long and 15 metres (49 ft) wide.

Adjacent to this area, and in a superb location overlooking the sea, are the remains of a monumental **Early Christian basilica**, thought to have been commissioned by Bishop Zeno, who in 431 represented the diocese of Kourion at

BELOW: mosaic of Kitsis.

the Council of Ephesus. The main part of the church had three aisles and the nave included a choir stall, set in front of the apse on a slightly raised level, and at one time separated by a choir screen. On both sides of the aisles you can still see long halls, the so called *catechumena*.

The entrance hall *(narthex)* in the west, which lies sideways, stretches across the total width of all five aisles. Going further west you come to the deacon's rooms, and the bishop's private rooms. Going north brings you to an **atrium court**, which is surrounded by columns, with a watertank in the middle and further rooms on three sides. The baptistry used to be on the eastern side. Inscriptions and the remnants of the mosaic floor can still be seen.

At the southern end of the gravel path you come across the **theatre**, first built in the Hellenistic period, but whose present size is the result of 2nd-century Roman extensions. Despite its size, it remains a rather modest building with a mere 3,500 seats. (By contrast, the theatre at Salamis can accommodate an audience of 17,000.) It was probably not restored by the Christians after the severe earthquake in AD 365 and so fell into decline.

Another complex of buildings worth visiting on account of the mosaics is the **annexe of Eustolios**, next to the theatre. The mosaics are thought to date from the 5th century. Fragmentary inscriptions refer to Eustolios (the builder), and Apollo (the former patron). It was probably originally a Hellenistic private villa, which was converted into public baths at the end of the 4th century. Christian influences can be seen in the floor mosaics: floral, geometric and animal motifs rather than portraits of people; and one of the inscriptions in the floor mosaic makes it clear that the building did not need defensive features because it was already "surrounded by the most honourable symbols of Christ".

Map on page 144–5

The most important motif (in the frigidarium) is the bust of a woman holding a measuring rod which, according to the inscription, represents Ktisis, the personification of the creation.

BELOW: Sanctuary of Apollo.

Map on page 144-5

The area around the Temple of Apollo is believed to be the oldest settlement in Kourion, founded by Dorians from Argos in the Peloponnese.

RIGHT: Kourion, bathed in dawn light.
BELOW: admiring the Sanctuary of Apollo Hylates.

The long oval of the **stadium**, of which only the foundations are extant, lies between the areas described above and the Sanctuary of Apollo, and covers some 229 metres (750 ft), of which the actual arena itself measures 186 metres (610 ft). The rest of the area was occupied by the seven rows of seats, which could accommodate a total of 6,000 visitors.

The **aqueduct pipeline**, which comes from the mountains and which provided the city of Kourion with water, passes the Sanctuary of Apollo and proceeds along the southern wall of the stadium. To the west, a little way back, is the ground wall of an Early Christian basilica, dating from the end of the 5th century or the beginning of the 6th century. According to archaeological discoveries, it was built to replace a pagan temple.

The hill is surmounted by the **Sanctuary of Apollo Hylates** (open daily; entrance fee; tel: 25-997049), the protector of the woodland. The imported Greek god was merged with the long-established Cypriot god of vegetation. The Pafos and Kourion gates lead into the sacred area of this syncretistic deity, who was worshipped only in Cyprus.

The passage to the Kourion gate is flanked by a bathing area and a square building with a courtyard in the middle (the *palaestra*). The south side of the trapezium-shaped courtyard, into which both gates lead, borders on five right-angled rooms, supported by columns and complete with stone seats.

From here a passage strikes north at a right angle, past buildings which have a stoa in front. The passage is lined by two walled-in **worshipping areas** *(temenoi)* and leads directly to the Temple of Apollo itself.

The smaller *temenos* on the eastern side has a small round altar in the middle. Excavations indicate that it was built as early as the 7th century BC. The middle of the larger *temenos* to the west is occupied by a fascinating circular monument measuring 18 metres (59 ft) in diameter. Said to be unique in the Mediterranean, it is dedicated to the "protector of the trees". The complex was probably built in the 1st and 2nd centuries AD.

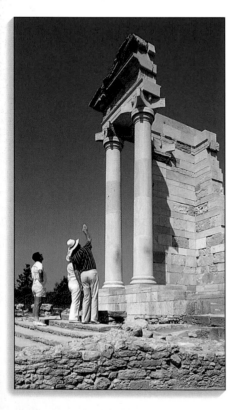

Episkopi

The name of nearby **Episkopi ❾** signifies that this village became the seat of residence of the bishop when the residence at Kourion was abandoned in the wake of the Arab invasions.

The village contains the **Kourion Museum** (open Mon–Wed and Fri 9am–2.30pm, Thur 3–5pm, except July and Aug; entrance fee; tel: 25-932453), which displays selected discoveries from Kourion and its surrounding area, where evidence has been found of Early Stone Age settlements, such as Erimi and Sotira, and the Bronze Age settlement of Phaneromeni. One of its most fascinating, and moving, exhibits is a skeleton group of a young man and woman with a baby lying huddled together in a vain effort to survive the earthquake that levelled Kourion in 365.

Some 20 km (12 miles) west of the Sanctuary of Apollo, off the old coast road to Pafos, is **Pissouri Bay**, which has the best sand beach between Kourion and Geroskipou. As always in Cyprus, that means it gets busy and is lined with tavernas (some of them very good, if rather expensive) and hotels. ❑

FROM LIMASSOL TO LARNAKA

Map on page 144–5

The journey from Limassol to Larnaka offers a wide variety of attractions, including the remains of Early Christian basilicas and prehistoric houses, lacemaking, ceramics and monastic peace

onsidering the important role **Amathous** ❿ (open daily; entrance fee) played in the ancient world, both as a port and the seat of residence of the local kingdom, it is somewhat surprising that archaeologists didn't begin excavating the site until 1980. What has been uncovered so far, on the coast about 8 km (5 miles) east of Limassol, has been very promising: it includes an Early Christian basilica on the bumpy coastal road, and the ruins of a sanctuary dedicated to Aphrodite on the **Acropolis Hill**, rising behind the road.

Other parts of the lower city, which probably stretched from the foothills of the Acropolis Hill to the south as far as the coast, have still to be excavated. Parallel to a river bed in the west, are the remains of a wall which ran from the southwestern edge of the Acropolis to the sea. On the other side of the wall, not far from the Amathus Beach Hotel, local archaeologists came across a burial ground from the Archaic period. Remains of the old harbour site have been located under the sea.

According to legends recorded by Tacitus, the city was founded by Amathus, the son of Aerias, although Amathousa, mother of King Cinyras from Pafos, is also credited with giving her name to the city. For quite some time, it was an important trading base for the Phoenicians, and during the Ionian rebellion it sided with the Persians. It remained an important port until the time of Richard the Lionheart, who destroyed it. The reason why the ruins give so little impression of the splendour of its ancient past is that, as so often in history, their stones served as building material for the projects of later eras – this time for the construction of the Suez Canal.

LEFT: Stavronouni monastery.
BELOW: Lefkara is famous for its lace and silver shops.

Fresh water and black sand

About 5 km (3 miles) inland from Amathous is Germasogeia Dam ⓫ and Germasogeia Lake, one of Cyprus's biggest freshwater reservoirs. The fluctuating level of the water behind the dam gives a good indication of the current state of Cyprus's reserves of drinking water.

A few miles beyond the ruins of Amathous, a side street leads from the main Larnaka-to-Nicosia road to the convent of **Agios Georgios Alamanos**. The monastery was founded at the end of the 12th century, but its buildings, positioned in the side of the mountain, were erected more recently. Outside the monastery wall a stall offers visitors a selection of icons painted by the nuns.

The next bay up the coast from Agios Georgios Alamanos, **Governor's Beach** ⓬, is known for its black sands. A salient side-effect of its unusual colour is that the sand soaks up even more of the sun's heat than do most beaches – so watch out for

toasted feet here. Keep going east on the coast road and you will arrive at **Zygi**, a fishing harbour with a line of good seafood restaurants along the shore.

Prehistoric houses

The motorway from Limassol to Larnaka crosses an area believed to have been inhabited from the the Early Stone Age; the round houses, which are characteristic of this period, have been found in the village of **Kalavasos** ⓭ and in the more famous **Choirokoitia** ⓮, both of which are situated just to the north of the motorway. The motorway also crosses the Late Bronze Age cemetery of **Agios Dimitros**, near Kalavasos. In Agios Dimitros two royal tombs have been discovered – including one belonging to a queen, which contained gold-decorated grave goods.

The round houses of Choirokoitia (open daily; entrance fee), which measure up to 10 metres (33 ft) in diameter, are packed tightly together and stretch over a steep slope halfway between Limassol and Larnaka. They were discovered in 1936, but excavations were halted in 1939 and not restarted until 1975, since when they have been ongoing. This settlement, probably the oldest on Cypriot soil, dates from the 7th or 6th millennium BC.

Its location was probably selected for its natural defensive qualities: the Maroni River flows around the hill in a large loop, thereby providing extra protection. The proximity of the river also ensured that there was an adequate supply of water, and its detritus provided building materials for the lower layers of the rotundas. Only the carefully constructed foundations of the rotundas, measuring up to 1 metre (3 ft) high, have survived. At one time lancet arches made from air-dried tiles stood on top of them.

BELOW: remains at Amathous.

Equally conspicuous is a wall-like construction that dissects the settlement. The theory that this is the foundation of a paved path, designed to make the steep climb easier for people and animals alike, has not been confirmed. It seems more likely that the wall marks the boundary of the settlement before it expanded. Its people lived from hunting, but also kept sheep, goats and pigs as domesticated livestock, and carried out a modest amount of farming. The discovery of objects crafted from obsidian rock is, in the view of some historians, proof of trading links with Asia Minor – the rock is not otherwise found on the island. The dead were buried either in lined graves under the floors of the buildings, or outside the houses. The grave goods which accompanied them reveal the religious beliefs of the inhabitants. In the last phase of the settlement in the 4th millenium BC, when the first metal objects (made of copper) appeared in graves, the locals also produced ceramics with typical "comb" patterns. Most of the discoveries are in the Cyprus Museum in Nicosia.

Villages and monasteries

If, instead of returning from Choirokoitia to the motorway you continue north along the approach road, you will eventually climb up to the village of **Vavla** ⓯ (after about half an hour). Signposts will direct you not just to the village but also to **Agios Minas** (St Minas; open Mon–Fri; group visits only), the convent in the village. This was founded in the 15th century, but owes its present appearance to its rebuilding in 1740. The nuns sell icons, honey that is famous all over the island and grapes, grown in greenhouses outside the convent walls.

Beyond Vavla the road meanders gently downhill, passing picturesquely sited Kato Drys, believed to be birthplace of the Cypriot national hero Agios Neofytos

Map on page 144–5

Lace is on sale in many places in the area.

BELOW: bathing below the ruins.

(born in 1134), before joining a road that leads to the twin villages of Lefkara, which are situated at around 600 metres (1,970 ft) above sea level in the foothills of the Troodos Mountains.

Kato Lefkara ⓰ is the smaller and lower-lying of the two villages. Most tourists, however, come to visit **Pano Lefkara** ⓱, usually to see and buy the elaborate cotton lace which is produced here. In summer, the narrow streets between the quaint-looking stone houses with red-tiled roofs are transformed into open-air workshops, because the women of the village prefer to practise their craft out of doors. The local men sell the filigree craftwork produced by their wives – named *Lefkaritika* after the place of their production – all over the island and beyond.

The local tradition of lacemaking is said to have been started by Frankish and Venetian noblewomen who spent their summers in cool Lefkara, and whiled away their time making lace. Leonardo da Vinci is said to have admired the fruits of their craft and bought an altar cloth for the cathedral in Milan when he visited the village in 1481. Historically there is no evidence that he was actually here. In the **House of Patsalos**, a small local museum (open Mon–Sat; entrance fee; tel: 24-342326) has now been set up for lace and the region's equally famous silver work.

The **Tou Timiou Stavrou** (Holy Cross) church contains an exquisite silver cross, dating from the 13th century, which is the focal point of the annual Festival of the Holy Cross held on 13–14 September.

It is worth visiting **Kato Lefkara** to see the 12th-century, mid-Byzantine frescoes in the **Archangel Michael** church. In 1865 a cache of sacred objects, including a bishop's mitre, was found in a hiding place under the floor. The items date from 1222, when the bishop of Limassol was banished here.

BELOW: welcome to Stavrovouni.

The monastery of Stavrovouni

Take a steep, winding asphalt road to reach the oldest monastery on the island – the **Stavrovouni monastery** (the Mountain of the Cross; open Sept–Mar 8am noon, 2–5pm, Apr–Aug 8am–noon, 3–6pm) – which lies at 668 metres (2,192 ft) above sea level.

Women are prohibited from entering the monastery, as indicated by the sign at the start of the ascent, where the venerable monk, Father Kallinikos, paints and sells superb icons in a little hut. Photographic equipment has to be surrendered at the entrance to the monastery, and taking pictures is also forbidden on the stretch of the approach road which borders military territory.

By the last S-bend before reaching the monastery there is a small **chapel**. Beyond the monastery gate, a steep set of steps leads past the gardens to the monastic cells and the main church. Below and to the left of the fortified complex, is the **Constantine and Helena chapel**. This was constructed in the 17th and 18th centuries, virtually on the foundations of the main church.

The Empress Helena, mother of Constantine the Great, is regarded as the founder of the monastery. According to the legend, she was stranded here in AD 327 in the course of a return journey from Jerusalem, and erected a cross made from cypress wood on the monastery hill. The cross was supposed to contain a nail from the cross of Jesus, and was therefore preserved as a relic. It is is said to have hung freely over the earth, without any form of suspension, until it was stolen by invading Mamelukes. Today a splinter of this cross is preserved in a silver cross in the church.

The view on a clear day from the monastery hill to the Troodos Mountains and over the extensive Mesaoria Plain to the Mediterranean is magnificent.

Map on page 144–5

It is worth organising your trip from Larnaka to the Stavrovouni monastery so that you can also visit the Chapelle Royale just outside Pyrga.

BELOW: icon painter Kallinikos plies his trade.

Chapelle Royale

The **Chapelle Royale** (Royal Chapel; open daily; entrance fee) lies just outside the village of **Pyrga** ⑲. This small place of prayer, which is dedicated to Agia Ekaterina (St Catherine) and was extensively restored in 1977, acquired its name when, in 1421, the identity of its founder was confirmed to be the Latin king Janus (1398–1423). Janus and his wife, Charlotte of Bourbon, can be recognised on one of the paintings, in which they are depicted kneeling on either side of the crucified Christ and wearing crowns. In addition, the coat of arms of the House of Lusignan appears on the ribs of the vaulting. Other scenes, of Mary and the baby Jesus, the raising of Lazarus, the Last Supper, the washing of Christ's feet, and Christ's ascension, are all easily recognised. Each scene is supported by inscriptions in old French, spoken in Cyprus at the time. Of the three doors that originally led into the little vaulted building, which had no apse, two were later walled in. On the lintel above the southern entrance is a representation of a wheel, the emblem of St Catherine. About 6 km (4 miles) southeast of Pyrga you can see the ruins of a Cistercian monastery.

Classical styles are still popular when it comes to pottery.

BELOW: picturesque village of Pyrga.

Kornos and Kiti

It is also worth making a detour to **Kornos** ⑳, just west of Pyrga and not far from the motorway. Kornos is a centre for ceramic production, in particular the large jars known as *pitharia*, formerly used for storing water, oil and wine, and now used mostly as oversized flower pots.

In the village of **Kiti** ㉑, the descendant of the ancient settlement of Kition, you can find the **Panagia Angeloktistos** church (literally "built by the angels"; open daily 8am–noon, 2–4pm; free). From an Early Christian basilica, which

Map on page 144–5

once stood here, only the apse now remains, on to which a domed cruciform church was added in the 11th century – itself later rebuilt. Amazingly, the 6th-century mosaic decorations in the earlier apse have survived. They show the standing figure of Mary, with the baby Jesus on her arm, flanked by the two archangels, Michael and Gabriel. Although this motif dates from the time when the theological controversy about the worship of idols (known as the "iconoclastic controversy") had been settled, the style of the portrayal of the figures along the arch of the apse (first discovered in 1952) suggest that it came from an earlier period. Indeed, so imposing is the style of the mosaic that it has been compared with those of the 6th-century Byzantine emperor, Justinian, Empress Theodora and their courtiers at the Church of San Vitale in Ravenna, Italy.

Later pictorial representations, such as frescoes from the mid-18th century, can be found in the church of **Agios Georgios of Arpera**, 2 km (1 mile) northeast of Kiti, not far from a dam on the River Tremithos. The church's founder, the Greek dragoman Christophakis, immortalised himself and his family here, in a picture that hangs over the northern portal.

Place of pilgrimage

Hala Sultan Tekkesi ㉒ (open daily; free but donations expected) lies within sight of the international airport at Larnaka, on the southern shore of Larnaka Salt Lake. (*Tékké* is the Turkish term for a Muslim monastery). Umm Haram, the holy woman associated with the site, is reputed to have been an aunt of the prophet Mohammed, on his father's side.

Accompanying her husband on the Arab invasion of Cyprus in AD 674, she fell from her mule, broke her neck and died. It was her tomb that gave the

BELOW: looking across the lake to Hala Sultan Tekkesi.

Map on page 144–5

mosque (constructed over her burial place at a later date) its import as a place of pilgrimage for Muslims. Umm Haram is known reverently by the Turkish population as *hala sultan* ("great mother").

Another tomb lies in a neighbouring room. Buried under an alabaster cenotaph with golden inscriptions is Chadija, the grandmother of the late King Hussein of Jordan. Chadija died in Cyprus in 1930. The picturesque mosque, situated in a palm grove with fountains, owes its appearance to the Turkish governor of 1816.

In **Larnaka Salt Lake** ㉓, which borders the mosque to the east, you can see colonies of flamingos and migrating birds in winter. Fortunately the birds remain unaffected by the salt-mining once practised here as extraction was confined to the period from the middle of summer to the onset of the autumn rains. But the noise and pollution from encroaching Larnaka and the nearby international airport are environmentally most unfriendly, and could be responsible for the decline in the number of flamingos. The summer heat causes the water to evaporate and the level to fall so low that the salt crust residue could be mined. The export of salt was a flourishing business in the time of the Franks in the Middle Ages. The practice was stopped when it was discovered that emissions from the airport pollute the salt.

On the left, a few hundred metres along the approach road from the airport to the *tékké*, archaeological digs have been underway since 1972. A Swedish team is uncovering the remains of a Middle and Late Bronze Age settlement, thought to have rivalled Kition in importance. Among the most interesting discoveries is a bathing area, otherwise unknown in Cyprus in this period, and Cypro-Minoan inscriptions.

In 1978 a treasure trove containing 23 objects of solid gold came to light. Some of these pieces – into which agate, carnelion and rock crystals had been intricately worked – show distinct Egyptian influences. Informative documentation of the archaeological findings is provided in the museum at Larnaka Fort. According to this, the area was settled around 1600 BC and developed steadily until its abrupt destruction in the early 12th century BC, when it was swallowed up by the severe earthquake that destroyed Egkomi and Kition. ❑

RIGHT: time to sit and reflect.

LARNAKA AND THE SOUTHEAST

Larnaka has managed to retain some of its historic character, despite its popularity as a gateway for tourists to the holiday resorts of southeastern Cyprus

Maps:
Area 174
City 176

After Nicosia and Limassol, Cyprus's third-largest city is **Larnaka ❶**. The major port of Kition *(Citium* in Latin, *Kittim* in the Old Testament) is known to have occupied the site of today's Larnaka, though extensive urban development has prevented archaeologists from uncovering more than a small part of Kition's remains. The ancient tombs which were found here seem to be the source of the city's modern name: Larnaka comes from *larnax*, a Greek word for sarcophagus. During the period of Frankish rule, when the salt mines in the large salt lake west of the port were its main source of industry, the town was known as "Salines" or "Salina".

Port town

Today oil is the city's main export. The second-largest port on the island, Larnaka serves as an important berth for tankers. Larnaka is also popular with yacht owners on account of its relatively cheap charges for winter mooring.

Under the Ottomans, Nicosia was the island's capital but most of the consulates and embassies were based in Larnaka, along with representatives of foreign trading companies. With 13,000 inhabitants, Larnaka was even larger than the capital for a short time. Reminders of that period are the 33 arches on the road to Limassol that formed part of an aqueduct built between 1746 and 1750 by the Ottoman governor. This 10-km (6-mile) pipeline, fed by springs not far from the River Tremithos, supplied water to Larnaka until 1939.

Larnaka city

The events of 1974 brought profound changes to the city. Following the closure of Nicosia's international airport, the airport at Larnaka was developed to take its place. Thousands of Greek Cypriot refugees arrived from the occupied north of the island. Despite the migration of the city's Turkish residents in the opposite direction, the net effect was to treble the city's population to its current 70,500. The Turkish community had settled mainly in the coastal areas in the southern parts of the city, as the street names testify. The fort marked the northern boundary of this area. Opposite the fort, you can still see the **Djami Kebir ❹**, the "large mosque", which had previously been the Latin Holy Cross church.

The city's main thoroughfare is the wide coastal road (known at its beginning as Leoforos Athinon, and further up as Odos Ankara), which stretches southwards from the port and the marina to the

PRECEDING PAGES: inside Agia Napa monastery. **LEFT:** Agios Lazaros church (interior) and (**BELOW**) the entrance.

fortress. In its northern part it is an attractive seafront promenade, bordered by palm trees, ornamental streetlamps, and chic cafés with outdoor terraces. Parallel to the coastal road is an inviting (and usually crowded) sandy beach.

The southern end of the beach and the promenade is marked by **Larnaka Fort** ❸ (open Mon–Fri; entrance fee). According to inscriptions above the entrance, this fort was constructed in 1605. Early in the 20th century, during the period of British rule, prisoners were interned here. In one of the buildings there is a small **Medieval Museum**, whose exhibits include documentation on the Swedish excavations from Hala Sultan Tekkesi. The inner courtyard of the fortress sometimes serves as an excellent open-air theatre.

If you make your way to the north of the fort, away from the coastal road and towards the centre of the city, you will arrive at the church of **Agios Lazaros** ❻ after a few hundred metres. The extension of this street to the west leads on to the church of **Agia Faneromeni** ❼, built in 1907. It has two ancient stone graves but these are likely to interest only real enthusiasts of antiquity.

In the former church, the Lazarus whom Christ resurrected from the dead is supposed to be buried in an accessible crypt to the right of the main altar. After the miracle, the resurrected Lazarus is said to have travelled to Cyprus where he was ordained as a bishop by St Barnabas. According to the legend, Lazarus served as a bishop for a further 30 years.

Icons of the saint are carried through the streets in an annual procession on the Sunday before Easter. The sacred building over the tomb, a multi-domed mid-Byzantine church, was founded by Emperor Leo VI (886–912), following the discovery, in 890, of a stone sarcophagus bearing the name "Lazarus". The relics of the saint were immediately transported to the Byzantine capital, Con-

A marble bust of Kimon, the Athenian commander who, in 450–449 BC, attempted to regain Cyprus for the Greeks, and who died on the island during his campaign, stands on the Larnaka waterfront.

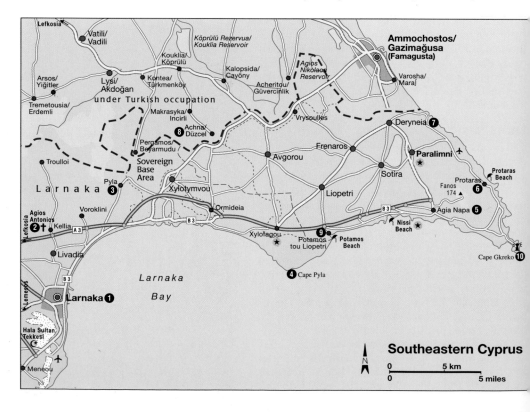

Southeastern Cyprus

stantinople. From there, in 1204, they were taken by plundering crusaders to Marseille, the French city which also claims Lazarus as a former bishop.

After the Ottoman conquest of Cyprus, the Christians succeeded, in 1589, in buying the church back. It underwent extensive restoration in the 17th century, and was extended by the addition of a bell-tower. Among the most notable features of the church are its baroque, wood-carved iconostasis, and the Corinthian capitals at the base of the vaulted roof.

Behind the church is a small cemetery in which privileged 19th-century European diplomats and businessmen are buried. One of the most notorious foreign representatives, holding the offices of both American and Russian consul at the same time, was Luigi Palma di Cesnola. This accredited diplomat, who had been working in Cyprus since 1865, took treasures from a number of ancient graves in Larnaka and the surrounding area with the full permission of the Ottoman authorities. He exported his valuable discoveries abroad, mainly to the United States. The Cesnola collection now forms a large part of the stock of the New York Metropolitan Museum of Art.

A trio of museums

Continuing inland along Odos Agiou Lazarou and Odos Stadiou brings you to Larnaka's **Municipal Park** ❺, a fairly small triangle of trees, grass and flowers that makes a good place of escape from the summer sun. Embedded in the park is the **Museum of Natural History** (open Tues–Sun; entrance fee; tel: 24-652569), which counts among its exhibits a number of interesting dioramas, including one of pink flamingos at Larnaka Salt Lake in winter.

A local amateur archaeologist and art collector, Demetrios Pierides (1811–95)

Map on page 176

Larnaka seafront promenade is a popular place for a stroll.

BELOW: the tomb of Agios Lazaros.

Pierides Museum: a rare 19th-century home which houses an interesting and varied collection.

created a remarkable private museum in Larnaka, the **Pierides Museum** ⑤ (open daily; entrance fee; tel: 24-817868). The collection of exhibits, extending from the Early Stone Age to medieval times, is housed in the family's private house at 4 Odos Zinonos Kitieos, one of the few remaining examples of resplendent 19th-century villas in the town.

The **Larnaka Archaeological Museum** ⑥ (open Mon–Fri, closed Thur afternoon in July and Aug; entrance fee; tel: 24-304169) in Plateia Kalogrenon is hard-pressed to compete with the rich and representative collection in the Pierides Museum. Nevertheless it is worth a visit. Among the ceramics and smaller objects in the display cases on the right of the entrance room, and the free-standing statues to the left, are a number of exquisite exhibits.

To the right of the museum is the Catholic **Convent of St Joseph** ⑥, built in 1848, with an impressive wrought-iron fountain.

Kition

In the open-air area behind the museum are excavations of the ancient city of Kition. Archaeologists believe they have discovered the acropolis of the city, although only a few relics have survived. Unfortunately the British forces levelled the hill of ruins – known to the locals as Bamboula – in 1879 to obtain the materials needed to reclaim a marshland area on the island.

BELOW: large congregations gather in Agios Lazaros church.

Excavations at other sites in the northern part of Larnaka have led to the discovery of a number of remains from the ancient city of **Kition** ❶ (open Mon–Fri 3–5pm, except July and Aug; entrance fee) – for example, at the junction of Odos Agiou Epiphaniou and Odos Kimonos. The main archaeological area, however, lies further north, and includes, along with the foun-

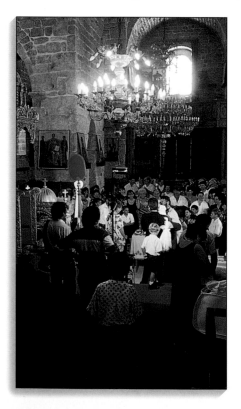

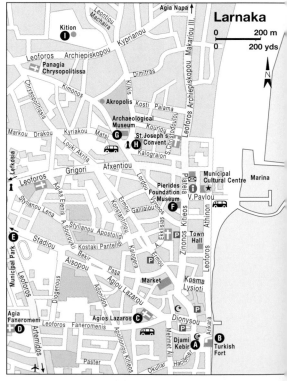

dations of an important temple, a bronze-processing factory. Cyprus was an important supplier of copper during the 2nd century BC, particularly for the Hittite Empire in Asia Minor (in whose cuneiform script the island appears as *Alaschia*), but the bronze-processing factory in the north of Kition is more recent than that.

The excavation area is very confusing for visitors as a result of the various building phases from different historical periods which lie next to and on top of each other. For example, the original shrine from the Bronze Age was replaced by a temple for the goddess Astarte when the Phoenicians settled here in the 10th century BC and developed the city as an export harbour. The new temple quickly acquired importance well beyond the region. After being rebuilt a number of times it finally burned down in 312 BC.

The Phoenicians extended their power over the island, from Kition outwards. In the 5th century BC they were able to conquer a number of other local city-kingdoms such as Idalion, Tamassos, Golgoi, Amathous and, between 450 BC and 411 BC, Salamis. Their success was due not least to the support of their Persian allies. Zeno (*circa* 336–264 BC), the founder of the philosophical school of Stoicism, was also born in Kition *(see page 33)*.

Archaeologists distinguish between three main periods in the history of Kition. The first phase, characterised by two temples with altars, separated by an artificially watered **Holy Grove**, probably began in the early 13th century BC and ended with the city's destruction around 1200 BC. The city was then re-built by the Mycenaeans. On the site formerly occupied by the shrine a large **temple complex** was built, measuring 34 metres (110 ft) by 22 metres (72 ft), thereby making it one of the largest of the Late Bronze Age temples in Cyprus.

Map on page 176

Just in case you forget that you're in the Mediterranean.

BELOW: older Larnaka residents have witnessed many changes to their home town.

Map on page 174

Between the temple and the nearby city wall there were extensive copper and bronze-processing plants which were directly accessible from the temple. In other shrines, which have been excavated a little to the east of the main temple, ivory carvings and the skulls of bulls have been discovered. The seafaring population, who lived from the export of copper, gave a stone anchor as an offering.

Although the city was rebuilt after severe damage, following the earthquake of around 1075 BC it was virtually depopulated. The third and last phase of the city's history was heavily influenced by the Phoenician invaders who built the large **Astarte temple**. The Phoenicians took advantage of the favourable location of the city and turned it into a naval base. The extent to which the Assyrians had previously influenced the history of Kition can only be guessed: a basalt stele of the Assyrian king Sargon II (721–705 BC), on which he boasts about his power over the island, was discovered here. This now lies in a museum in Berlin.

Byzantine frescoes

The church of **Agios Antonios** ❷, which lies on a hill to the north of Larnaka, is worth a visit on account of its mid-Byzantine frescoes. The oldest of the wall paintings date back as far as the early 11th century, making them some of the earliest Byzantine frescoes in Cyprus.

If you travel along the bay of Larnaka from the main city to the east, you can reach the village of **Pyla** ❸ by leaving the coastal road at the vortex of the bay and turning north. Pyla has achieved a degree of fame since the Turkish invasion in 1974: here, right on the Greek-Turkish demarcation line, is the only place on the island where the Greek Cypriot and Turkish Cypriot populations still live side by side, albeit under the supervision of the UN peacekeeping force. The village square has both a Greek *kafeneion* and a Turkish coffee shop. In the upper floor of a restaurant a blue-helmeted member of the UN peacekeeping force keeps guard, whilst on a rock spur directly above the village the Turkish military has set up a colossal silhouette of a Turkish soldier ready for battle with fixed bayonet.

You come to the cape of the same name, **Cape Pyla** ❹ on the far side of Larnaka Bay. ❑

RIGHT: Larnaka's old port, still thronging with boats.

AGIA NAPA

Since the 1970s, the formerly tranquil fishing village of Agia Napa has been turned into a typical Mediterranean hotel city and is now one of the hottest spots for clubbing

Map on page 174

The Cypriots call the flat expanse of land south and southwest of Famagusta, the Kokkinochoria, "the red villages". Nowadays, the name tends to conjure thoughts of the sunburnt tourists who populate its beaches, but initially it came from the fertile *terra rossa*, the soil tinged red by the presence of large amounts of iron and other metallic oxides.

At the beginning of the 1970s there was little here apart from potato crops. Visitors might have explored the coast to the west and north of Cape Gkreko with its string of idyllic sandy bays, and those interested in religious art and local crafts would have found the 16th-century monastery at **Agia Napa** ❺, the pretty village churches of **Liopetri**, **Sotira** and **Frenaros**, the 16th-century church of **Agios Angonas** (near Ormideia on the road to Avgorou) and the basketmaking community of Liopetri.

The southeast corner of the island was at that time little more than an unexciting hinterland for the tourist centre of the then undivided Cyprus, the hotel suburb of Varosha in the south of Famagusta.

A twofold invasion

None of the other formerly rural areas was transformed so thoroughly by the events following the Turkish invasion of 1974. The strengthening links with the urban centre of Famagusta were suddenly impeded by an impregnable demarcation line. The suburb of Varosha is today a ghost town, serving only as a pawn of the Turkish Cypriots in their negotiations with the Greek Cypriots. Its buildings are falling to pieces after decades of neglect.

By far the most important result of the invasion and division of the island, however, was the influx of refugees from the area around Famagusta. It led to a sudden quadrupling of the resident population. Large refugee settlements were created near the formerly rural villages and in the open countryside, for example in **Vrysoulles**. Within sight of their former home of Acheritou, now on the Turkish side of the border, nearly 2,000 refugees were given new detached family houses. Many of the refugees were soon able to find employment. To compensate for the demise of Famagusta and Varosha, hotels began to spring up like mushrooms in the latter part of the 1970s, in particular in Agia Napa, Paralimni and **Protaras** ❻.

Migrant workers

A third of Cyprus's tourist industry is concentrated here. The booming construction and tourist industries have long since absorbed all the local workers and consequently the town must draw on a daily influx of commuters from the economically depressed Turkish-

LEFT: Nissi beach, near Agia Napa. **BELOW:** the tourist industry has taken over this part of the island.

Agia Napa offers plenty of fun for children.

occupied part of the island. No one really knows how many commuters there are – especially now that the borders are in effect open – but what is clear is that though the borders were once almost hermetically sealed to all but the migrant workers, the now allowable two-way traffic through two crossing points near Agia Napa is bound to have a positive effect on the economies of both sides of the slowly fading dividing line.

Away from the beach

Agia Napa's leading, indeed almost its only, historical attraction is its 16th-century **monastery**, sandwiched between pizza parlours and boutiques, and the **Folk Museum** with its samples of prehistoric threshing boards. Supporting its firm commitment to the sea, Agia Napa has developed a number of maritime attractions. Cyprus's highly regarded and culturally highbrow Pierides Foundation has established a **Marine Life Museum** (open Mon–Sat; entrance fee; tel: 23-723409) on the premises of Agia Napa Town Hall. Such sedate attractions can't, however, disguise the fact that Agia Napa has become one of the hottest party and rave scenes in the Mediterranean, where the music and action doesn't stop from April to October.

Demarcation line

BELOW: you'll find no shortage of bars and bright lights.

There is hardly anywhere better than the surrounds of Agia Napa to appreciate the division of Cyprus. From a high platform at a café on the northern outskirts of **Deryneia** ❼, you can look with binoculars across the demarcation line, past Greek Cypriot, UN and Turkish positions, to the ruined hotel towers of **Varosha**, the abandoned suburb of Famagusta. The 33 hotels that line the long narrow

beach are derelict but the return of Varosha is an issue to which Greek Cypriots attach a symbolic value that transcends even the practical benefits of reset-
tling its 40,000 former residents here – an aspiration that could be realised only
after rebuilding the whole town. For the time being, however, it remains a nego
tiating pawn and figures high on the agenda of intercommunal discussions.

Anyone making the trip along the demarcation line on the former connecting
road between Larnaka and Famagusta, should also take a look (from a distance)
at the deserted village of **Achna** ❽, immediately behind the Turkish positions.

Near Achna the Turkish Green Line borders the territory of the British military
base of Dhekalia, one of two on the island. Here is a miniature Britain, complete
with a military hospital, housing estates, a golf course, clubs and pubs.

Not many visitors go to Agia Napa to immerse themselves in Cyprus's tragic
recent history. West of the resort, at **Makronisos Beach**, surrounded by toast-
ing bodies, there is a complex of Hellenistic and Roman rock tombs (open permanently; free), whose excavation was paid for by local hoteliers. Just 4 km
(2½ miles) further west on the Larnaka road is **Potamos tou Liopetri** ❾ fishing harbour, a typically colourful Mediterranean scene, with a fine family-run
seafood restaurant beside the boats.

Going east from Agia Napa, but still within cycling or even walking range, is the
scenic **Cape Gkreko** ❿, a great place for snorkelling and scuba-diving. Unfortunately the cape's tip is occupied by military satellite communications gear.

The cape can be reached on foot in just under two hours from Agia Napa, but
sections of the path cross quite rough ground. There is no proper footpath along
the east coast to Protaras and Pernera. Some of the testing trails around the
cape are popular with off-road motorbike riders.   ❑

**Map
on page
174**

TIP

The Agia Napa area
offers beach holidays
with every possible
amenity, but if you're
looking for isolated
bays, traditional
villages and authentic
cuisine, you should
probably head
somewhere else.

BELOW: home of
Cyprus potatoes.

WINDMILLS AND LIMESTICKS

The red soil of this area made Kokkinochoria one of the
richest agricultural regions on the whole island. Water
used to be abundant here. Creaking wind pumps, a feature
typical of the region, drew water from under the ground
and it was even stored in a lake during the winter. But
intensive agriculture has caused the water table to sink
and for many years now the area has needed the added
benefits of artificial irrigation. Most of the windmills have
long since been replaced by motor pumps drawing water
from deep bore holes. And today water is received mainly
via a pipeline from a new dam upstream from Limassol.
The farmers of Avgorou and Xylofagou have specialised in
growing potatoes and now harvest up to three crops a
year. Growing demand made the Cyprus potato one of the
island's most important exports. However, in recent years
competition from low-cost countries has caused production to slump.

A less palatable export from this area is pickled birds.
Migratory birds like to stop and rest here but for some,
especially the small fig-eating Blackcaps, this is fatal. Leg-
islation has been passed outlawing the use of limesticks
and fine mesh nets to trap the exhausted birds, but with a
ready market the cash rewards are a tempting incentive.

PAFOS AND THE WEST

For anyone wanting to trace the Hellenistic and Roman worlds of Cyprus, Pafos will provide some of the highlights of their tour. This is also an area of considerable scenic beauty

Map on page 188

The Pafos district, in the west of Cyprus, can look back on a truly glorious past. In the ancient world **Pafos** ❶ (Paphos), a centre for the fertility rituals of the goddess Aphrodite, became a centre of pilgrimage for the entire Hellenistic world. "The Paphian" was one of several names given to Aphrodite. According to mythology, she rose out of the foaming waves off the coast. Here, more than in any other area of Cyprus, you continually encounter spectacular evidence of the past, and no doubt the earth hides further treasures for archaeologists to discover in the future.

Craggy coast

The beauty of this area lies particularly in the dramatic changes that occur between its craggy coastline, steeply terraced vineyards, and the dense pine forests on the slopes of the Troodos Mountains. As the moist west winds from the sea get trapped on the edges of these mountains, this part of Cyprus gets more rainfall than the eastern or central areas. Bizarre cloud patterns decorate skies even in summer. The sea wind brings a warm, even climate to the coastal plain, so bananas and other tropical fruits thrive. The Troodos Mountains also form a natural barrier with the rest of the island.

In the 19th century the Pafos district had a reputation for lawlessness. Livestock rustling, which was common, sometimes led to bloody family feuds.

The district remained virtually untouched by the modernisation and industrialisation which had such a far-reaching effect on Nicosia and Limassol. Instead it remained a somewhat backward, poor hinterland, from which many people began to migrate. Pafos became the most sparsely inhabited district in Cyprus: in 1982 it was home to just nine percent of southern Cyprus's population.

All that changed with the opening of Pafos International Airport in 1984 and the rapid development of tourism. Nowadays Pafos ranks a close third behind Agia Napa/Protaras and Limassol in terms of the number of hotel beds, and it is developing at a faster rate.

A journey through the Pafos area provides insights into the variety of settlements in Cyprus, and into modern-day rural life. Nowhere else on the island is as interesting in this regard. Rich agricultural villages, dilapidated mountain settlements, communities destroyed by earthquakes, Turkish Cypriot villages sliding into ruin, refugee settlements and smart holiday villages are all here.

Pafos is one of the smallest of the Cypriot district capitals, with just 40,000 inhabitants. The urban communities in the surrounding countryside amount to a further 20,000 people.

PRECEDING PAGES: bringing in the grapes.
LEFT: Tombs of the Kings, Pafos.
BELOW: vineyards near Pafos.

Western Cyprus

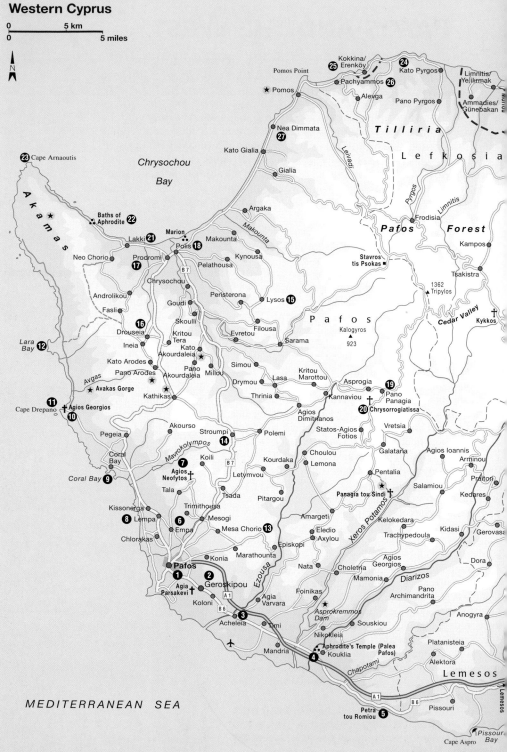

0   5 km

0   5 miles

N

Cape Arnaoutis 23

Chrysochou

Bay

Pomos Point

Kokkina/Erenköy 25   24 Kato Pyrgos

Pachyammos 26

Limnitis/Yeşilırmak

Pomos ★

Alevga

Pano Pyrgos

Ammadies/Günebakan

Nea Dimmata 27

Tilliria

Kato Gialia

Lefkosia

Gialia

Akamas

Baths of Aphrodite 22

Argaka

Leivadi

Frodisia

Pafos   *Forest*

Lakki 21   Marion

Polis 18   Makounta

Makounta

Kampos

Neo Chorio   Prodromi 17

Kynousa

Stavros tis Psokas ■

Tsakistra

Androlikou

Chrysochou

Pelathousa

Peristerona

Fasli

Goudi

Skoulli

Filousa

Lysos 15

Pafos

1362 ▲ Tripylos

Cedar Valley

Drouseia 16

Kritou Tera

Evretou

Sarama

Kalogyros 923

Kykkos †

Lara Bay 12

Ineia

Kato Akourdaleia ★

Simou

Kritou Marottou

Kato Arodes

Pano Akourdaleia

Millou

Drymou

Lasa

Kannaviou

Asprogia

Pano Panagia 19

Pano Arodes

Avakas Gorge ★

Kathikas

Thrinia

Agios Dimitrianos

20 Chrysorrogiatissa

Cape Drepano 11   10 Agios Georgios

Akourso

Stroumpi

Statos-Agios Fotios

Vretsia

Pegeia

14

Polemi

Choulou

Galataria

Agios Ioannis

Armminou

Coral Bay

Mavrokolympos

Koili 7

Kourdaka

Lemona

Pentalia

Praitori

Coral Bay 9

Agios Neofytos †

Letymvou

Panagia tou Sindi †

Salamiou

Kedares

Tala

Tsada

Pitargou

Kissonerga

Trimithousa

8 Lempa

Mesogi 6

Mesa Chorio 13

Amargeti

Kelokedara

Kidasi

Gerovasa

Empa

Eledio Axylou

Trachypedoula

Chlorakas

Konia

Marathounta

Episkopi

Nata

Agios Georgios

Dora

Pafos 1

2

Geroskipou

Choletria

Mamonia

Diarizos

Anogyra

Agia Parsakevi †

Koloni

Agia Varvara

Foinikas

Pano Archimandrita

Acheleia 3

Timi

Asprokremmos Dam

Souskiou

Platanisteia

Nikokleia

Aphrodite's Temple (Palea Pafos)

Mandria

4 Kouklia

Chapotami

Alektora

Lemesos

MEDITERRANEAN SEA

Petra tou Romiou 5

Pissouri

Cape Aspro

Pissouri Bay

Xeros Potamos

Ezousa

The town of Pafos

Modern Pafos is divided into two distinct parts: the lower town, **Kato Pafos**, with its little harbour, and the upper town, **Ktima**, once the original town centre, which lies to the north on a 170-metre (557-ft) high rocky ledge.

The remains of the ancient city of **Nea Pafos** (New Pafos) are in modern Kato Pafos. Nea Pafos was founded around 320 BC and King Nikokles, the last ruler of the city-kingdom of Pafos, moved the capital here from Palea Pafos (Old Pafos), which is now an archaeological zone around the village of Kouklia, 16 km (10 miles) southeast of present-day Pafos. Shortly after the city's foundation, Cyprus fell into the hands of the Hellenistic Egyptian Ptolemies, and in the 2nd century BC Pafos became the capital of the Ptolemaic governor. After 58 BC, when the period of Roman rule over Cyprus began, Nea Pafos remained the capital as seat of the island's Roman proconsul.

One important event which is said to have taken place here, and which was to be of lasting significance for the Christian world, concerns the missionary work of the apostles Paul and Barnabas: on their visit to Pafos in AD 47 they converted the proconsul Sergius Paulus to Christianity. If this myth is historically true, Cyprus was the first Christian-ruled area. Many of the archaeological treasures of Nea Pafos also date from Roman times. They include the splendid mosaics in the Houses of Dionysos, Theseus, Aion and Orpheus *(see page 191)*.

Kato Pafos

The focal point of life in Kato Pafos is the little **harbour** ❶ with its string of tavernas. The catches of the fishing cutters in the harbour basin are among the largest on the island. Across the harbour lies the **Fort** ❷ (open daily; entrance fee), built in 1592 by the Turks. The new tourist zone of Kato Pafos, complete with hotels, restaurants and discos, stretches along Leoforos Poseidonos away from the harbour, as well as north along the road to Pegeia (Peyia).

The barren, rocky coast is not especially conducive to swimming. All the same, the relatively late development of tourism has led to much better planning. Unlike in Limassol, building here is subject to strict control. Despite this, the coastline north and south of Pafos is rapidly filling with tourist-related developments. There might be a couple of hotels less than would have been the case in "pre-enlightenment" days, but since the space saved is occupied by villas and apartment complexes, the effect in terms of the amount of concrete poured is marginal. Pafos may have some way to go before it reaches the level of over-development of Agia Napa and Limassol, but it's getting there fast. Kato Pafos in particular has a burgeoning, neon-lit nightlife zone, with discos, pubs, fast-food eateries, karaoke bars, and lots of noise and bustle. The entertainment here is fast-paced and can be quite wild on summer evenings, but it tends to stop this side of rowdiness.

The town's Department of Antiquities is permanently holding its breath as excavators on the building sites make potentially valuable discoveries that yield yet more secrets of the distant past.

Map on page 190

A new friend.

BELOW: one of the many tourist-related developments in Pafos.

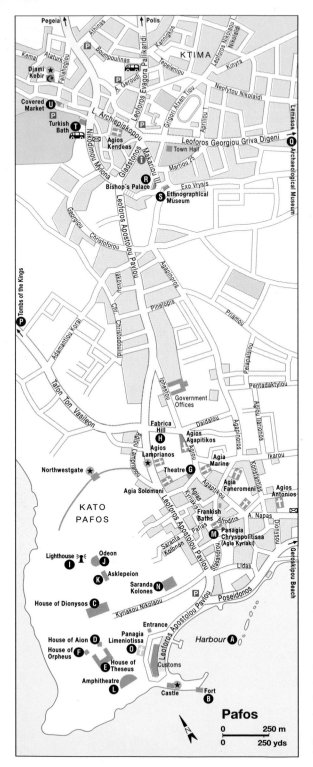

Pafos

0   250 m
0   250 yds

Archaeological Pafos

The ancient city of Nea Pafos covers some 95 hectares (235 acres). The main archaeological area lies to the west of Odos Apostolou Pavlou, which connects Ktima with modern-day Kato Pafos.

Nea Pafos was founded at the end of the 4th century BC by King Nikokles. Shortly after its foundation, Cyprus fell into the hands of the Egyptian Ptolemies. Around the time of the 2nd century BC, Pafos became the new capital of the island. In 58 BC, Cyprus was conquered by the Romans, and thenceforth was ruled by a Roman governor. Pafos remained the capital of the island. The public buildings and the luxurious houses which have come to light during the excavations have revealed the important role played by Pafos during the time of the *Pax Romana*.

Nea Pafos was affected by a number of earthquakes in the 1st century BC and then again during the 1st and 4th centuries AD. In the 4th century, following a series of devastating quakes, the city was razed to the ground, and its inhabitants fled. The city of Salamis was then made the new capital of Cyprus under the name of Constantia.

After the Arab invasions of the island in the 7th century, the decline of Nea Pafos continued at a steady pace, interrupted only by short periods of prosperity during the time of the French Lusignans and the Venetians, when a number of Gothic buildings were constructed. During the Ottoman period (1572–1878) the inhabitants began to migrate to the hinterland – now occupied by the modern town of Pafos (Ktima) – with the result that the coastal region became deserted.

An indication of Nea Pafos's importance was given by UNESCO when it added the entire ancient city to its list of World Cultural Heritage Sites. The excavated Roman villas of Nea Pafos and now part of the Pafos Archaelogical site (open daily June–Sept 8am–7.30pm Oct–May 8am–5pm; one fee covers entry to all sites; tel: 26-940217), with their wonderful floor mosaics, are of particular interest. The most famous are the House of Dionysos, the House of Aion, the House of Theseus and the House of Orpheus. These names were given to the houses by archaeologists, and refer to the figures represented in their respective mosaics.

Map
on page
190

The House of Dionysos ◉

The House of Dionysos came to light in 1962, when a chance discovery of the floor mosaic led to further excavations. The building dates from the end of the late 2nd or early 3rd century. It consists of an *atrium* (courtyard), from which corridors lead off in four directions. The most impressive features are their mosaics of mythological scenes and geometric shapes.

Just to the left of today's entrance is a mosaic from the surrounding area that features a depiction of Scylla, a mythological monster that is part woman, part fish and part dog. It is the oldest mosaic to have been found in Cyprus, and is peculiar in that it is made entirely of black and white pebbles. On the western side of the atrium are four scenes from Greek mythology. The first one on the left shows the death of Pyramus and Thisbe. The next shows Icarus learning the art of wine-making from Dionysos. To the left of Icarus you can see the nymph Akme, and on the right-hand side is a group of figures drinking wine. The neighbouring scene shows Poseidon and Amymone, and in the fourth scene

The large reception or dining hall *(triclinium)* to the west of the atrium shows the reception of the triumphal procession of Dionysos on his return from his Indian adventure. The rest of the room is decorated with scenes from the grape harvest. Other mosaics depict mythical figures such as Narcissus, Hippolytus, Phaedra, Ganymede with the eagle, and allegories of the four seasons.

ABOVE AND BELOW:
mosaics inside the
House of Dionysos.

The House of Aion

Excavations began on the House of Aion in 1983 and have so far uncovered only a small number of rooms. The largest of them, probably the reception hall, is decorated with a large mosaic depicting five mythological themes. The first picture at the top on the left shows the queen of Sparta, Leda, with the scheming Zeus in the form of a swan. In the next picture, at the top on the right, you can see the young Dionysos sitting on Hermes's lap, before being handed over to Tropheus, while the nymphs prepare Dionysos's first bath. The middle – and largest – picture shows a famous beauty competition, known as the Judgement of the Nereid. The winner of this contest is Queen Cassiopeia, who is seen being crowned by a winged female figure. The centre of the ensemble is dominated by the figure of Aion, the symbol of eternal life and judge over all people. The picture at the bottom on the left shows the triumphal procession of Dionysos, although only the chariot has survived the ravages of time. The last picture shows the aftermath of a musical competition between the satyr Marsyas and Apollo, god of music – Marsyas is being led away to his death after losing.

However extensive the development in the rest of Pafos, the headland between the harbour and the lighthouse is unlikely to be touched; the area is thought to contain as many archaeological treasures as it has already revealed.

The House of Theseus

The House of Theseus is near the House of Aion. It was built in the 2nd century and has undergone numerous alterations over the course of the centuries. Its mosaics date from the 3rd and 5th century. Its size and, above all, its architectural plan have led archaeologists to conclude that it must have once served as the residence of a Roman governor. The house consists of a large inner courtyard, from which the rooms radiate.

The most impressive mosaic decorates one of the vaulted rooms on the south

BELOW: the first bath of Achilles, House of Theseus.

side. Dating from the 3rd century, it was restored in the 4th century and has a beautiful geometric motif. The medallion at its centre portrays the battle between Theseus and the Minotaur in the Labyrinth of Crete. Next to this are varied depictions of the island of Crete.

Map on page 190

On the floor of the large room on the southern side of the villa is another interesting picture. This shows the new-born Achilles having his first bath. Next to his parents, Thetis and Peleus, are his two trophies and the three Fates. The mosaic dates from the 5th century.

The House of Orpheus Ⓕ

The House of Orpheus is situated to the west of the House of Theseus. Systematic excavations begun in 1982 have so far uncovered a building with many rooms, which are laid out around an atrium, itself encircled by colonnades (peri-style), with baths in the northeastern corner. The original building dates from the end of the 2nd century or the beginning of the 3rd century – when Nea Pafos was at its zenith. Like most of the buildings in the area, the house was decorated with rich floor mosaics and splendid frescoes.

The most important mosaic decorates a room on the northeastern side. This shows Orpheus with his lyre, surrounded by figures, and playing his heavenly music. The inscription under Orpheus is probably the name of the owner or founder of the house. Two further mosaics, on the floor of a room to the south, are also worth finding. The first shows with impressive simplicity the battle between Hercules and the mythical lion Nemea. The other shows an Amazon standing against a blue background, carrying a horse's bridle in her left hand and a double axe in her right.

BELOW:
taking a break.

The lower rows of seats in the Roman Odeon have been restored.

BELOW: an eager lemon-seller, Pafos.

The public buildings

The **Theatre** (open permanently; free), which lies in the northeastern corner of the old city, above the hill known as **Fabrica** ⓗ, is one of the most important buildings in this region. It is possible to visit the upper rows of the *koilon*, which are carved into the rocks. The lower part of the *koilon*, the orchestra and the stage, were all built out of stone. An inscription on one of the stone seats indicates that the theatre dates from the Early Hellenistic period.

On the western side of Fabrica Hill you can visit a complex of underground chambers (open permanently; free) which have been carved into the rocks. The sheer size of some of these rooms is staggering and their original purpose has never been satisfactorily explained.

Further west still, on the other side of the main road, is the so-called **Guard's Camp** (open permanently; free). This consists of two underground rooms, cut out of the rocks, one of which is rectangular and the other circular. It is thought that they had nothing to do with the camp, but belonged to a subterranean altar from the Hellenistic period.

On the other side of the main street, on a hill, is the **Northern Gate** of Nea Pafos. Another hill in the west can be identified as the **Northwestern Gate**. These gates probably formed part of the city wall which King Nikokles built at the end of the 4th century BC. The wall began and ended at the harbour, and it is still possible to make out its full length. Close to the sea the wall was built from massive stones, augmented in certain places by rock hewn out of the sea bed. In certain places the wall included multi-sided towers.

Not far from the Northwestern Gate you can see both the wall and the towers. Traces of the gate's door have survived, together with the ramp which led to the sea. There are also a number of emergency exits known as sally ports, which connected Nea Pafos with the plain outside.

The hill in the west, where the **Lighthouse** ⓘ now stands, seems to have been the Acropolis of Nea Pafos. To the south of the lighthouse are the remains of some buildings, whilst the Roman **Odeon** ⓙ dating from the 2nd century, lies on the slopes of the hill. The lower row of *koilon* around the semicircular orchestra have been restored. Only the foundations have survived from the stage house *(skene)*. The audience would enter the Odeon via two side entrances and a corridor to the rear of the *koilon*.

To the south of the Odeon you can visit the **Asklepeion** ⓚ which was the healing centre and altar of Asklepios, the god of medicine. A corridor connects this building to the Odeon. Its architectural plan consists of a centrally-located arched hall, surrounded by two rectangular rooms. The building dates from the 2nd century.

The surviving foundations of a row of Corinthian columns reveal that the *agora*, dating from the 2nd century, was located to the east of the Odeon. It consisted of a courtyard with rows of columns. From this courtyard you could ascend, via three steps, to the stoa and the shops, which lay behind. A number of columns, capitals and other remains have survived. A little way to the south of the Odeon-Asklepeion

complex you can find evidence of a small **Hellenistic altar**. All that remains now are its foundations, carved into the rock, and the steps which led up to it.

Beyond the city boundaries to the east is the altar of **Apollo Hylates** (open permanently; free), from the end of the 4th century BC. The altar consists of two rooms, both carved into the rocks. Two engraved inscriptions, one over the entrance and the other on the inside, reveal that the altar was dedicated to the god Apollo. From various inscriptions that have been uncovered we know that Aphrodite, Zeus, Artemis and Leto were also worshipped in Pafos.

Also worth seeing are the remains of the Roman **Amphitheatre** ❶: these consist of a hill with an oval-shaped bowl in the middle, which lies to the north-west of the fort.

Byzantine and medieval

Without doubt the most impressive building of the Early Christian period is the **basilica**, known as **Panagia Chrysopolitissa** ⓜ, in the eastern part of Pafos, adjacent to the modern church of **Agia Kyriaki**. The basilica, an imposing building constructed at the end of the 4th century, has undergone extensive reconstruction. It is one of the largest early Christian basilicas to be found in Cyprus. Originally it had seven aisles, but this number was reduced to five during the reconstruction work of the 6th century. The nave was fitted with a double floor, a characteristic which is found only in Cyprus. Four granite columns still support the eastern part of the roof.

In the western part of the church is the **narthex** and the atrium with a fountain in the middle surrounded by rows of columns. A corridor leads in a south-westerly direction to a building which is thought to have served as a residence

Map on page 190

BELOW: Chrysopolitissa basilica dates from the Early Christian period.

of the bishop of Pafos. The most important decorations in the basilica are the floor mosaics, which date from various periods. They consist mainly of plant and geometrical motifs, but near the shrine three pictures, depicting inscriptions and stories from the Old Testament, have survived from the 4th century.

Many of the floors were provided with new geometrical patterns during the 6th century. The floor of the nave must have been particularly impressive as it was embellished with multicoloured stone slabs *(opus sectile)*. A column on the site known as **St Paul's Pillar** is, according to the legend, said to be the one to which St Paul was tied and scourged.

The basilica survived until the middle of the 7th century, when it was destroyed during the Arab invasions. A small church was then built on the same spot. This was also destroyed, in 1500, in order to make space for the current Agia Kyriaki church.

During the Frankish and Venetian periods (1192–1571) Pafos was the seat of residence of the Latin bishops and, as a result, a number of important new buildings were constructed. One of them lies directly northeast of the Agia Kyriaki. Here are the remains of the **Franciscan church**. From the foundations it is possible to recognise a building with three aisles, which was probably constructed at the end of the 13th century or at the beginning of the 14th century. The architectural feature of two arches above a double column is especially interesting.

On the main road to Kato Pafos are the meagre ruins of the **cathedral of the Latins**, built in the 13th century. All that remains now is its southwestern corner. On the way to the mosaics, on the right-hand side on a hill, are the remains of a medieval castle known as **Saranda Kolones** (open permanently; free),

BELOW: St Paul's Pillar, scene of the saint's beating.

which means "the 40 columns". It was named after the old granite columns that were incorporated into the castle but which previously lay scattered over the area. The central section of the castle is surrounded by a mighty wall and moat. The castle has four massive corner towers. In the central courtyard the roof was supported by arches; some of the *pessoí* (supporting piers) were later converted into toilets.

A large kiln can still be seen. This is said to have served as a heater *(praefurnium)* for water. There are also a number of stalls here. The outer wall was protected by eight towers of different shapes. In the centre of the wall were seven steps which ended in an emergency exit leading to the moat.

We can only speculate about the origins of the castle – we can't even give a date to its construction. We do know that it was devastated by an earthquake in 1222, and that later, in the 13th century, during the period of the Lusignans, it was replaced by a smaller **fort** (open daily; entrance fee) near the harbour. What can be seen here today are the remains of a much more imposing building that was constructed around the core of a Frankish fortress. The Venetians had the fortress extended, but they abandoned the edifice when they realised, in 1570, that they would not be able to defend it from the invading Ottomans. An inscription directly above the main entrance reveals that the fortress was eventually restored by the Turks.

Behind the restaurants at the harbour are the remains of an early Christian basilica, **Panagia Limeniotissa** ⊙, which was probably built in the 4th or 5th century. The building was divided into three aisles by two rows of columns; the narthex and the atrium were to be found in the western section. A number of floor mosaics can still be seen. Particularly worth seeing, in a room in the north-

Map on page 190

Time for a snooze.

BELOW:
the massive arches
of Saranda Kolones.

east of the building, is a wonderful example of an *opus sectile*. The Arabic inscriptions from the second half of the 7th century indicate that the Arabs made use of this room during their periodic invasions.

The Necropolis

According to ancient tradition, cemeteries *(necropoleis)* were always situated outside the walls of a city. In Nea Pafos the enormous necropolis extends from the town in all directions. The graves of the northwestern necropolis are known as the **Tombs of the Kings** ℗ (open daily; entrance fee; tel: 26-306235). The name is an indication of their imposing character rather than a reference to the regality of their inmates. In fact, they were used by the nobles of the Ptolemaic dynasty as family graves. The tombs, which are carved into the rocks, were built over a period of some 600 years, between the 3rd century BC and the 3rd century AD. They are small, cubic graves without any form of decoration. There are over 100 tombs in all, of which the largest display an impressive architectural plan, having been cut into the rocks with the greatest precision.

The two most important **peristyle tombs** can be reached by ascending a flight of stairs that eventually leads into an open central courtyard – the atrium. The tombs are arranged around the courtyard and the columns exemplify the Doric style. Traces of a number of frescoes reveal that the rocks were intricately painted at one time. A neighbouring tomb throws up a different architectural form, consisting of a compact cube in the centre, which is surrounded by wide corridors. Unfortunately, only a small section of the decoration and its coloured stucco has survived.

BELOW: Tombs of the Kings.

The necropolis served as a place of refuge during the persecution of the

island's first Christians. Tomb number 5 was later converted into a kiln and was used for firing medieval ceramics. Tomb number 6, on the other hand, was used as a chapel, and it is from this that the region takes its name, *Palioeklissia*, ("the old church").

Pafos Archaeological Museum

Away from the hustle and bustle of the tourist trade, the **Pafos Archaeological Museum** ⓠ (open daily, to 1pm only on Sat and Sun; entrance fee; tel: 26-940215) is the first large building you encounter as you arrive in the upper town, Ktima, from Limassol.

The first hall of the museum features discoveries from the Neolithic and Chalcolithic periods (8000–2500 BC), the Bronze Age (2500–1050 BC), and metal objects and pieces of golden jewellery from a number of other periods. In the centre of the hall is the mummy of a girl, which dates from the 3rd century BC. This fascinating artefact was discovered in the village of Lempa.

The museum also exhibits an important collection of ceramics from the Chalcolithic period. The ceramics have a red pattern on a white background and are among the earliest and most beautiful such objects to be found on Cyprus. In addition, a collection of surgical tools from Roman times is worth seeing. These items came from a tomb now lying under the Annabelle Beach Hotel.

In Pafos, not all the art is ancient.

In the second hall discoveries from the Geometric (1050–750 BC), Archaic (750–475 BC) and Classical (475–325 BC) periods are displayed. Besides the Cypriot vessels with their beautiful paintings and sculptured decorations, you can see black-on-red receptacles which were imported from Attica. The most significant of the statues are the ones which come from the altar of Aphrodite

BELOW: exhibits inside and out at Pafos Archaeological Museum.

in Palea Pafos, which display characteristics typical of Archaic sculpture. Egyptian, Phoenician and Greek influences can be clearly recognised. The wonderful tomb relief in white marble, only parts of which have survived, is of Greek origin, while the tomb columns to the side come from Cyprus.

In the same room you can see a row of inscriptions in the Cypriot dialect, as well as the spelling of the Greek language spoken in Cyprus before the introduction of the Greek alphabet at the end of the 4th century BC. One of the glass display cases contains a collection of bronze and copper coins, most of which came from the mint in Pafos.

In the third hall there are glass and clay pots, along with sculptures and idols from the Hellenistic (325–58 BC) and Roman (58 BC to AD 330) periods. Two rectangular **sarcophagi** in the shape of a house are particularly impressive. Between them is a lion, another example of Attic work, which was found in Nea Pafos. Amongst the sculptures, the beautiful **head of the Egyptian Queen Isis**, with its characteristic locks of hair, is outstanding, as is the **statuette of Asklepios**, the god of medicine, which has survived in perfect condition. One of a collection of lamps *(lynchnas)* was modelled in the shape of a ship from the House of Orpheus and features the embossed form of Serapis, the Egyptian deity. In another display cabinet look out for a number of primitive clay "hot-water bottles", which were moulded to the shape of feet, hands and other parts of the body that they might be required to warm.

In the fourth room objects from the Roman and Byzantine periods (4th–10th centuries) are displayed. The local Roman pottery and the Byzantine amphora come from the House of Dionysos. Particularly worth checking out are two marble **trapezophora**. The first shows the drunken Hercules surrounded by

BELOW: covered market in Pafos.

Map on page 190

the Erotidis. The other, only part of which has survived, depicts Orpheus and the beasts. A number of Christian inscriptions in marble, and another in the form of a mosaic are derived from local basilicas. The columns, with their Arabic inscriptions, come from the basilica of Limeniotissa, and are rare evidence of the Arabic presence in Cyprus.

In the last room are discoveries from the Frankish (1192–1489) and Venetian (1489–1571) periods, including a collection of handsome glazed ceramics. One display case contains examples of glazed Cypriot pottery, which was famous in its time. Another features ceramics imported from East Asia, Syria, elsewhere in the Middle East, Italy and Spain.

Also derived from foreign sources is the **Group of Four Angels**, which was discovered during excavations of the Latin church near the church of Agia Kyriaki in Kato Pafos. The angels' bodies are made of limestone, their wings are of terracotta and their decorations of multicoloured marble. The Frankish **tombstones** are also highly important, not least due to their inscriptions, which reveal vital information about the nobles who died in Cyprus.

Ktima offers the quintessential charm of a Cypriot town. Its role as a commercial centre for the area ensures plenty of lively activity.

Ktima

On Leoforos Georgiou Griva Digeni are the particularly striking buildings of the **Gymnasium** (a high school built in 1960), the **Academy of Economics** (former-ly a school that was built in 1928) and the gateway to the stadium.

The school buildings, which are extraordinarily grand for a small town like Pafos, reflect the value which Greek Cypriots continue to place on classical learning. There is also a symbolic dimension: educational institutions here have always been central to Hellenic dreams of liberation. One of the reliefs in the

BELOW: the Pafos Gymnasium.

Map on page 190

Exhibit at the Ethnographical Museum in Ktima.

BELOW AND RIGHT: a couple of local characters.

courtyard of the gymnasium, for example, shows a schoolboy trying to kill a wild lion with a stone. This represents the heroic struggle of young Cypriots against the British colonialists towards the end of the 1950s.

If you turn off towards the town park and the town hall, you come to the **Bishop's Palace** ®. Archbishop Makarios fled here after the Greek officers' coup of 15 July 1974. It was from here that the radio broadcast his historic denial of reports disseminated by the coup's leaders that he was already dead. Pafos's **Byzantine Museum** (open Mon–Sat, to noon only on Sat; entrance fee; tel: 26-931383) is within the grounds of the bishopric. Although not particularly interesting, unless you have an abiding interest in Christian iconography, the museum's collection of icons is nevertheless the most impressive in the Pafos area, with works dating back to the 12th century and a collection of ecclesiastical metal artworks from 17th–20th century.

Not far from the palace, the **Ethnographical Museum** ⑤ (open Mon–Sun, to 1pm only on Sun; entrance fee; tel: 26-932010) is housed in an interesting town house. Its eclectic collection of exhibits ranges from Stone Age artefacts to items representing the present day. One highlight is the museum building's own **chapel**, which is situated in a Hellenistic rock tomb discovered in the basement. An 18th-century wooden bridal chest recalls just one folk tradition that was widespread until the late 20th century.

A little further to the north on a slope below a car park is the recently renovated **Turkish Bath** ⓣ. Until around 1955 this *hamam* was used by both Greek and Turkish Cypriots. In later years there was no such harmonious coexistence: on 7 March 1964 widespread fighting broke out between Greek and Turkish nationalists. There were deaths on both sides and hundreds of hostages were taken. As a result of the battle, the Turkish Cypriots were forced to withdraw to a heavily protected area. A mosque which stood on the square above the Turkish bath was pulled down by the Greeks after Turkish gunmen had fired on civilians from the tower of its minaret.

To the east of the **Covered Market** ⓤ you come into the new part of **Ktima**, with its main shopping street, **Leoforos Archiepiskopou Makariou III**. To the north and northwest of the market the Turkish street signs indicate the former Turkish area. The narrow streets, with their many nooks, crannies and dead ends, used to have a timeless appeal.

Today, however, the commercial centre of Pafos is changing rapidly, with burgeoning shops, shopping malls, workshops, restaurants and cafés occupying the former Turkish buildings (which probably would have collapsed through neglect if they had been left unoccupied). The streets are still narrow, and thus quite unable to cope with modern levels of traffic. If travelling in a car, don't expect to move very fast.

Although some of the old atmosphere can still be appreciated, particularly in the more tranquil side streets, Pafos is a victim of what is euphemistically known as progress. In all likelihood, at some point in the near future, it will probably be realised that Pafos has "developed" into another Limassol. By then it will be too late to do anything about it. ❏

OUTSIDE PAFOS

*Pafos provides an excellent jumping-off point for exploring
the island's "wild west" – towards Limassol via Palea Pafos,
or north to Cape Drepano, Polis and the Akamas Peninsula*

Map on page 188

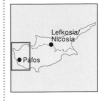

The road from Pafos to Limassol passes through the southern coastal plain, now the most fertile part of the whole region. Fields of bananas, citrus fruits, avocados, grapes, early potatoes, sesame and peanuts flank both sides of the road. All these crops need considerable irrigation. The water is brought from a dam on the lower reaches of the Xeros Potamos (to the west of Kouklia), which is part of the Pafos irrigation project. This, one of the largest such schemes on the island – it covers 5,000 hectares (12,500 acres) – is an ambitious project that was completed in 1974. The profits from the area's production, derived mainly from exports, have led to a substantial improvement in living standards in this formerly economically backward region.

Pafos to the Rock of Aphrodite

Beyond Pafos is the sign for **Geroskipou** ❷ ("Holy Grove"). What was once a tranquil garden on the pilgrimage route from Nea Pafos to Aphrodite's shrine at Palea Pafos, is now a busy suburban village. Only a few decades ago numerous mulberry trees and one of the largest silk-spinning mills in Cyprus were here. Wild fennel still grows in abundance in Geroskipou. Other specialities of the area include Cypriot (or Turkish) delight, the sweet *loukoumia*, which is made from grape syrup, and *halloumi*, a cheese made from the milk of goats that are fed on thyme-rich pastures.

The church of **Agia Paraskevi** (open Mon–Sat 8am–1pm, 2–5pm, Sun 10am–1pm; tel: 26-961859) in Geroskipou is not only a masterpiece of Byzantine sacred architecture, but also one of the most important monuments from the Iconoclastic period (the first half of the 9th century). The church, with its five domes, follows the architectural pattern of Peristerona, and is modelled on the multi-domed 6th-century Justinian church of St John in Ephesus.

In the dome above the sanctuary rare frescoes with Byzantine motifs have survived from the Iconoclastic period. Only a few fragments of frescoes with figures from the end of the 12th century (such as the head from the Assumption of the Virgin on the northern wall, centre aisle) survive. Most of the works from this epoch were painted over in the late 15th century.

Near **Acheleia** ❸ a signpost points to one of the experimental farms run by the Ministry of Agriculture. Projects centre on pig-rearing and attempts to produce exotic fruits. The areas of cultivation formerly belonged to a feudal estate dating from the Lusignan period. Later, in the middle of the 15th century, the Venetians commandeered large areas for growing cane sugar. According to one legend, sweet-toothed buffaloes swam here from Egypt, attracted by the exquisite juice of the sugar cane.

LEFT: icon in the Agios Neofytos monastery.
BELOW: mosaic in Palea Pafos.

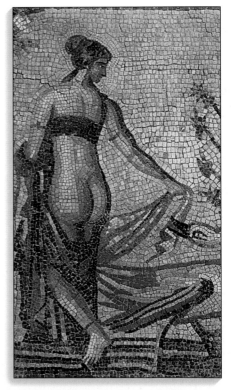

Palea Pafos

Palea Pafos ❹ is situated 16 km (10 miles) southeast of Nea Pafos. According to legend, the city was founded by King Agapenor from Tegea in the Peloponnese. The city owes much of its considerable fame to the Sanctuary of Aphrodite which, according to various writers, including Homer, was the most revered temple of the ancient world.

The Sanctuary of Aphrodite

The temple (open daily; entrance fee; tel: 26-432180) comprises a mixture of buildings from the Late Bronze Age and the Roman period. From the original buildings it is the enormous stone blocks in the southwestern corner which particularly catch the eye. Most of these blocks were drilled through by farmers from the surrounding environs who were searching for the mythical treasure of Aphrodite. A large part of the extant ruins and mosaics come from the construction that took place during the Roman period.

A number of Roman coins and cameos indicate what the temple looked like in its original form. It consisted of three parts, and in the middle there was probably a *baetylos* – an abstract representation of a goddess. According to ancient sources, the cult of Aphrodite was not represented by the statue of a woman. Indeed it is thought that the grey-green conical stone, now in the museum of Palea Pafos, was the symbol of the goddess. Between the temple and the medieval *kastro* (fortress), a path leads in a northwesterly direction into a small **Roman House**, of which only a room with floor mosaics and a bath has been excavated. In the centre of the geometrical mosaics is a picture of Leda and the Swan. This is a copy; the original is kept in the Cyprus Museum in Nicosia.

BELOW: the temple of Aphrodite, Palea Pafos.

Map on page 188

Medieval manor house

During the Frankish period Cyprus became famous for its sugar production. The area around Palea Pafos was one of the biggest sugar cane and sugar-processing centres on the island. The medieval feudal **manor house** (open daily; entrance fee included with Sanctuary of Aphrodite ticket) served as the headquarters of the district administration of the sugar-processing industry. Built in the 13th century, and altered during the period of Ottoman rule, it consists of a large courtyard surrounded by four buildings. On the eastern side, the large rectangular hall, half underground and surmounted by four small cross-vaulted domes, dominates the layout.

The small local museum has two rooms. On the ground floor is a mosaic brought here from a Roman building in Palea Pafos. On the upper floor, above the large rectangular hall, the discoveries from the area around Palea Pafos are arranged in chronological order. In the area around the temple room, and even more emphatically in the neighbouring plain (known locally as Stavros), excavations have unearthed the remains of water mills which are still in good condition. These water mills were used to power the sugar-processing factory.

Banana trees are a rather unexpected sight in the area around Pafos.

Rock of Aphrodite

A few kilometres after the turning that leads to Palea Pafos the fertile coastal plain comes to an end. The road now runs through an area of deserted, barren land along the edge of an imposingly steep coast. A number of enormous rocks and boulders appear below, looking as if they were tossed up by a raging sea. It is behind one of these rocks, **Petra tou Romiou** ❺ (Rock of Romios, but better known as Aphrodite's Rock), that Aphrodite, born from the sea foam, is

BELOW: birthplace of Aphrodite.

supposed to have stepped out of the waves. The view to Petra tou Romiou can be enjoyed from the tourist pavilion lying just inland here.

Pafos to Cape Drepano

From Pafos, roads lead northwards to the cove of Coral Bay and Pegeia village. The villages of Chlorakas, Empa and Kissonerga, along the way, have been swallowed up by the ever more invasive sprawl of Pafos. Extensive developments of holiday homes and apartments spread inland, their charms advertised to sun-hungry northern Europeans by means of massive hoardings. **Panagia Chryseleousa**, a domed cruciform church with a domed narthex extension, lies right in the middle of **Empa ❻**. You can get the key to the church – which contains interesting frescoes from the end of the 15th century and a valuable iconostasis from the 16th century – from the village priest.

Ancient texts at Agios Neofytos.

BELOW: Agios Neofytos monastery.

Further uphill, beyond Tala village, is **Agios Neofytos monastery ❼** (open daily; entrance fee). In 1159 a 25-year-old monk by the name of Neofytos settled as a hermit not far from Pafos. He cut a hermitage in the rock with his own hands, and by about 1200 a sizeable community had evolved around it. Even during his lifetime, the hermitage attracted pilgrims. Neofytos was renowned far and wide for denouncing the injustices of the Byzantine tax collectors. His bones, removed from his tomb in 1750, are in a wooden sarcophagus. His skull is preserved in a silver reliquary.

The rock grotto was painted in two distinct phases and styles at the end of the 12th century. In 1183 artists from Constantinople painted frescoes in the neoclassical style, and then in 1196 the "monastic" frescoes were painted, as was usual in monastic churches then. The paintings in the **Neofytos Rock-**

Map on page 188

Grotto are among the most important on the island. The few paintings from 1503 are in traditional rural character.

In the 16th century a large monastic development, now inhabited by Orthodox monks, was built to the east of the rock face. In the **northern aisle** of the monastic church some artistically valuable frescoes from the beginning of the 16th century have survived. In terms of their style and execution these are excellent examples of Italo-Byzantine art.

At **Lempa** ❽, a handsome little village overlooking the sea that has in recent years become something of an artists' colony, a **neolithic village** (open daily; free) has been excavated. Replicas of the inhabitants' circular dwellings have been constructed on the site. Beyond Kissonerga, the coast road passes through banana plantations.

The beautiful sandy cove of **Coral Bay** ❾ is a good bet to satisfy those disappointed by the quality of beaches near Pafos. But don't expect to find peace and quiet here. Coral Bay, and the neighbouring Corallia Beach, are popular with locals and tourists alike, and are served by a bus that travels to and from Pafos. Indeed, Coral Bay is yet another resort that now features a large tourist complex. Built between the beach and the main road, it has apartments, shops and restaurants, few of which can be recommended.

On the other side of Pegeia, around **Agios Georgios** ❿, you can find quieter beaches and tavernas, some of which have accommodation. **Pegeia** is the focus of intensive villa and holiday-apartment development and, not surprisingly, it has all but lost its village character. Around the central square, however, is a cluster of fine village tavernas. At **Cape Drepano** ⓫ are the excavated ruins of a 6th-century Christian basilica with floor mosaics. There is no public access but they can be seen from behind the surrounding fence.

You can, by contrast, visit the nearby modern church of Agios Georgios (St George), which stands on a clifftop overlooking the sea beside a tiny, and far older **Byzantine chapel** of the same name. Small strips of cloth hung on a nearby tree indicate the chapel's importance in the beliefs of local people. Lovers are supposed to come here to discover the outcome of their amorous affairs. St George is said to help shepherds and goatherds whose animals have gone astray.

Agios Georgios is a good starting point for a tour of the uninhabited **Akamas Peninsula**. This is a difficult journey best undertaken on foot or in a four-wheel-drive vehicle. A bumpy track leads along the coast as far as **Lara Bay** ⓬. Here an ambitious environmental project hopes to conserve the island's endangered green turtles. The track continues northwards before heading inland finally meeting the tarmac again at Neo Chorio village.

Between Pafos and Polis

From Ktima the road winds upwards in a northerly direction into the beautiful Pafian hill country. Wine is the main product of this area's soil. Every turn-off along the road to Polis produces its own special reward: there is nowhere better to see authentic rural life. Be prepared for a degree of adventure – some "roads" turn out to be no more than tracks strewn with

BELOW: St George and the Dragon, church of Agios Georgios.

potholes. Often the only alternative is to walk. The village of **Mesa Chorio**
to the east of the main road by the turn off to the monastery of St Neofytos, was
famous for its camels. The tradition of transporting wine and sultanas to the
coast for shipment to Egypt continued until World War II.

At the large village of **Stroumpi** 🔟 you reach the ridge of the range of hills
separating Pafos from Polis. The wine from Stroumpi has a particularly good
reputation and features in Lawrence Durrell's *Bitter Lemons*. Stroumpi was
also near the epicentre of an earthquake that destroyed large parts of the Pafos
district in September 1953. After the quake the British colonial administration
erected simple prefabricated shacks for the homeless. In recent years the inhabitants who still remained in these huts were given detached family houses by the
Cypriot government.

The two possible routes for continuing to Polis can be combined to make an
interesting circular tour. The first option is via the main road to Polis, which follows the fertile valley of the River Chrysochou, descending all the way. Adventurous travellers may want to make a detour from this route to the east in the
direction of **Lysos** 🔟. In this area of barren but nevertheless dramatic landscape you will come across a series of Turkish settlements which were abandoned by their inhabitants in 1975 in the aftermath of the Turkish invasion.
Slowly but surely, the empty houses are falling into decay.

The alternative route leads from Stroumpi via Kathikas through mountain
vineyards to the ridge of a further range of mountains with excellent views over
the Akamas Peninsula and the western foothills of the Troodos Mountains. The
beautiful village of **Arodes**, with its two communities (Kato and Pano), traces
its name back to the medieval feudal rule of the Knights Hospitaller. The village

BELOW: countryside
near Stroumpi.

was named after the island of Rhodes, where the order had its headquarters.

The village of **Drouseia** ⑯ reflects on an even earlier history: the ancestors of the current inhabitants came here from Arcadia in the Greek Peloponnese. This wave of Arcadian immigrants is responsible for the remnants of Homeric Greek in the Pafian dialect. *Drouseia* is the dialect word for "cool" or "fresh", and indeed a cool wind from the Akamas blows almost constantly through the bizarre rock formations above the village. In the Droushia Heights Hotel it is possible to enjoy this rural idyll in comfortable accommodation.

Hikers should take the little stony road which winds its way from Drouseia into the eastern part of the Akamas via the abandoned Turkish villages of Fasli and Androlikou, and down to **Prodromi** ⑰ and **Polis** ⑱.

The villages at the southern end of the Akamas Peninsula have suffered a massive wave of emigration as a result of the meagre living conditions in the area. An "agro-tourist" project set up by Friends of the Earth will, it is hoped, open up new horizons for communities such as Kathikas, Kritou Tera, Theletra and Akourdaleia. The intention of the project is to promote "gentle tourism". For example, the inhabitants of the villages have been given special low-interest loans to renovate their houses in traditional style so that one part of the renovated building can be rented out to visitors.

By such methods Friends of the Earth hopes to encourage a form of tourism that will be in harmony with the structure of the growing settlements. The other underlying idea is to guarantee that the financial benefits of the tourism industry are enjoyed by as many of the local people as possible.

The lovely village of **Pano Panagia** ⑲ and the nearby **monastery of Chrysorrogiatissa** ⑳ (open daily; tel: 26-722457) make enjoyable destina-

Map on page 188

Carob tree.

BELOW: bindweed in the hedgerows.

tions for day excursions from Pafos or Polis. The journey ascends to more than 800 metres (2,600 ft) to the western edge of the forest belt encircling the Troodos Mountains. Both of the possible routes to Pano Panagia passes through extraordinarily beautiful landscapes. The shortest way from Pafos is via Polemi and past the pretty village of Kannaviou. More impressive, however, is the road winding from the southern coastal plain in the direction of Timi. There are fantastic views over the Xeros Potamos Valley, whose river is one of the few Cypriot rivers not to turn into a desiccated wadi in summer. The villages of **Nata**, **Axylou** and **Eledio** further to the north were destroyed by the devastating earthquake of 1953. Only a few members of the older generation still live in the settlements built by the British following the disaster.

Icons and vineyards

The founding of the monastery of Chrysorrogiatissa in 1182 followed the discovery of an icon. Indeed many other monastic buildings in Cyprus were conceived by such a find. This one is reputed to have been painted by the apostle Luke himself. The current monastery church was built in around 1770, and its splendidly carved iconostasis contains the reputedly miracle-working icon of *Panagia Chrysorrogiatissa*. This somewhat unpronounceable name means "Our Lady of the Golden Pomegranate" and symbolises the nurturing breast of the Virgin Mary. A large part of the monastery had to be rebuilt after a fire in 1966.

One of the main reasons for visiting Chrysorrogiatissa, aside from its historic art, is to enjoy the monastic grounds and their setting. The abbot here has his own vineyards, and the wine he produces is highly regarded by connoisseurs. You can buy it in the monastery itself or in the adjoining taverna.

BELOW:
Chrysorrogiatissa
monastery, near
the village of
Pano Panagia.

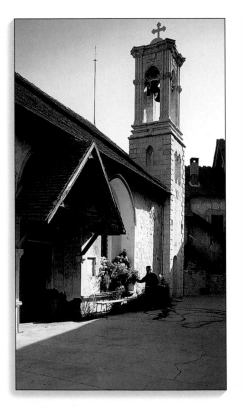

BIRTHPLACE OF AN ARCHBISHOP

The village of Pano Panagia has a particular claim to fame. It was here in 1913 that Michalis Mouskos was born, the eldest son of a farmer and goatherd. His entrance as a novice into the monastery of Kykkos was the first step in what was to be an extraordinary career, during which he was to become "Makarios III", Archbishop of Cyprus and, from 1960 until his death in 1977, the president of the island republic.

Metal signposts in the village point the way to the house of the parents of Makarios III. The traditional architecture of the house, typical of the area, makes a visit especially worthwhile. People and animals alike entered the house through the single door at the front. The whole family lived in the large front room, where you can see a collection of old furniture and ceramics. The smaller room at the rear was used as a stall for the animals. The reasoning behind this design was to make it more difficult for rustlers to steal livestock. A museum (open daily; free) and a larger-than-life sculpture of Makarios are further proof of the pride the inhabitants of Panagia feel for their most famous son.

The important landmarks in the life of this charismatic church leader and statesman are documented with the aid of photographs, mementoes and insignia.

Polis to Akamas

Polis ("city") is the abbreviated version of **Polis Chrysochou** ("city of the golden land"). There are a number of different interpretations of the origin of the eponym golden, all of which probably contain a degree of truth. One cites the extraordinary fertility of the land by virtue of the River Chrysochou, now augmented by water from a number of dams.

The main product of the Lusignans and Venetians was cotton, obtained from the large feudal estates. But the rich copper deposits in the area, which have been mined since ancient times, are another possible explanation for the name. And it is said that veins of gold really were discovered here during the Ottoman period, though they were declared as vitriol for export purposes as a means of evading Turkish tax laws.

A timeless scene of rural life near Pafos.

Golden past

Certainly the region has experienced golden times during its history. The ancient city-kingdom of Marion, founded by Ionian Greeks in the 7th century BC, was located east of Polis. You can see excavated items from the site in Polis's small **Marion-Arsinoë Archaeological Museum** (open Mon–Sat; entrance fee; tel: 26-322955). Look out for: two sets of gold spiral earrings with each piece ending in a woman's head; terracotta funeral statuettes; and a funerary stela from 480 BC of a young woman tenderly holding a bird. By the time of the British takeover there was little sign of economic prosperity. A report of the district commissioner of Pafos in 1879 castigated local highwaymen, robbers and murderers. Another type of larceny was endemic at the end of the 19th century: thousands of ancient tombs were opened and plundered, with their contents invariably being taken abroad.

BELOW: Polis church.

The British travel writer Colin Thubron, who visited Polis during his walking tour of the island in 1972, described it as a desolate, unfriendly spot: "I strolled among an unsmiling people down streets lined with deserted shops and houses with damaged roofs which were hanging down… It was the only town I saw in which the owls dared to come in at evening and cry from the rooftops."

Maybe it is its shabby charm which has made Polis into a last refuge in coastal Cyprus (at least in the south) for those whose idea of fun doesn't involve giant hotels. Polis, however, is building small hotels and holiday villas as fast as concrete can be trucked in, to cater for "alternative" tourists and Cypriots looking for a refuge from foreign tourists. Prices are rising, and though Polis retains some of the quaint good looks and laid-back attitudes that once made it an insider's tip for the backpack set, there's no saying how long that can last.

But as it stands, in Polis you can still find cosy, candlelit tavernas, music from Theodorakis, and laid-back discos. On the beach there is still room to move and the hinterland has a wildly romantic quality. Tourists have brought prosperity, and a large proportion of the population has benefited from the visitors' purchasing power. Polis is making up for lost time to catch up with the rest of Cyprus.

A few miles west of Polis is the Akamas Peninsula, the most westerly part of Cyprus. This stretch of land is named after the mythical son of Theseus, and founder of the city-kingdom of Soli. The untamed landscape, with its steep slopes and deep gorges, is one of the last areas on the island to remain untouched by human hand. Enthusiasts describe it as the last authentically Homeric landscape of the Hellenistic world.

Given its lack of development, the Akamas Peninsula has become a vital haven for all sorts of flora and fauna. Unfortunately the natural qualities of the region are now acutely threatened. Entrepreneurial Cypriots have long since recognised the potential for tourism – particularly on the coasts that feature fantastic sandy bays – and are quickly acquiring the land.

That the further development and eventual destruction of the Akamas Peninsula has so far failed to materialise is due solely to the indefatigable work of Cypriot environmental campaigners. Conservation groups such as the Friends of the Earth have been campaigning for the Akamas, bringing to the attention of the Cypriot people the danger of further environmental destruction on the island. Other organisations have also expressed their concern. The European Union has included the Akamas within its Mediterranean protection programme, and the Cypriot government has announced a long-term intention to turn the area into a national park.

Progress towards this goal is painfully slow, however, and "eventually" seems to recede ever further over the political horizon. In a case that acquired near scandalous proportions in 1997, planning regulations in the Akamas area were "relaxed" by the government to permit the building of a huge resort hotel by a company partly owned by the family of a government minister.

BELOW:
a lane in Polis.

One nature conservation project, with lessons for the entire Mediterranean area, has been underway since the middle of the 1970s: Lara Bay, which lies on the western coastal edge, serves as a breeding ground for two threatened species of turtle (the green turtle and the loggerhead turtle). The Cypriot fishing authorities are collaborating with the World Wildlife Fund for Nature on the Lara Project, which aims to protect the spawning and newly-hatched young turtles – both from natural enemies and unthinking bathers.

Fish tavernas

From Polis the asphalt road runs in the direction of Akamas via the tranquil fishing village of **Latsi/Lakki ㉑** where there are a number of good fish tavernas. Until recently Latsi was a commercial diving base, in particular for diving for sponges.

On both sides of Latsi there are beautiful sand and pebble beaches. Further to the west you come to the **Baths of Aphrodite ㉒**. Underneath a rock overhang, a cool spring emerges from the rocks and pours into a natural pool. It is here that Akamas is said to have caught Aphrodite unawares as she was bathing naked; the goddess is supposed to have fallen in love with the simple-minded voyeur. Others, however, say that the location of this mythical event was an altogether different spring in the far west of the peninsula. Either way, wherever the *fontana amoroza* (fountain of love) is located, those who drink from it are supposed to fall head over heels in love with the next person they see.

The asphalt road ends next to a tourist pavilion near the Baths of Aphrodite. If you happen to be travelling on a motorbike suitable for cross-country treks, you can ride on to **Cape Arnaoutis ㉓**. But if you want to appreciate the

Map on page 188

A restaurant in Latsi advertises its menu.

BELOW: the harbour at Latsi.

unspoilt quality of the Akamas, you should leave your vehicle here and proceed on foot. The scenery is particularly beautiful in spring when the slopes are covered with gorse and sage. For hikers, the Cyprus Tourism Organisation has designed nature trails, complete with information boards.

From Polis to Kato Pyrgos

The coast northeast of Polis, as far as the demarcation line with the Turkish-occupied part of the island near Kato Pyrgos, is the most remote from the cities on the south coast.

Before the division of Cyprus it was possible to get to **Kato Pyrgos** ❷ relatively quickly from Nicosia via Morfou and Karavostasi, but since 1974 the area of northern Tilliria can be reached only via Polis and via a winding route from the Kykkos monastery *(see page 227)*. The border situation has mitigated against excessive development so tourists can still find deserted pebble beaches. In Kato Pyrgos there are three cosy hotels, and in other places private rooms are let.

The coast road to Kato Pyrgos is blocked by the Turkish military enclave at **Kokkina** ❷, and traffic is forced into the Tillirian hills to circle around it, with Greek Cypriot and UN military positions clearly visible on the bare heights. Just before here, at **Pachyammos** ❷, the modern church of Agios Rafaelis has been built in a beautiful location overlooking the sea. Agios Rafaelis is notable for an interior covered with contemporary frescoes.

From Polis you can drive past the now closed administrative buildings and the loading areas of the Limni mine. When, in 1979, the supplies of copper concentrates and iron pyrites were exhausted, the mines were closed down, thus end-

BELOW: beaches close to Pafos, like Coral Bay, are very popular.

ing a centuries old mining tradition that dated as far back as the Roman times.

The road, flanked by farmhouses, proceeds further along a small strip of irrigated land that runs parallel to the coast. It is hard to imagine that the whole coastal area was virtually uninhabited at the beginning of the 20th century. Until then it was mainly the domain of pirates and slave traders.

The local population preferred to settle further inland, in the area of the modern-day Pafos Forest, living from their goats, charcoal burning and other types of forest farming. These ways of earning a living, destructive as they were for the forests, did not meet with the approval of the British Forestry Commission. Whole villages were moved out, including the 14 families from the village of Dimmata. In 1953 they were given arable land and British-style brick houses in **Nea Dimmata** ㉗. These houses are still inhabited today.

Empty villages

The main road now follows a large arc inland to the mountain region, skirting the village of Kokkina. This village was already a refuge for Turkish Cypriots from the Turkish villages of the surrounding area during the Greek-Turkish dispute of 1963–64. The inhabitants of the now empty villages of Alevga, Sellain t'Api and Agios Yeorgoudhi were evacuated to Kokkina by UN troops to protect them from the attacks of General Grivas and his National Guard. The Turks

After the Turkish invasion of 1974 Turkish troops also held the area around Kokkina, even though it wasn't directly connected with the rest of the occupied north. Kokkina, whose civilian population was evacuated to the North, has remained a Turkish enclave guarded by three different border posts manned by Greek, Turkish and UN soldiers. ❏

Map
on page
188

TIP

The last part of the journey to Pyrgos is worth tackling but the border barricades that prevent visitors from travelling along the coast road beyond Pachyammos don't make it easy.

BELOW: the remote Akamas coast is a tranquil location.

AKAMAS PENINSULA – THE WILD WEST

The ruggedly beautiful Akamas Peninsula is one of the last truly natural places in Cyprus. Achieving National Park status would ensure its protection

Covering some 70 sq km (27 sq miles) the Akamas Peninsula juts out into the sea like a mighty bastion defending the natural riches within. Its coastline is jagged and treacherous, while inland forests of Aleppo pine mixed with juniper crown the rough range of hills that runs along the peninsula's spine. Some 530 plant species, almost one-third of Cyprus's indigenous total, grow in the Akamas, and in springtime the colours are those of a giant Expressionist palette. Some 168 species of birds have been observed in the area, and butterflies, snakes and other reptiles are abundant too.

There are those who ply their way wimpishly through this exhilarating landscape by four-wheel drive vehicle, but only your own legs will give you a real taste of the Akamas.

The most popular walks are along two sign-posted trails known as the Aphrodite and Adonis trails, which begin at the Baths of Aphrodite. There are also various unmarked trails, which you can pick up at the Baths, or at Neon Chorion village or Lara Bay, on the west coast. The longest of these take you along the east coast or over the hills past the Fontana Amoroza to Cape Arnaoutis: these are 20–30-km (12–19 mile) round trips so are for the serious walker only. Make sure you take plenty of water and a hat, and be prepared to sweat a great deal.

SOFT OPTIONS

The virtually unfrequented beaches of the Akamas, although mostly composed of pebbles or rock, are among the best places in Cyprus for sunbathing and swimming, but beware of razor-sharp rocks. For the laziest Akamas experience of all, consider hiring a powerboat at Latsi.

▷ **UNSPOILT CHARACTER**
Untouched – so far – by the developer's hand, the Akamas offers spectacular views and a remarkable diversity of vegetation, wildlife and geology.

△ **HAVE A BANANA**
The warm, well-irrigated and relatively sheltered hinterland of the Akamas makes it an ideal place for the cultivation of bananas.

▽ **NATURAL AVENUES**
The Adonis and Aphrodite nature trails are both about 8 km (5 miles) long. The going is fairly easy and will take 2–3 hours depending on your pace and the heat.

DEVELOPMENT THE LAONA WAY

The Laona Project was conceived by the Cyprus branch of Friends of the Earth to demonstrate the feasibility of ecologically sound development in the Akamas Peninsula and the nearby Laona plateau.

Increasingly vocal and increasingly desperate – given the runaway environmental destruction which has washed over much of the coastline in a concrete tidal wave – Cypriot environmentalists and their international supporters are trying to draw a line in the sand around the Akamas. Securing the interests, above all the economic interests, of the local people is essential to the successful protection of this region, so the project aims to revitalise the declining economies of area's villages. Technical and financial assistance are offered to restore traditional properties for visitor accommodation and small-scale industry. Pictured above is one such restored house.

There is powerful opposition to any attempt to slow the development juggernaut, but this project is one of the area's last and best chances.

◁ **TURNING TURTLES**
The continued protection of the beach at Lara Bay, the last refuge for endangered green and loggerhead turtles, is a *cause célèbre*.

▽ **BATH TIME**
It is forbidden to dip in the Baths of Aphrodite, where the goddess is said to have bathed and which are said to be a source of eternal youth.

▷ **JUST VISITING**
The hoopoe (*Upupa epops*), a migrant visitor to Cyprus's shores, is just one of the many winged attractions in the Akamas. Its colourful plumage and distinctive call announce its arrival. If you're lucky, you might also see kestrels, falcons or vultures wheeling overhead.

THE TROODOS MOUNTAINS

The Troodos Mountains rise up like a gentle giant over the western part of Cyprus. Some of the island's most stunning scenery is here, together with a treasure trove of Byzantine masterpieces

Map on page 224

The remoteness of the Troodos Mountains, together with careful forestry policies, have ensured the preservation of a large forest area in the central part of the Troodos. This forest once extended to the plains, and is unique in the eastern Mediterranean in terms of both its extent and its beauty. The dominant tree in the Troodos Mountains is the Aleppo pine, which accounts for 90 percent of the total stock. It is only in the upper reaches, above 1,500 metres (5,000 ft), that the bizarre silhouettes of the black pine predominate.

Place of refuge

The inaccessible nature of the mountain area has made it a place of refuge since early times. Byzantine churches and monasteries here survived the period of Ottoman rule more or less undamaged. It is therefore possible to find a wealth of Byzantine art treasures in the Troodos.

In the 20th century the Troodos area became a refuge of another sort: first as a summer destination for wealthy foreign visitors and now as a holiday and weekend retreat for native Cypriots. The average temperature on Mount Olympus is around 15°C (60°F) lower than in Nicosia. In July the temperature is unlikely to exceed 27°C (85°F).

Every August convoys of cars bring families looking to escaping the sticky heat of the cities into the Troodos Mountains. Camping and picnic spots are often filled to bursting point. Moreover, Cypriots tend to take a substantial part of their household equipment with them on any outing. The mountains now attract a growing number of visitors who enjoy a network of well organised hiking and trekking trails that make a refreshing antidote to the often heavy commercialism on the coast.

The Troodos area acts as a cloud trap for the prevailing westerly winds and therefore receives a relatively high level of precipitation of 800–1,000 mm (31–39 in) – three times as much as on the plains. In mid-winter, areas higher than 1,400 metres (4,600 ft) above sea-level are covered with snow, which in some years can reach a depth of more than 3 metres (10 ft). Between January and March skiers flit about on the slopes of Mount Olympus. Even in Ottoman times people knew how to take advantage of the snow, which they transported to Nicosia to use as a cooling agent.

On the right track

The Cypriot Forestry Commission maintains a network of good (although not always asphalt) roads throughout the forest area, most of which are also suitable for walking tours. Those who drive into the

PRECEDING PAGES: members of Kykkos monastery. **LEFT:** rich interior of Asinou church. **BELOW:** icon inside Kykkos monastery.

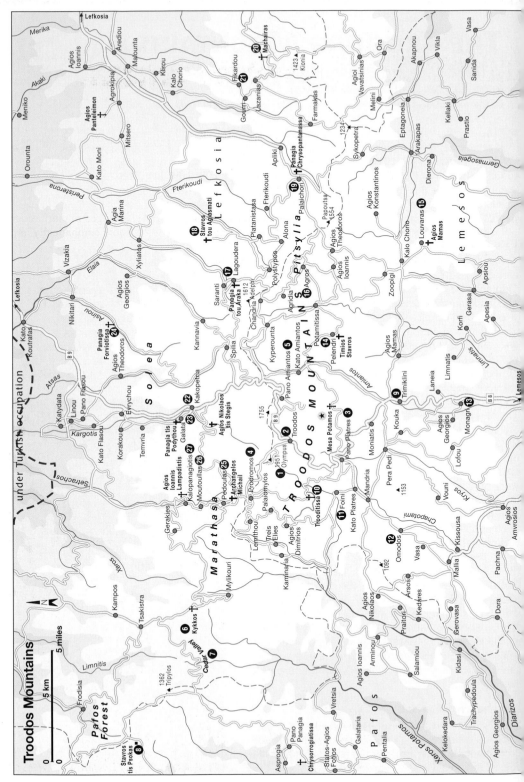

Troodos Mountains

N

5 miles

5 km

0

0

remote forest areas (for example the Pafos Forest) in winter and spring should enquire at the local forestry stations about the state of individual roads. Roadworks, landslides or high water levels can make even some of the best roads impassable. Among the particular attractions of the landscape are the cultivated valleys and hills surrounding the high forests. In the middle of all the vineyards, orchards, and olive and carob plantations, quiet, unspoilt villages nestle into the scenery.

Map on page 224

Around Mount Olympus

Mount Olympus ❶ is, at nearly 2,000 metres (6,500 ft), the highest peak of this range and indeed the highest mountain in Cyprus. It takes its name from the famous home of the gods in northern Greece. The Cypriots use the more modest name of *Khionistra*, which is a reference to the snow *(khioni)* that lies here in winter. Apart from a fine view on a clear day, the mountaintop has little to offer. The large white "golf ball" of the British military radar station near the peak, visible for miles around, has become a symbol of the area.

The unmissable golf ball atop Mount Olympus.

The village of **Troodos** ❷, at the foot of Mount Olympus, is not particularly attractive, unlike the mountains whose name it shares. Without a settled resident population, it is just a loose conglomerate of tavernas, souvenir shops, accommodation for visitors and venues where Cypriot civil servants and British soldiers come to enjoy themselves. During the short winter season, from January to March, this is the main centre for skiing in Cyprus, with four ski runs, a ski school and shops that hire out the necessary equipment.

Nearly 3 km (2 miles) from Troodos, in the direction of Platres, is the summer residence of the president of Cyprus. The main building was constructed in 1880 under the supervision of a 26-year-old French poet, the then unknown Arthur Rimbaud, and was designed as a summer residence for the British governor.

BELOW: workmates.

For nature-lovers

With the aim of providing genuine nature-lovers with more than just holiday camps and fast-food snack bars, the Cypriot tourist authorities, together with the Forestry Commission, have laid out a number of nature trails in the upper reaches of the Troodos Mountains.

The paths are easy to follow and provide the most vivid and impressive information about the flora and fauna of the area, and also the damage which has been done to the natural habitat. The paths pass strawberry plants and junipers and various evidence of forestry practices and features: areas scarred by forest fires, signs of reafforestation and gnarled trees from which resin has been extracted, as well as disused quarries, strange rock formations and impressive views across the mountains, villages and coast.

Hill resorts

The villages of **Pano Platres** ❸ (or simply Platres) and **Prodromos** ❹ near the summer palace of the British governor were the most salubrious of all the hill resorts of the 1940s and '50s. These resorts were modelled on the hill stations in India that were built as summer retreats for British colonial administrators. When the British departed, the upper social classes of the Near East started to spend their summers in the comfortable, but expensive, hotels here. Wealthy traders of Greek origin from Alexandria and Cairo frequented the area. King Farouk of Egypt once owned a summer villa near Prodromos. Well-to-do Israelis also congregated here. At that time, when beach tourism had yet to become popular and mass tourism was unknown, the hill resorts were among the most important tourists centres in Cyprus, in terms of the number of visitors, and the number of nights they stayed.

Coming to Platres and Prodromos today, you see only a few reminders of the old days. The colonial rulers have long since disappeared from the island, and the development of air travel has opened up other destinations to affluent Levantine holiday-makers. The once noble hotels are now showing distinct signs of shabbiness, and the clientele they attract during the short summer season has none of the grandeur of bygone guests.

Devastation

A very different, less glittering history can be found in **Pano Amiantos ❺**, on the eastern slopes of the upper Troodos. *Amiant* is the local name for asbestos, which was mined here in ancient times. In the past 100 years the mountain has been extensively levelled, first by pick-axes and then by bulldozers, in order to extract the fireproof material. The 10,000 men who worked here turned the mountain into a barren lunar landscape.

BELOW: early spring brings a profusion of wildflowers.

The workers endured terrible conditions, not least of which was their constant contact with the dangerous asbestos fibres. This was in marked contrast to the luxurious indolence enjoyed by visitors to nearby Platres. Eventually asbestos

TROODOS NATURE TRAILS

The four Troodos nature trails can be found in a state forest classified as a National Forest Park (see the map of trails on the inside back cover):

• **Atalante Trail** (10 km/6 miles): This begins at Troodos. After 3 km (2 miles) there is a spring with drinking water. The destination is the main road from Troodos to Prodromos, near a disused copper mine.

• **Persephone Trail** (3 km/2 miles): The starting point is Café Meli on the southern side of the main square in Troodos. The end of the trail has a good view.

• **Kaledonia Trail** (2 km/1¼ miles): Begins near the summer palace of the president, and follows the route of a river to a small but beautiful waterfall. It continues along a small forest road to the Psilo Dendro restaurant above Pano Platres. The restaurant is popular with tourists (its trout is recommended). This trail gives the best impression of the upper reaches of the forest vegetation.

• **Artemis Trail** (7 km/3 miles): The beginning and end of this trail is on the Troodos–Prodromos road, just above the turning which leads to Mount Olympus.

Information about flora and fauna is provided in a small, free brochure, *Nature Trails of the Troodos*, available from local tourist offices.

became as outmoded as summer holidays in Platres. At the end of the 1980s the quarrying was brought to a halt, but the mountainside remains a sad scene of devastation, and there are fears that carcinogenic asbestos fibres can be carried by the wind and might infiltrate water supplies.

Map on page 224

Madonna worship

The most famous of all the monasteries in Cyprus is **Kykkos** ❻ (Panagia tou Kykkou; Our Lady of Kykkos), which is revered all over the Orthodox world. The iconostasis of the monastery church contains an icon of the Madonna, which is supposed to have been painted by St Luke. The monk who founded the monastery received this icon in the 12th century from the Byzantine emperor Alexius I Comnenos, after he had cured the emperor's daughter of a severe illness.

Over the course of the centuries the monastery has been destroyed by fire on several occasions. The current building probably dates from the 19th century. Although there is little historical art to be found here the monastery is worth a visit on account of the showy extravagance of its church and its grounds. Yet for all their brilliance, the dazzling marble and gold-plate are no more than modest expressions of the true wealth of the monastery.

At the beginning of the 19th century, when the tax burden on the Orthodox population was particularly excessive, many farmers donated their property to the church to relieve themselves of the tax burden which the land represented. Such donations brought Kykkos property in lands as far afield as Russia and Asia Minor. Enormous expanses of expensive land in modern-day Nicosia, which could be used for construction, belong to Kykkos.

Mosaic detail from inside Kykkos monastery.

BELOW:
Kykkos courtyard.

Numerous pilgrims visit the monastery, particularly at weekends. They come to worship the icon of Luke and to pay their respects at the tomb of Archbishop Makarios III. Makarios entered the monastery as a 12-year-old novice in 1926 and later became its abbot. After his death in 1977 his mortal remains were buried on Throni Hill, above the monastery. In recent years the monastery authorities have added a series of buildings in which Cypriot visitors (but not foreigners) can stay overnight free of charge. Visitors also come to see the excellent **Byzantine Museum** (open daily; entrance fee; tel: 22-942736) with its stunning collection of ecclesiastical and Byzantine artefacts.

The mass of rock which makes up the central upper Troodos arose some 100 million years ago. The oldest part of the mountains is surrounded by a ring of younger rocks.

Cedar Valley

The monastery of Kykkos is also the starting point for a trip to the famous **Cedar Valley** ❼, at the foot of Mount Tripylos in the heart of the Pafos Forest. The area was named after a type of *cedrus brevifolia*, which is larger and more beautiful than the Lebanese cedar, itself a symbol of the Levantine state. This type of cedar grows only in Cyprus, and it is only in Cedar Valley that the majestic tree is found in significant numbers.

With a bit of good fortune you might also come across a moufflon in or around Cedar Valley. This Cypriot species of Mediterranean wild sheep is both rare and shy. Just as the species was on the point of extinction, successful attempts were made to breed it in captivity. A small boost to this laudable campaign was provided by the national airline, Cyprus Airways, which adopted the moufflon as its emblem. For a virtually guaranteed sighting of one of these charming animals you should visit the reserve in the idyllically located Forest Station of **Stavros tis Psokas** ❽ in Cedar Valley. Stavros tis Psokas, the head-

BELOW:
Cedar Valley.

quarters of the largest forest division of the Pafos Forest, was the first of the Cypriot forestry stations to be set up, in 1882. It has a resident population of around 60 moufflons.

There are two possible ways of proceeding from Pafos or Polis to Stavros tis Psokas and into Cedar Valley: from Pafos, via the village of Kannaviou, and from Polis via Pomos on the north coast to a turn-off called the Lorovouno Junction, south of the Turkish enclave of Kokkina.

Map on page 224

The southern foothills

On the way from Limassol to Platres or the monastery of Kykkos you should take time to explore the southern foothills of the Troodos Mountains, with their wide variety of landscapes and pretty villages. Here you can find peace and tranquillity in a shady *kentron*, such as near the famous Royal Oak, an ancient oak tree growing near **Trimiklini ❾**.

En route you might see the rustic **Trooditissa monastery ❿**, in a beautiful location of pine forests at the top of a steep gorge near Platres. Founded in the 13th century, the monastery's buildings date mostly from the 18th century, and house a silver icon of the Virgin. Prayers to the holy icon give hope to childless couples wishing for a child. Trooditissa's treasures also include a leather belt with silver medallions, which is said to be an infallible charm against infertility. Unfortunately, visiting this once freely open monastery is now all but impossible.

A splendid variety of local wines and spirits can be found in the Troodos Mountains. As well as producing the excellent local wine and distilling the fiery *Zivania*, the locals also make a range of grape-based liqueurs such as *Palouzé*, *Sudjuko* and *Loukoumi*.

BELOW: moufflons.

Fresh *loukoumades*, small doughnuts dipped in syrup, can be purchased in **Foini** ⓫ (Phini), a pretty village which is worth visiting on a number of counts. The main attraction, the local **Folk Art Museum of Phanis Pilavakis** (dedicated to Cypriot folk art), features information about the production and use of the large clay *pithoi*. The potters of Foini used to be famous for their skill in producing these storage containers.

Farther south, on the road to Limassol, is the restored wine village of **Omodos** ⓬. Its whitewashed houses with blue doors, shady vine arbours and well tended flowers are reminiscent of Greece's Cyclades islands. Unfortunately, Omodos is a shade too knowing to be altogether genuine. The government-financed restoration has enhanced its attributes beyond their original quality, leaving it looking different from all other Cypriot villages.

Still, a stroll through the streets and a visit to its arts and crafts and souvenir shops is pleasant enough. You can visit traditional private homes, some of which have their own wine press, but be warned that, if you accept an invitation to step inside, you will be expected to buy the wine or crafts on offer. The handsome **Timios Stavros Monastery** in the centre of the village is said to have been founded in 327 by St Helena, mother of the Roman emperor Constantine, but most of it dates from the 19th century. Its church has a hemp fibre said to be a Crucifixion relic donated by St Helena. Monks no longer live here.

On the direct Limassol-Platres road you can visit the church of **Panagia Amasgou monastery**. This barrel-vaulted one-roomed chapel, which has the additional protection of a barn roof, lies 3 km (2 miles) outside **Monagri** ⓭. The key is kept by the village priest. Inside are fragments of frescoes from the 12th and 13th centuries. On a more easterly route southwards off the Troodos, pass-

BELOW:
Troodos foothills.

ing through **Pelendri** ⓮, the 14th-century church of **Timios Stavros** is embell-ished with fine religious frescoes. Farther east, at **Louvaras** ⓯, the one-roomed chapel of **Agios Mamas** has a complete cycle of frescoes, dating to 1495, by the Lebanese artist Philippos Goul.

Map on page 224

The eastern foothills

Pitsilia is the name of the eastern Troodos chain. Of its many forested peaks, the highest, at 1,550 metres (5,100 ft), is Papoutsa. Like other remote areas, Pitsilia suffers from the emigration of its young people, but serious attempts have been made to reduce the exodus, and to prevent the decline of the houses and meadows.

In 1977 the government initiated the Pitsilia Integrated Rural Development Project to improve local living conditions. New, wide arable terraces were laid out, small dams, reservoirs and water supply systems were built, and the road network was improved considerably. A high school was built in **Agros** ⓰, and a gymnasium and a health centre in **Kyperounta**. New life has since returned, particularly in large villages such as Agros and Pelendri. Many of the residents, however, work in Nicosia or Limassol.

Troodos cherries.

Agros offers visitors a special treat in May and June, when farmers unload baskets of rose petals in the village, from which rose-water is distilled. The rose water makes an excellent gift.

Byzantine masterpiece

Several of Cyprus's finest Byzantine churches lie in the eastern Troodos, includ-ing one that is widely considered to be the masterpiece of Byzantine art: **Pana-gia tou Araka**, with frescoes from 1192, at **Lagoudera** ⓱. The church lies

BELOW: Panagia tou Araka church at Lagoudera.

Christ Pantokrator
*inside Panagia tou
Araka church,
Lagoudera.*

BELOW: many
churches in the
Troodos look more
like barns than
places of worship.

just outside the village to the west and looks more like a barn than a church. This is typical of Troodos churches, since the mountain weather, particularly the heavy snowfalls, led to the construction of barn-like gable roofs for extra protection. The iconographic cycles of frescoes, traditionally painted in the dome, were housed on the raised long walls and on the gable surfaces.

The simple cruciform domed church contains works of the neoclassical style painted by artists from Constantinople. The name of a painter, Leon Authentou, is included in the donor's inscription. The most important iconographic themes are represented: in the **sanctuary**, with its semicircular apse, is the Virgin Mary in majesty with child, flanked by the two archangels, Gabriel and Michael. Below this are seven medallions with the busts of saints. (The third from the right is the Cypriot saint Irakleidios.)

In the vertical section of the apse are the Twelve Early Fathers, including the Cypriot St Barnabas to the right of the middle window, and (under the window on the left), the bust of the Cypriot St Spyridon, who became the patron saint of Corfu at the end of the 15th century. In the vault above the sanctuary is Christ's Ascension, on the northern wall below are St Simeon Stylites Thaumaturge and St Onufrios; on the southern wall is a portrayal of St Simeon Stylites Archimandrite.

On the eastern pendentives of the dome (the triangular supporting vaults between the piers and the drum of the dome) is a scene of the Annunciation with the Archangel Gabriel and Mary, whilst between them hangs a medallion depicting the beardless Christ Emmanuel. The western pendentives show the Evangelists Mark and Matthew (left) and John and Luke (right). On the piers of the drum are twelve life-sized figures of the prophets from the Old

Map on page 224

Testament, while the dome itself is filled with an impressive *Christ Pantokrator* (Christ as lord of the universe) surrounded by medallions with angels; on the east side is a medallion with the "empty throne" ready for Christ's reign over the world after the Day of Judgement. In the vertex of the vault are four medallions decorated with the busts of martyrs, below an *Anastasis* (Christ's descent into Hell following the Crucifixion) and the Baptism of Christ. On the lunette is a mural of the Virgin's Presentation in the Temple, below which are life-sized depictions of saints whose expressive faces are unusually realistic for this kind of art: Sabbas, Nicholas, Simeon with the baby Jesus, John the Baptist, and *Panagia Eleousa* (Mary with the Angels). A beautiful Assumption of the Virgin can be seen on the lunette of the southern recess. Located below is the *Panagia Arakiotissa*, which as *Panagia Amolyntos*, the Mother of God with the Instruments of the Passion, has become a model for numerous portrayals of icons.

Next to this on the right is a larger than life portrayal of the Archangel Michael, and on the underside of the arches are excellent representations of saints (for example St Antonios on the right). On the south side of the west vault is a portrayal of the Nativity, and below St Peter and various other saints.

Frescoes and icons

Stavros tou Agiasmati ⓯ church is situated about 5 km (3 miles) north of the village of **Platanistasa**, in a remote mountain area. Its gable roof has a cycle of frescoes by Philippos Goul from 1494 which is well worth seeing. (Before visiting the church be sure to collect the key from the *kafeneion* in the village.) One special iconographic feature in the church is the fresco-cycle entitled *The Discovery of the Holy Cross* (in the arched recess of the north wall).

BELOW: monastery of Machairas.

The small chapel of **Panagia Chrysopantanassa** has just one room. Located in the village of **Palaichori ⓳**, 6 km (4 miles) southeast of Platanistasa, it contains a number of frescoes from the first half of the 16th century. Particularly worth seeing is a detailed iconographic cycle portraying the life of Christ.

On the eastern edge of Pitsilia is the **monastery of Machairas ⓴** (open Mon, Tues and Thur; group visits only), a popular day-trip destination for Cypriots, especially during the summer months when its shady location is much appreciated. Like so many Cypriot monasteries, the 12th-century building is supposed to mark the site where a miraculous icon was found. Under the gallery on the upper floor, the history of the monastery is recorded in illustrated texts.

The undisputed hero of the monastery is not a devout man of the church, but Grigoris Afxentiou, a secular rebel. Afxentiou, one of the leaders of EOKA at the time of the struggle for independence, was tracked down by British soldiers to a hideout in a cave just below the monastery in March 1957. He bravely fought the foreign troops, but was killed when his refuge was set on fire. The place where Afxentiou died is now decorated with wreaths and the Greek flag. It has become almost as important a place of pilgrimage as the grave of Archbishop Makarios at the monastery of Kykkos. In the monastery of Machairas a little museum has been set up in memory of the heroic fighter. Visitors with a taste for the macabre can see his partly charred remains.

Conservation

On the road just north of Machairas is a cluster of restored conservation villages. **Fikardou ㉑** is the official one, its folk architecture coming under the auspices of the Department of Antiquities to ensure that its wooden-balconied Ottoman-

BELOW: Lazanias.

period houses are not replaced with nondescript modern villas.

Nearby **Gourri** is equally rustic and unspoiled, while **Lazanias**, situated between Gourri and Machairas monastery, is not only rustic and unspoiled but so tranquil it seems that its inhabitants have all departed.

Map
on page
224

The Solea and Marathasa Valleys

The Solea and Marathasa valleys that cut into the northern slopes of the Troodos Mountains run parallel to each other. They comprise one of the most beautiful areas on the island, even though the lower reaches of the valley and the local connections to the sea have been cut off by the demarcation line and cannot be reached from southern Cyprus. The patchwork landscape, dotted with tightly packed gabled houses, is enchanting. Each season has its own particular appeal: in spring, for example, the upper Marathasa Valley becomes a white sea of cherry blossom. Not least of the region's attractions, concealed under the rather inconspicuous "barn roofs" of local churches, are the most important religious art treasures of the Byzantine era.

Kakopetria ㉒ in the Solea Valley is a particularly popular Sunday destination for citizens of Nicosia, who come specially to eat its famous trout. Parts of the village have been undergoing extensive restoration in recent years in a successful attempt to preserve the traditional local building style.

Local priest, guardian of his church's treasures.

Village of springs and Byzantine art

Further out on the Nicosia road, past Kakopetria, is **Galata** ㉓. This mountain village boasts plentiful springs and no fewer than four Byzantine churches. All are worth visiting, but two are particularly impressive. (As is so frequently

BELOW: decorative panels in Panagia Theotokos, Galata.

the case in remote areas, the keys can be obtained from the priest; the best place to find him is in the *kafeneion* near the bridge with the plane trees.) **Panagia Theotokos** is also known as the Archangelos Michail church, after a larger-than-life statue of the archangel which keeps guard over the main portal. The church houses a detailed cycle of Christian works, and the quality of the paintings is impressive. The frescoes, which were painted in 1514, are the work of the Cypriot artist Symeon Axenti.

Panagia tis Podythou church has a number of Italo-Byzantine frescoes from 1502. The influence of the Venetian epoch (1489–1571) is noticeable in the case of the portrayals of the Mother of God and the Communion of the Apostles in the apse. The dramatic portrayal of the Crucifixion in the western gable is very moving, although there is nothing Byzantine about it.

Northern constellation

A constellation of Byzantine churches can be seen off the northern face of the Troodos Mountains. Taking the right fork from Troodos village (the Nicosia road) you come first to **Agios Nikolaos tis Stegis** (St Nicholas of the Roof; open Tues–Sun; donations), which lies some 3 km (2 miles) outside the village of Kakopetria, and contains Byzantine paintings from 11th–17th century. The art from the 11th century includes Christ's Entry into Jerusalem and the Transfiguration, which is portrayed in one large composition together with the Raising of Lazarus. The Comnenian style of the 12th century is represented by the Virgin Mary's Presentation in the Temple, the 40 martyrs, the Day of Judgement and so on. Art from the 14th century includes various excellent works in the nave, particularly the Nativity and the two soldier saints, Theodoros and Georgios.

BELOW: the *Raising of Lazarus* depicted in Agios Nikolaos tis Stegis near Kakopetria.

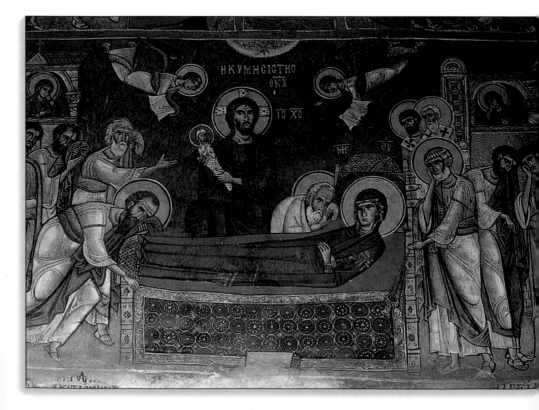

At least a good 16 km (10 miles) further along the Nicosia road, via a diversion through **Nikitari** village, is the Byzantine church of **Panagia Forviotissa** ㉔, also known as **Panagia tou Asinou**. The church is a veritable museum of Byzantine art. The quality of the paintings from various epochs gives a very good impression of the art of Byzantine Cyprus. The key for the church is obtained from the village priest in Nikitari. He accompanies visitors to the church, so a small gratuity is always welcomed.

The little one-roomed chapel, dating from the turn of the 12th century, was adorned with Comnenian paintings by artists from Constantinople in the years 1105–06, in accordance with the style of the capital.

At the end of the 12th century a **western narthex** (entrance hall) was added with semicircular apses to the north and south. After the narthex had been built, the **southern portal** was walled up, and towards the end of the 12th century or at the beginning of the 13th century a picture of St George on his horse was painted on the inside of the portal.

Archangelos church in Pedoulas.

There are five different layers of paintings in the Asinou church, from four epochs. Some paintings from 1105–06, for example the Communion of the Apostles and Christ's Ascension, are in the sanctuary. In the nave and on the western wall are portrayals of Christ's Entry into Jerusalem, the Last Supper and the death of the Virgin Mary. The 40 martyrs and various saints are depicted on the north wall. St George in the southern apse of the narthex dates from the end of the 12th century and the beginning of the 13th century. All the other paintings date from 1332–33, including the Mother of God in the apse and the patron's picture with St Anastasia in the narthex (to the right of St George). A booklet explaining the frescoes is available.

BELOW: the fine interior of Panagia Forviotissa, also known as Panagia tou Asinou.

Map
on page
224

Back at Troodos village, and taking the left fork towards the Marathasa Valley and Pedoulas, you can visit the **Archangelos Michail church**. The gable roofed church of the Archangel Michael is situated in the lower part of **Pedoulas** ㉕. The frescoes in the nave are the work of a certain "Adam" from 1474. The cycle depicts rarer themes such as Pilate, and Peter's denial of Christ.

Preserved traditions

In the Marathasa Valley, which until a few decades ago was extremely remote, a number of interesting traditions have been preserved. You can, for instance, still sample the valley's traditional speciality – aromatic dried cherries, which were once enjoyed as far away as Egypt.

In **Moutoullas** ㉖ the mineral water of the same name is bottled, and *sanidhes* and *vournes* are produced from sandalwood. *Sanidhes* are traditional long planks with a number of hollows (usually 11), in which the bread dough was placed to rise. *Vournes* are wooden bowls also used in breadmaking. Just a few decades ago such items could be found in every Cypriot kitchen. Only selected parts of pine trunks were used, and the carpenters' demand for wood was so great that they were regarded by the British forestry officials as one of the biggest threats to the Troodos forests.

Moutoullas and beyond

On the western edge of Moutoullas is the tiny church of **Panagia Moutoullas**. This is the oldest known church with a gable roof in Cyprus. Its frescoes, some of which have not been well-preserved, date from 1280. The most interesting is the fresco of the donors. The carved doors are also worth closer inspection.

RIGHT: local people are often kind and helpful.
BELOW: enjoying a closer look at the mountains.

Two kilometres (1 mile) or so beyond Moutoullas is **Kalopanagiotis** ㉗, a Marathasa Valley town noted for the Byzantine monastery of **Agios Ioannis Lampadistis**. The monastery is situated in the valley on the opposite side of the river to the village. (Get the key from the village priest, who can usually be found at the church or in the nearby *kafeneion*.) Its colossal barn roof incorporates a collection of sacred Byzantine architecture spread over three centuries – from the 13th century to around 1500.

The paintings in the domed Orthodox church of **Agios Irakleidos** have survived from the first half of the 13th century, from the Early Comnenian period. Their expressiveness, lines and colours indicate that they were painted by artists from Constantinople. The Entry into Jerusalem is particularly outstanding.

The scenes in the main church date from the period around 1400 and show good examples of traditional painting. The **narthex**, which was built later, was decorated with frescoes in the style of Constantinople, before the city was conquered by the Ottomans in 1453. According to one of the inscriptions, the painter was a refugee from Constantinople who painted this part of the church shortly after the fall of the city.

The 15th-century **Latin chapel** in the north of the complex is the work of a Venetian. Its frescoes of the Acathist Hymn were painted in 1500 and show strong Western influences in terms of their style. ❏

BYZANTINE LANDMARKS AND PROUD TRADITIONS

Cyprus's churches and monasteries are among the island's foremost tourist attractions – nowhere more so than in the Troodos Mountains

Cyprus's Orthodox priests and monks climbed into the Troodos Mountains to flee the coast with its invaders and worldly towns. Tourism and UNESCO have followed them there, and nine Byzantine churches have been designated as World Cultural Heritage Sites.

Looking more like barns than churches, none appears very promising from the outside. Their true glory lies in the magnificent interior frescoes, dating from the 11th to 14th centuries. The creators of these paintings may have been influenced by the style of now-vanished frescoes in the churches of the distant capital, Constantinople, and other religious centres, but it seems that Cyprus's own creative energies were the primary impulse. To these can be added influences from Christian churches from the Levantine mainland, including from what is now Lebanon.

KEYS OF THE KINGDOM

It used to be well nigh impossible to get into the churches, since the key-holding priest was almost invariably absent. But nowadays there is often a keyholder on site from dawn to dusk. Taking a tour of the churches is another matter. A few, such as those at Galata, are close together, while others are at the end of long and dusty trails. If you are keen to see all nine UNESCO churches you need at least two days, beginning at the central axis of the Troodos: the road from Platres to Kakopetria and Kalopanagiotis.

▷ **BULWARK OF FAITH**
Agios Neofytos monastery is a popular outing from Pafos – as it has been since the 1100s, when the monk Neofytos *(see page 208)* retreated to his cave here.

△ **BAPTISM OF CHRIST**
The frescoes in the Michail Arkhangelos church, Pedoulas, are credited to a 15th-century artist known only as Adam.

△ **LAZARUS RISING**
Under the twin roofs of Agios Nikolaos tis Stegis, near Kakopetria, is a suite of superb murals including this *Raising of Lazarus*.

▷ **CAVE PAINTINGS**
High up on a cliffside near Pafos, the murals of Agios Neofytos illuminate the interior of the cave, which was the saint's refuge.

THE PICK OF THE BUNCH

The nine UNESCO churches in the Troodos are:
- *Agios Ioannis Lampadistis, Kalopanagiotis* – three churches in one, from the 11th to 18th centuries.
- *Archangelos Michail, Pedoulas* – a timber-roofed church with post-Byzantine frescoes.
- *Panagia Forviotissa, Nikitari* – arguably the most unmissable of the nine.
- *Panagia tis Podythou, Galata* – with exquisite frescoes of the Crucifixion and Our Lady.
- *Panagia tou Araka, Lagoudera* – a 12th-century church with fine frescoes including the Last Supper.
- *Panagia tou Moutalla* – tiny church full of murals.
- *Stavros tou Agiasmati, Platanistasa* – with fine 15th-century frescoes.
- *Timios Stavros, Pelendri* – biblical murals in a 14th-century church.
- *Agios Nikolaos tio Stegis, Kakopetria*. An 11th-century church with frescoes and a double roof.

▷ **HEAVENLY VIEW**
An image of Christ Pantokrator (Lord of the Universe), gazing down from inside the dome – as if from Heaven itself – is characteristic of many Byzantine churches.

▽ **ACROBATIC ARTISTS**
The frescoes in Agios Mamas church at Louvaras, many by the renowned Lebanese fresco painter Philippos Goul, show how artists skilfully used even the most awkward spaces.

▷ **UNLIKELY BEAUTY**
Pictured here and top right is Panagia Forviotissa, also known as Panagia tou Asinou, which has perhaps the most beautiful frescoes in all the UNESCO-recognised churches in the Troodos mountains.

NICOSIA AND AROUND

*Nicosia is a divided city, split into two utterly separate communities
by the buffer zone known as the Green Line. Despite its status as
a capital city, South Nicosia sees relatively few tourists*

Lefkosia/
Nicosia

I n 1873 Ludwig Salvator, the Archbishop of Austria, described the city in *Lefkosia, the Capital of Cyprus*: "When, having climbed up the gentle hills, you first catch sight of Lefkosia, with its slender palms and minarets, and the picturesque mountain range in the background on the scorched plains of Cyprus, it is reminiscent of a scene out of the *Arabian Nights*. A jewel of orange gardens and palm trees in an area otherwise devoid of trees, an oasis (by dint of its embankments) – created by human hand. And in the same way that the contrast between the city and its surroundings stands out clear and harsh, the spirit of contradiction can also be felt within the city. Venetian fortifications and Gothic buildings crowned by the half-moon of Turkey; Turks, Greeks and Armenians mingling together colourfully on this ancient land, each other's enemies but united in their love of this piece of earth which is their common home."

PRECEDING PAGES:
Nicosia, ancient
and modern.
LEFT: Laïki Geitonia,
a restored district
popular with visitors.
BELOW: Venetian
fortified walls.

A divided capital

Today, however, **Nicosia ❶** bears little resemblance to this description. The Ledra Palace Hotel is damaged from shelling, and surrounded by barbed wire. To the right of Leoforos Markou Drakou are the remains of a burnt-out villa, just 100 metres from the Venetian Walls of the old city.

The walls are still functioning as a bulwark, 400 years after they were built. They are now part of a heavily guarded border. And for many years the Ledra Palace has served as a barracks for the units of the UN peacekeeping troops. Leoforos Markou Drakou is blocked by barbed wire and blue-and-white painted concrete walls. However the pedestrian traffic leading to and from the Ledra Palace crossing is now quite busy with visitors from both sides crossing freely up to midnight daily. Only official vehicles belonging to diplomatic and UN personnel are allowed to cross. The crossing facilities have been tidied up in recent times with separate channels for foreigners, Greek Cypriots and Turkish Cypriots. The crossing opens at 8am daily and closes at midnight. Records of foreigners crossing from the Greek Cypriot side are virtually non-existent so it is an easy matter to simply walk though and onwards through the covered walkway to the Turkish-Cypriot checkpoint. The main concern of Greek Cypriot police seems to be with any purchases you may make in the north. Don't be tempted to stock up on cheap goods such as tobacco or drinks as they will be confiscated when you return.

At first sight, the two halves of the city appear to have virtually nothing in common. Greek Cypriot and Turkish soldiers still face each other in dugouts and the Green Line cuts the streets and water pipe-

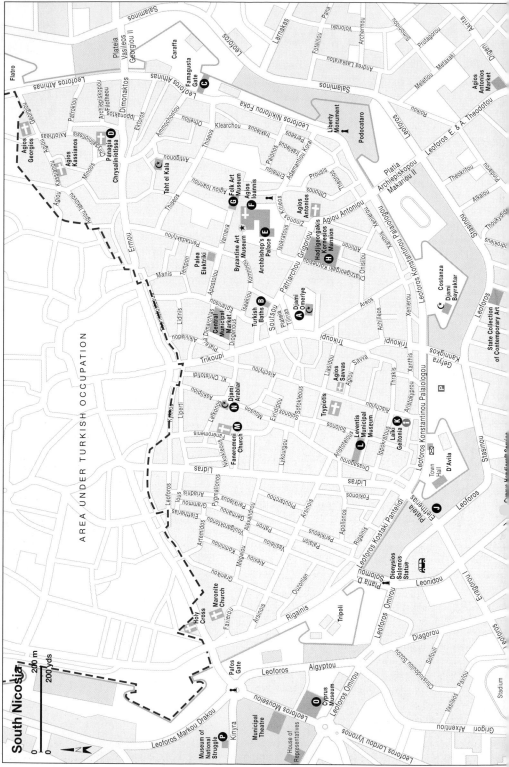

South Nicosia

AREA UNDER TURKISH OCCUPATION

lines in two. The former international airport is cut out of the action by the Line, and the city is still effectively divided into two disparate parts.

Past glories

At the entrance to Odos Hermes in the old city, you can recognise the faded victory slogans of the Olympiakos football team, which once had its home here. *Olympiakos 3 Omonia 2* has been painted on the wall with an unsteady hand, along with the date – 8 June 1961. A hundred metres further on, near a post of the Cyprus National Guard, the buffer zone begins. Unlike in the rest of the island, the division of Nicosia didn't start with the Turkish invasion of 1974, but in 1964. On Christmas Eve 1963 civil violence broke out in the city. The Greek Cypriots demanded that the newly formed Republic become part of Greece, the so-called *enosis*. The Turks, on the other hand, fought for *taksim*, the division of the island. Neither of the two demands could be realised at the time, and yet the common state divided along ethnic lines.

The prosperous Greek Cypriot majority live in large apartment blocks or in their own detached houses in the new part of the city. In the old city centre many houses become more dilapidated every year. First the plaster crumbles away, then the roof begins to leak. The inhabitants have no money for the repairs, and the owners no longer care. Many valuable buildings from the Ottoman era now stand empty. In some, only the ground floor is inhabited, because the upper floor is in danger of collapsing.

The city authorities have renovated a small area of the city: Laïki Geitonia, the "popular neighbourhood", could be a model for the restoration of the old city. The only problem is that virtually nobody lives there: it has been turned into an

Map on page 246

The captal of Cyprus is called Lefkosia by the Greeks and Lefkosha by the Turks. Nicosia is the old name given to the city by the Crusader-era conquerors.

BELOW: a quiet backstreet of Nicosia.

CROSSING THE GREEN LINE

In Nicosia it is painfully clear that the line dividing north from south cracks open a unity that was centuries in the making. The Green Line, created by the United Nations, is so called not because of the grass and wild flowers that grow through the asphalt surfaces of no-man's land, but because it was drawn with a green pen on a map in UN peacekeeping headquarters. Everything must remain as it was then. UN patrols check regularly that the opposing troops do not change the position of their sandbags or dug-outs and no-one has ever been allowed to remove their belongings from the area in between.

Visitors to the Republic of Cyprus may cross freely to the north as long as they are back by midnight. There are no particular formalities on the Greek Cypriot side, though police stationed at the various pedestrian channels will normally ask to look briefly at your ID. From here walk the 800 metres to the Turkish Cypriot side where you will fill in a brief form with your name and passport number. This will be stamped and handed back to you for retrieval later when you return The whole process should take no longer than 10 minutes – as long as there are no queues. Cars, including hire cars, must now be taken across at the Agios Dometios crossing, some 4 kilometres to the west of Ledra Palace.

enclave of expensive restaurants and souvenir shops. However, the process of restoring the living spaces of the old city has begun, particularly in the zone around the Archbishop's Palace. Although for some of the old Ottoman architecture it is too late – some buildings have literally bitten the dust – the calm beauty of those that have been renovated shows what is still possible if the will and the money exist. Most of the streets are narrow, the shutters of the houses pulled down. From the outside there is little indication of the beauty of the old buildings. Life here has always gone on within the rooms hidden from the outside: the traditional houses of the Levant face inwards, with arcades and inner courtyards in which palms or orange trees grow.

Minarets and church towers rise above the mainly one or two-storey houses of the old city. And palm trees too, hundreds of them, either standing in line along the city walls, or in groups of twos and threes, casting their flat shadow on the narrow streets and courtyards.

From the Selimiye mosque in the north, the wind blows the *muezzin*'s call to prayer as far as Odos Patroclos. For the inhabitants of this area, the minarets of the cathedral of St Sophia, the coronation church of the Middle Ages, visible from a long distance, are tantalisingly close.

Daily life

Although the citizens in the two halves of Nicosia have some restrictions on how they may visit each other, have two different religions, and speak different languages, they have more in common than most of them would like to admit. In the south as in the north the men invariably spend their spare time in one of the small coffee-houses. All Nicosians – like all Cypriots in general –

BELOW:
drinking partners.

have a passion for extensive company. In the gestures that are used, in the customs of daily life, in the strong sense of family identity – life is much the same everywhere in the narrow streets of old Nicosia. In both north and south the carpenters are busy in their open work-places, and you can watch the chair-makers as they go about their business. Owners sit in front of their small shops and wait for customers, cats patrol their territories. It would be wrong to say that time has stood still in old Nicosia, but the clocks certainly seem to go slower than elsewhere.

City history

Nicosia was founded in AD 965 under Byzantine rule, although the area was settled well before that. In the 7th century BC the city of Ledra, one of the Cypriot city kingdoms, was sited here. Under Greek and Roman rule Nicosia – which at that time had the name *Leukos* – was an important trading centre. Its upswing from the 9th century onwards was largely due to the fact that the coasts were plagued by pirates. Nicosia had the advantage of lying inland and so remained protected from such attacks.

Under the Lusignans (1192–1489) the city became the seat of residence of the Catholic archbishop and capital of the crusader state of Cyprus. At that time there were around 20,000 people in Nicosia, a considerable number for the time. The population was a colourful mixture: along with the Greek Orthodox majority and the Catholic feudal lords, there were Nestorians, Copts, Armenians and Jews. Gothic churches and cathedrals were built at this time.

A large palace, built in the 14th century, served as the seat of government for the French nobles. Unfortunately little is known about its architecture, not even

Map on page 246

Drinks on the hoof: a man delivers coffee by bike in Nicosia.

BELOW: Venetian fortified walls.

Greek sculpture known to everyone in Cyprus as the head on the CY£5 note.

BELOW: the Archbishop's Palace.

its exact location. Like many other buildings, the palace fell victim to the Venetian military planners. Between 1567 and 1570 they built a circular fortified wall with 11 bastions. To maintain a free field of fire, all the buildings outside the new city boundaries had to be erased. Churches and palaces, cemeteries, domestic dwellings and monasteries were all burned to the ground. The engineers responsible for the wall also diverted the River Pedieios (which had previously flowed straight through the city) around the new city wall. The only entrance to the city was through one of the three heavily fortified gates.

The purpose of this bulwark was to repel the Ottomans. Yet this hastily erected fortification, praised as being of the most perfect design, proved to be no serious obstacle at all for the Sultan's troops: after a two-week siege they conquered Nicosia. The Venetians and the Catholic feudal lords were either killed or driven out, and the Ottoman soldiers and settlers from Anatolia moved in.

Favourable impressions

"Nicosia is the capital of Cyprus and lies under the mountains in the middle of a wide plain with a wonderful, healthy climate. As a result of the perfect air temperature and the healthy climate, the King of Cyprus and all the bishops and prelates of the Kingdom live in this city. A large number of the other princes, counts, nobles, barons, and knights also live here. They busy themselves each day with spear-throwing, tournaments and, above all, with hunting." Thus wrote the pilgrim Ludolf von Suchen in 1340.

The walls have been maintained as a symbol of the city. On the bastions, which are named after influential Italian families, the cannons of the defenders once stood. One of them, *Flatro*, remains a prohibited military zone even

today. The Greek and Turkish posts now stand facing each other at this point, separated only by a small UN building in the middle. In all other respects, however, the walls have lost their purpose; during the period of British colonial rule, gaps were cut in the wall, so that streets could connect the old and new parts of the city.

Religious buildings

It is only a few steps from the Greek Orthodox Archbishop's Palace in the Agios Ioannis quarter to Taht el Kala with its mosque. The Faneromeni church is just a few metres from another tiny mosque. And from the church of the Armenians to the Arab Ahmet mosque is also not far. Yet nowadays the mosque in Taht el Kala is closed, and the Armenian church lies in the middle of the Turkish military no-go area. The Armenians were driven out of their traditional area and now live outside the city wall in the new city.

The **Djami Omeriye** Ⓐ or Omeriye mosque (open daily; free, although a donation is appreciated) is the only place in the Greek Cypriot south of the city where the *muezzin* still calls the faithful to prayer five times a day – for the benefit of the Arab tourists and the few remaining Lebanese refugees. The Agios Loukas church in the north has been turned into a secular cultural centre. Nevertheless, the intricate patchwork of churches and mosques shows just how closely integrated the Christian and Muslim communities used to be. There are 18 mosques and 13 churches in the 24 districts of the old city. Hardly any of these districts had an ethnically homogeneous population before the invasion: Sunni Muslims, Greek Orthodox and the small Armenian and Maronite minorities all lived together peacefully.

Map on page 246

BELOW:
the main square.

The Omeriye mosque, like several other mosques in the city, has a Christian past. The former Augustinian church was dedicated to John de Montfort, who accompanied St Louis on the Fourth Crusade and died here in 1249. It was destroyed by Mustapha Paşa during the Ottoman conquest, and a mosque dedicated to the prophet Omar, whose final resting place Mustapha Paşa thought it occupied, was erected on the site. It is possible to climb to the *muezzin's* platform of the minaret, from where there is a superb view of the divided city. On one side, opposite the old **Turkish Baths** Ⓑ, it is still possible to trace elements of Gothic style. The tiny Djami Arablar or Arablar mosque, encircled by flowers near the Greek Orthodox Faneromeni church, was formerly a chapel.

Ottoman *caravanserais*, churches built by the Lusignans, the Greek Orthodox Panagia Chrysaliniotissa church in Byzantine style – Nicosia is a vast open-air museum, now divided and threatened with decline.

Foreign conquerors have left their mark all over the city and even in the 1950s and 1960s, certain cardinal sins were still being committed by builders – ghastly concrete buildings were put up in a number of streets and a tower-block was erected in the middle of the old city.

City gates

Two of the three former city gates have survived. In the north the smaller Keryneia Gate (formerly the Porta del Provveditore) spans a major roadway through the city wall. In the south the massive **Famagusta Gate** Ⓒ (formerly the Porta Giuliana) has been restored in the most exemplary fashion. The Pafos Gate – known by the Venetians as the Porta Domenica – has been reduced to a simple roadway for traffic through the city wall.

TIP

Art exhibitions, concerts and lectures take place at the restored Famagusta Gate in the old city walls.

BELOW: the Famagusta Gate.

Churches and palaces

When the Ottomans conquered Nicosia, they changed only the Gothic churches of the Venetians into mosques. The Orthodox places of worship remained untouched: some of the churches of the Orthodox Greeks still survive virtually unaltered. The most beautiful church of all is **Panagia Chrysaliniotissa** (open daily; free), in an area that is being extensively renovated near the Famagusta Gate in the carpenters' quarter.

In the middle of this dilapidated area is the unexpectedly grandiose **Archbishop's Palace** ❸ (occasional guided tours; entrance fee), a modern building completed in 1961. Directly in front of the Palace stands the **statue of the Archbishop and President Makarios** in solitary splendour, measuring around 6 m (20 ft) high. The statue of the guiding father of all Greek Cypriots was the subject of some controversy over its size and what some consider its monumental ugliness.

Near the Archbishop's Palace is a smaller predecessor – the **Agios Ioannis church** ❻, the cathedral of Nicosia, also known as the Cathedral of St John the Evangelist (open Mon–Sat, to noon only on Sat; free). Completed in 1662 on the site of a Benedictine abbey church that was destroyed by Egyptian raiders in 1426, Agios Ioannis is ornately decorated with murals, icons, chandeliers, the archbishop's throne, and a lectern in the shape of the Byzantine double-headed eagle.

In the **Old Palace**, part of the former Benedictine monastery, is the small **Ethnographic Museum** ❼ (open Mon–Fri; entrance fee; tel: 22-432578), whose exhibits comprise mainly everyday items. The right-hand section of the New Palace houses the **Byzantine Museum** (open Mon–Fri, Sat to midday;

BELOW: the interior of Agios Ioannis church.

entrance fee; tel: 22-430008) in which around 150 icons illustrate the development of 1,000 years of icon-painting, from the 8th century to the 18th.

The **Hadjigeorgakis Kornesios Mansion** , or the House of the Dragoman Hadjigeorgakis Kornesios (open Mon–Fri 8am–2pm, Sat 8am–1pm; entrance fee; tel: 22-305316), documents the life of a member of the upper classes during the period of Ottoman rule. Kornesios was one of the wealthy tax collectors appointed by the Sublime Porte in Istanbul. The interior of this building, which has been restored in Ottoman style with old furniture and carpets, is a testimony to the comfortable lifestyle which Kornesios enjoyed. But all the splendour didn't help him in the end: in 1809 he was executed in Istanbul as punishment for his various intrigues.

Preserving crafts and forests

On the southern edge of the city, close to the start of the motorway to Larnaka and Limassol, is the **Cyprus Handicraft Service** (open Mon–Fri; free; tel: 22-305024), at 186 Leoforos Athalassis. This is the main workshop of the government-owned foundation that aims to preserve Cyprus's endangered folk crafts. You can watch pottery, woodwork, embroidery and a range of other skills, and buy the excellent finished products at the CHS shop. Just across busy Leoforos Lemesou is the **Athalassa Forest**, a piece of Cyprus's re-created forest right on the city's doostep and a great place for picnics.

A walk round Greek Cypriot Nicosia

BELOW: lunching in Laïki Geitonia.

Begin this tour at **Plateia Eleftherias** near the centre of the old city, where the small Town Hall stands on one of the bastions of the city wall. From here it

Map on page 246

is only a few steps to Leoforos Konstantinou Palaiologou. Opposite the main post office is a small street to the left, and here you will find yourself in **Laïki Geitonia** , a reconstructed area of the old city with shady cafés, good restaurants and many souvenir shops. If you want to know more about the history of Nicosia, visit the new **Leventis Municipal Museum** ⓛ (open Tues–Sun; entrance fee; tel: 22-673375), which is nearby at Ippokratous 17.

A little further to the west you come to Lidras. This was once the most important area for shopping, although it wasn't always as busy as it is today: during the Greek Cypriot guerrilla struggle it was dubbed "murder mile" by the British, because numerous soldiers were ambushed and killed here. Nowadays, in terms of shopping, the street has been surpassed by Leoforos Archiepiskopou Makariou III in the new city. Lidras ends abruptly at the Green Line after a few hundred metres.

Shortly before the Green Line, on the right, you come to the Greek Orthodox **Faneromeni Church** ⓜ, where Archbishop Kyprianou, executed in 1821 by the Ottoman authorities, lies buried. The small **Djami Arablar** ⓝ, or Arablar mosque, is situated directly behind the church.

If you follow the Green Line to the east at a suitable distance (taking photographs is strictly forbidden) and go past the indoor market, you will come to a confusing maze of tiny streets, where you can watch various craftsmen at their trade. Continuing further, you come to the Archbishop's Palace. (The House of the Dragoman is situated a short distance away, in Patriarchou Grigoriou to the south.) If you follow the street to the west you will arrive at the Omeriye mosque and the Turkish bath.

When you want to go back to the beginning of this tour, follow Trikoupi to the

A piece of Greek memorabilia.

BELOW:
admiring glances.

city wall, and then go in a westerly direction along a palm-lined avenue. To the east, the way leads along the wall to the Famagusta Gate. After a further 100 metres you come to Ektoros on the left and then turn right into Chrysaliniotissa, which leads to the beautiful church of **Panagia Chrysaliniotissa**, a domed building in Byzantine style. (The whole walk lasts 2 to 3 hours.)

The oldest treasures on the island are in the **Cyprus Museum O** (open daily, to 1pm only on Sun; entrance fee; tel: 22-868888), a house built in classical style by the British in Leoforos Mouseiou. A representative selection of archaeological discoveries is on display in 14 separate rooms, stretching from the Stone Age (around 7000 BC) to the time of the Roman Empire. Mycenaean ceramics and tomb monuments, bronze statues, furnishings with ivory decorations, and coins and jewellery from over 5,000 years give an insight into the island's rich history. One of the most impressive exhibits is the collection of around 2,000 votive figures from the Sanctuary of Agia Eirini. Also on display is the famous marble statue from 1st century BC. **Aphrodite of Soli**, which has become a symbol of Cyprus, and a larger-than-life bronze nude statue of the Roman Emperor Septimus Severus.

What is missing, however, are the discoveries which the Europeans made in the 19th century and at the beginning of the 20th century. These were taken off the island and now adorn museums all over the world, including the Metropolitan Museum of Art in New York. Opposite the museum building is the City Garden and the Theatre of Nicosia. Around the corner, in Odos Kinyra, the **National Struggle Museum P** provides a reminder of the Greek Cypriot guerrilla struggle against the British. Photographs, mementos, pistols, even a gallows of the type used to hang EOKA fighters convicted of murder, are on display.

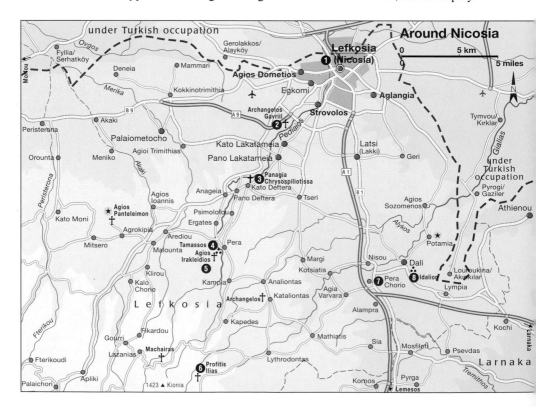

Outer Districts

Outside the centre, the city is growing in a more or less uncontrolled fashion (with the exception of the Turkish-occupied sector). Previously independent villages have been swallowed up by the sprawling suburbs. In the outer districts, the Republic of Cyprus has built large refugee settlements. Banks, businesses and the subsidiaries of many European firms have been drawn to Cyprus and Nicosia since the demise of Beirut as a business centre.

Maps:
Area 256
City 246

Collaboration

There are no official relations between the Republic of Cyprus and the self-proclaimed Turkish Republic of North Cyprus. Nevertheless the city fathers have proved that a form of practical collaboration is possible across the Green Line. In the mid-1980s they began cooperation on a project to develop a joint sewerage system, which is now finished and fully operational. The loosening up of Green Line crossings will no doubt presage further developments in bi-communal relations.

Now the much needed restoration of the valuable, beautiful buildings in the old city has also begun. However, it is a race against time and the old city's continuing decay.

Money is in short supply, despite help from international sources such as the EU and the World Bank. With the help of the UN development plan (UNDP) a common city development plan has been drawn up to avoid planning catastrophes, for example to make sure a situation can't arise where a park is spoilt by the construction of a new factory just over the border. The plan contains alternatives for each eventuality: one with and one without the Green Line.

Exterior detail, Agios Irakleidios.

BELOW: landscape near Tamassos.

Map on page 256

Around Nicosia

This subheading is, of course, a contradiction in terms: there can be no meaningful "around" Nicosia while the city is sliced in two and the two halves are all but inaccessible to each other.

Nevertheless, there are a few places within easy striking distance by car that are well worth seeing: Nicosia International Airport, for a start, although as it is now UNFICYP headquarters you can't actually get there. In 1974 the Cyprus National Guard successfully defended it against élite Turkish paratroops, and wrecked aircraft can be seen as you skirt its edge.

Take the road through Strovolos towards the eastern Troodos Mountains, and you will come to the monastery of **Archangelos Gavriil ②** (Archangel Gabriel), whose 17th-century church has a noted fresco of the archangel.

Further out, near the village of Kato Deftera, you come to **Panagia Chrysospiliotissa ③** (Our Lady of the Golden Cave). The church is in a natural cavern halfway up a cliff face, in a location that may have been used by early Christians. The faithful still climb up to leave votive offerings to the Virgin – wedding dresses seem especially popular.

Still further out on this road, at Politiko, are the ruins of ancient **Tamassos ④** (open daily, closes 3pm; entrance fee). There isn't a lot left of a city whose wealth was mentioned by Homer, and which won favourable reviews from Ovid and Strabo. Two Archaic tombs dating from the 7 BC (a third was apparently appropriated by local villagers in the 19th century for building materials), a jumble of low walls, and that's about it.

Near Tamassos, the nuns of **Agios Irakleidios monastery ⑤** (open daily; group visits only) look after the skull and handbones of St Heraclides, keeping them safe for posterity in ornate reliquaries. In a more tourist-friendly activity, they make honey and icons and sell them to visitors in their tranquil, flower-bedecked cloister.

Continuing on this road, in the general direction but slightly to the southeast of Agios Machairas, is another monastery, or in this case former monastery. **Profitis Ilias ⑥** lies amid countryside so rugged it seems hardly surprising that its monks gave up and pulled out. The Cyprus Forestry Department inherited the monastery's buildings and now runs it as a Forest Station, a great place for picnics and hikes.

A third direction to take from Nicosia is along the Nicosia–Larnaka motorway, turning off at junction 7 or 8 towards the village of Dali. You pass **Pera Chorio ⑦**, where the frescoes in the cemetery chapel of **Agii Apostoloi**, although not in good condition, are important because of their age and artistic quality. They were painted between 1160 and 1180 and are examples of the classic Comnenian style.

South of Dali is an archaeological site whose minimalist character marks it as being for enthusiasts only. **Idalion ⑧** (open permanently; free) was an important Bronze-Age city linked to the myth of Aphrodite and Adonis, and which has the scattered remains of temples to Aphrodite and Athena. A statue of Sargon II found here lends weight to Assyrian claims of domination over Cyprus in 8 BC. ❑

RIGHT: Tripioti church, Nicosia.
BELOW: a market vendor.

NORTHERN CYPRUS

Maps:
City 266
Area 268

*Day trips to Northern Cyprus are now easy to undertake and the
extra time allowed makes it possible to spend a relaxing evening in
a restaurant on Kyrenia harbour before heading back south*

Your picture of Cyprus will not be complete without a glimpse of the
northern part of the island. It is also useful to see first-hand how this part
has fared since 1974, and to draw your own conclusions about the truth of
the various assertions made by each side.

Some Turkish Cypriots claim that the Turkish military presence is still essential to protect the area and its population; others believe they are kept on
primarily for economic reasons. Matters are futher aggravated by chronic tension
– officially denied, but universally acknowledged – between the indigenous
population and Anatolian civilian settlers brought in after 1974. Many native
Turkish Cypriots feel discriminated against in comparison with the "new
Cypriots", and their numbers are steadily declining with emigration.

Visits to the north from the south are officially limited to between 8am and midnight. In a 16-hour day and evening visit there is really a choice of only two routes:
one in a westerly direction, and the other going east all the way to the end of the
Karpasia peninsula, following a brief walking itinerary through northern Nicosia.

Taxi-drivers and money-changers cluster just beyond the checkpoints, though
it's unwise to purchase too many Turkish lira. It may be worth hiring a car for the
day especially if you have the ability to make a late drop-off. This way you will
get to see more of the north in your time available.

PRECEDING PAGES:
Salamis; Keryneia/
Girne harbour.
LEFT: children take
part in a Turkish
Cypriot festival.
BELOW: Belediye
Market.

Northern Nicosia/Lefkosia

Before engaging a taxi for your tour of the north, you
might spend a couple of hours taking in the medieval
monuments and backwater atmosphere of northern
Nicosia within the walls. Immediately past the Zahra
(Mula) bastion, one of the five under Turkish-Cypriot
control, a minor breach in the walls allows you to slip
inside and follow quieter Tanzimat Sokak to the
Keryneia Gate ⒜ at the top of Girne Caddesi, logi-
cal start-point of a walkabout. The British left the gate
isolated when they demolished the walls to either side
in 1931 as a traffic-easing measure.

A few steps south along Girne Caddesi, on the left,
stands the **Ethnography Museum** (open Mon–Fri;
summer 9am–7pm; winter 9am–1pm and 2–4.45pm;
free), housed in the former **Mevlevi Tekke ⒝**. The
Mevlevi Dervish order was active here until 1953, long
after it was supressed in Republican Turkey; the multi-
domed hall on the street side shelters the tombs of the
16 sheikhs of the Cypriot order. Near the south end of
Girne Caddesi, **Atatürk Meydani ⒞** has been the
heart of the city since Ottoman times, and is still ringed
by banks, the British-built post office and law courts
and a baroque 19th-century mosque.

From Atatürk Meydani, Asmaalti Sokak leads
southeast past a functioning *hamam*, or Turkish bath,

towards a pair of *hans*, medieval inns for travellers. The smaller **Kumarcilar Hani** (open M Fri; summer 9am–7pm; winter 9am–1pm and 2pm–4.45pm; entra ee), is more typically Cypriot with its pointed-arch colonnade; the larg iyük Han ❺ (open daily; entrance fee) adheres more to Anatolian prototy with its free-standing ablutions fountain, perched on six columns in the cen ourtyard.

Still further sou t from here is the bazaar district, mostly pedestrianised to match the same ocess in South Nicosia as part of the overall masterplan. In the **Belediye Paz i ❻**, or covered market, by the Green Line, there are a few stalls selling craf or antiques, more interesting than the cheap jeans outside pitched at Turkish soldiers.

Immediately north, past the locked **Bedesten**, looms the **Djami Selimiye** ❼, formerly the Lusignan cathedral of Agia Sofia, begun in 1209 but still unfinished 150 years later. It is sometimes possible to climb one of the pair of 50-metre (160-ft) minarets added after the Ottoman conquest. Inside the west facade with its sculpted portal and giant rose window, inspired by French prototypes, the coronation of the Lusignan kings of Cyprus took place.

Directly east of the Selimiye stands the **Sultan Mahmut library** ❽ (open Mon–Sat 9am–4pm; entrance fee), with its collection of precious manuscripts and books – and a warden with the key to the **Lapidary Museum** ❾ (opening times as for library; entrance fee) across the square, essentially a warehouse for archaeological masonry established by the British. Star exhibit is the Gothic tracery window, rescued from a Lusignan palace at Atatürk Meydani that was demolished by the British.

Just north of here rises the **Djami Haydarpaşa** ❿ (open daily; entrance fee),

TIP

If you're tempted to make purchases at the Belediye Pazari, or anywhere else in the north, bear in mind that the goods are liable to confiscation when you return to the south.

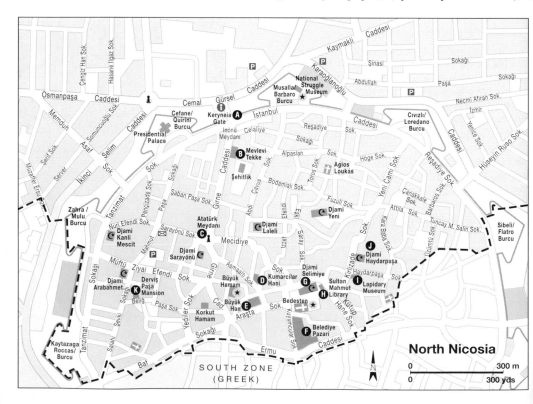

North Nicosia

originally the 14th-century church of St Katherine, perhaps the most under-rated Gothic structure in town; it now serves as an art gallery (open Mon–Fri 9am–1pm and 2–5pm, Sat 9am–1pm) and merits a look inside for its architectural details.

From the **Selimiye Meydani**, head west towards the minor gate near the **Zahra bastion**, admiring as you go the fine Ottoman houses of the Arabahmet district around the eponymous mosque. One of the oldest, the **Dervis Paşa mansion**  (K), once home to a local worthy who founded the first Cypriot Turkish-language newspaper, is now a minor ethnographic museum (open daily 9am–1pm and 2–5pm; entrance fee).

Maps:
City 266
Area 268–9

Western tour – Nicosia–Keryneia–Vouni

Heading northeast out of **Nicosia/Lefkosia** (1), the road runs towards Keryneia, signposted as "Girne". This initially crosses the **Mesaoria**, the fertile plain whose name means "between the mountain ranges": the two in question being the **Pentadaktylos (Besparmak)**, the legendary "Five-Finger" mountains to the north, and the **Troodos Mountains** on the south. During early spring this expanse becomes a vast carpet of flowers, quickly followed by golden corn or grain, reaped in June, leaving a brown, steppe-like landscape.

In 1191 a decisive battle took place on the Mesaoria that changed the historical course of the island. The fleet of Berengaria of Navarre, the fiancée of Richard the Lionheart, ran into a storm off the south coast of Cyprus, whilst her betrothed was fighting in the Crusades. Isaac Comnenos, the Byzantine despot of Cyprus, had taken Berengaria and Richard's sister prisoner, when Richard appeared to defend his kinswomen. Following his marriage to Berengaria in Limassol, the English king defeated the Byzantine army so decisively at Tremetousha, southeast of Nicosia, that the island remained under European Catholic rule for almost 400 years.

During the first three centuries of this era, under the Lusignan dynasty, various splendid public buildings were constructed. Many of these are still in good condition, including the Agios Nikolaos cathedral (Lala Mustafa Paşa mosque) in Famagusta and the beautiful Agia Sophia (Selimiye mosque) in Nicosia.

Three pre-existing Byzantine fortresses in the Pentadaktylos range were also reinforced during this period: the westernmost and best preserved of these, **Agios Ilarion** (2) (open daily 9am–4.30pm; entrance fee; tel: 0533-161276), is reached after a short side-journey west from the main highway, passing a Turkish military camp.

The present castle, on the site of a Byzantine monastery, is named after St Hilarion, a 7th-century Syrian hermit. The Lusignan nobility used it as a summer residence during the 13th and 14th centuries; magnificent jousting tournaments took place on the high plateau just below the castle pinnacle. It takes a good hour to scramble through the multi-levelled fortifications, from a Byzantine chapel near the bottom to the so-called royal apartments on the summit, with sweeping views over the north coast. The battlements and towers seem to grow naturally out of the steep

The unmistakable peak of Five-Finger Mountain, northeast of Nicosia.

BELOW:
the Mesaoria.

limestone rocks of the mountains. The roof and modern plastered additions to the structure suffered heavy damage in a 1995 forest fire, but a snack bar/café is now operating outside the main entrance.

Keryneia

Keryneia was founded by Greeks from Arcadia in the 10th century BC and numbered among the ten Classical city-Kingdoms of Cyprus, though little remains of this period.

Descending in wide arcs from the Agios Ilarion saddle, you arrive at **Keryneia/Girne ❸**, built around a seaside fortress which was reinforced by the Lusignans. Visitors to this small coastal town before 1974, with its circular harbour, compact and picturesque town plan and cosmopolitan expatriate society, may not recognise it today. Much of the town is an untidy sprawl of buildings indistinguishable from anywhere else on the Mediterranean coast; little remains of Keryneia's Hellenic past, or the days when it could barely muster 2,000 tourist beds. The visible architecture of the oft-painted old quarter curled around the harbour is Frankish-Byzantine, with Venetian and Ottoman additions. Much of the new construction is holiday accommodation, for Keryneia is the epicentre of the tourist industry in the north of the island. Only in the hillside village of **Karmi/-Karaman ❹**, where foreigners have been issued long leases to renovate abandoned houses, is there a faint echo of the former post-colonial bohemianism.

There are a few small museums in the narrow alleys around Keryneia's port, such as the **Icon Museum** (open daily; summer 9am–7pm; winter 9am–1pm and 2–4.45pm; entrance fee) in the deconsecrated church of Archangelos, and the **Folk Art Museum** (open daily; June–Sept 9am–5pm; entrance fee) in a Venetian-vintage house, however of most interest is the **castle** (open daily 8am–1pm and 2–5pm) on the eastern side of the old quarter. Its foundations were laid by the Byzantines after 7th-century Arab raids, but its present form is the work of

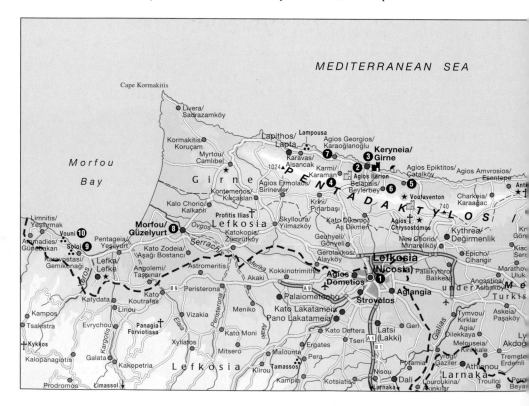

Venetian military engineers. In addition to their dissimilar bastions and earlier Lusignan living quarters, you can tour the dungeons where rebellious nobles and knights starved to death in 1310; more recently, Greek Cypriot EOKA fighters were imprisoned here by the British.

The highlight of **Keryneia Castle** is the **Shipwreck Museum** (open daily 9am–6.45pm; entrance fee) just off the courtyard, which features the oldest recovered wreck in the world: a Hellenistic cargo boat discovered at a depth of 33 m (108 ft) and salvaged, between 1968 and 1969, by a team from the University of Pennsylvania and the Cypriot Antiquities Service.

The wreck, 15 m (48 ft) long and 3 m (11 ft) wide, was a singled-masted boat travelling with a cargo of nearly 400 amphorae filled with wine, almonds and oil. The amphorae came from various potteries, indicating that the ship must have called at several ports en route. Radiocarbon analysis of the 10,000 almonds and the keel planks, along with the dating of two coins, indicate that the ship probably went down between 330 and 280 BC.

Sorting through the day's catch along the north coast.

Around Keryneia: beaches and Belapais

By now you may have had lunch overlooking the harbour, and be ready to break the journey with a swim at one of the excellent beaches to the east of Keryneia. In order of occurrence they are **Acapulco**, rather encroached on by the eponymous resort and army installations; **Lara**, 3 km (2 miles) east, with a single restaurant; **Alagadi**, or "Turtle Bay" after the creatures which nest here; and best of all **Onucuncu Mil** (Thirteenth Mile), the stated distance east of town.

Acapulco lies next to the highway veering inland towards the second of the mountain castles, **Voufaventon** unrestricted access but the 5-km (3-mile) access

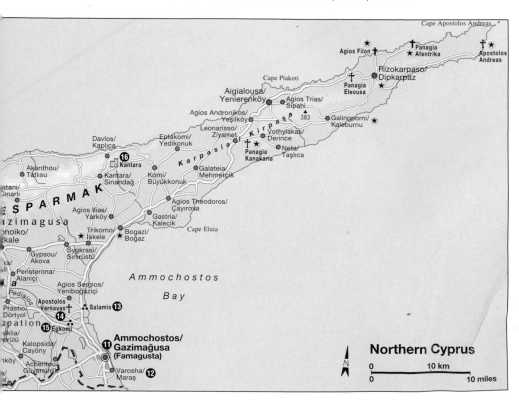

Northern Cyprus

*The ruined castle at
Voufaventon is in a
dramatic location.*

BELOW: the land-
scape around
Keryneia/Girne.

road is narrow and unpaved. From the high point of the bypass road to Famagusta via Kythrea/Degirmenlik, a rough track leads west to the trailhead for the 45-minute ascent to the castle. This does add a two-hour diversion to a tightly scheduled day so, instead, you may prefer to backtrack slightly from the beach to a pair of sites prominently featured in Lawrence Durrell's classic *Bitter Lemons*, a portait of the area in the 1950s. Just seaward of **Agios Epiktitos/Catalkoy** ⑤ stands the little shrine of **Hazreti Omer Turbesi** and, one cove west, Fortuna – the elaborate house built by Durrell's friend Marie; this is unfortunately now the residence of the Turkish military commander, and off-limits.

From Hazreti Omer a road leads inland to Agios Epiktitos (Catalkoy) and thence west to the abbey at **Belapais/Beylerbey** ⑥ (open daily; June–Sept 9am–7pm; Oct–May 9am–5pm; entrance fee), the third unmissable sight on this western tour, apart from the castles of Agios Ilarion and Kerynia. Lawrence Durrell put the village of Belapais on the touristic and literary map when he bought an old house here in 1953 and restored it, as related in *Bitter Lemons*; a plaque on the outer wall comemorates his stay, though the house has had several other owners since, and has been extensively modernised.

The abbey itself is one of the more beautiful and atmospheric Gothic buildings on the island, despite vandalism by raiding Genoese, medieval villagers and even the British. Founded early in the 13th century by Augustinians fleeing Palestine, it changed its affiliation within a few years to the Premonstratensians, whose brethren wore white robes – giving rise to the epithet "the white abbey". Under the patronage of Lusignan King Hugh III (1267–1284), Belapais reached its zenith, with the existing monastic church built at this time, and the monks accorded many privileges, such as the right to travel on horseback, armed

Map
on page
268–9

with gilded sword and spurs; other, less codified perks, such as the acquisition of personal riches and the taking of (multiple) concubines, were overlooked so that the place soon had a well deserved reputation for luxury and scandal. Despite such goings-on, the palatial abbey was known as "L'Abbaie de la Paix", adapted under the Venetians to "de la Pais" – from which it was a short step to the present name. During the Genoese-Venetian period the abbey went into decline, there were few monks left for the victorious Ottomans to drive out in 1570, after which the grounds were handed over to the Orthodox church.

The delicate 14th-century cloister is mostly intact; on its north side, perched at the edge of an escarpment, is the sumptuous refectory, where six bay windows look onto the sea, and (conditions permitting) the Taurus Mountains in Turkey. Because Belapais sees plenty of foreign tourists, the 13th-century church here is undesecrated, and much as the local Greeks left it when they departed under duress in 1976, the last group around Keryneia to do so; perhaps their tenacity and loyalty to their parish church owed something to the legend that the village was originally populated by the bastard offspring of the monks.

West of Keryneia

Some 8 km (5 miles) west of Keryneia is **Agios Georgios/Karaoglanoglu ❼**, site of the Turkish amphibious landing on 20 July 1974. A cluster of hideous monuments – including a cement structure resembling an artillery piece – marks the spot; nearby is a **"Peace and Freedom" Museum** (open Mon–Fri; summer 9am–2pm; winter 9am–1pm and 2–4.45pm; entrance fee) consisting of disabled Greek-Cypriot military equipment, and a wall-relief chronicle of atrocities perpetrated on Turkish-Cypriots by Greeks and Greek-Cypriots. For Turkey, the

BELOW: the ruined abbey at Belapais/Beylerbey.

landing marked the start of the "Peace Operation" – the "invasion and occupation" in Greek-Cypriot eyes, the "intervention" for the studiously even-handed.

The town of **Morfou/Güzelyurt**  47 km (29 miles) west of Kerynia, fourth largest settlement in the north, lies amidst extensive citrus groves; export of the fruit provides much needed income to the unrecognised state of Northern Cyprus. In the years immediately after 1974, there was an insufficient population for the labour-intensive job of tending citrus; most of the Turkish Cypriots who settled nearby were from the grape-growing areas of Limassol and Pafos. Apart from the combined natural history and archaeological museum (open daily 9am–5pm; entrance fee), the main sight is the originally Byzantine (but much altered) monastic church of **Agios Mamas**, where the venerated tomb of the saint is in fact a Roman sarcophagus a few centuries too old to have housed his mortal remains. But at intervals a magic unguent is said to have oozed forth from holes bored in the tomb, the liquid a panacea for earache and stormy seas. Mamas is more renowned as the patron saint of tax evaders; he was a hermit who successfully defied a Byzantine governor on the issue of a poll tax.

A 30-minute drive west of Morfou brings you to the ruins of ancient **Soloi**  (open daily 9am–7pm; entrance fee), just past the little modern port of **Karavostasi/Gemikonagi**. The name of Soloi is often spuriously linked to the Athenian statesman Solon, who supposedly urged King Philokypros to move the city from an inland site to this spot early in the 6th century BC; it seems almost certain, however, that there has been a settlement here since the late Bronze Age. One of the ten ancient city-kingdoms of Cyprus, it was the last to hold out during the 498 BC revolt against the Persians; later, under Roman rule, Soloi flourished again, courtesy of the rich copper mines just inland.

The town of Morfou/ Güzelyurt is famous for its citrus fruit.

BELOW: floor mosaic in the basilica at Soloi.

Map on page 268–9

The 2nd-century AD amphitheatre was dismantled by the British and its stone sent to line the Suez Canal and the quay at Port Said; the ugly structure of today is a crude 1963 restoration. More worthwhile is a 5th-century basilica to the east, which features extensive floor mosaics including a swan and waterfowl with dolphins. To the west lies the ancient *agora*, which has been fenced off since Canadian excavations were suspended in 1974; the Roman statuette of Aphrodite uncovered here is now in the Cyprus Museum in southern Nicosia.

Should time permit, you may want to continue 3 km (2 miles) west to the palace of **Vouni** ⑩ (open daily 10am–4.30pm; entrance fee), located on a hill 250 m (820 ft) above the sea. Its history is shrouded in mystery – even the ancient name is unknown – but it was apparently founded early in the 5th century BC by the pro-Persian king Doxandros of Marion (modern Polis) to watch over pro-Hellenic Soloi in the wake of the recent revolt. Following Kimon of Athens' campaign on the island, a Greek dynasty seized control and remodelled the palace, which in the event lasted only a few decades before being burnt down early in the 4th century BC.

The mud-brick walls of the upper storey were unable to withstand the fire and many centuries of erosion, so only foundations remain. The most comprehensible structures are a monumental seven-stepped stairway, a guitar-shaped windlass serving as a deep cistern, and the low remains of two temples, one of which has what is obviously an altar where many votive offerings were recovered.

Eastern tour: Nicosia–Famagusta–Salamis

A separate day-trip can be made to points of interest east of Nicosia, scattered along the east coast in the district of Famagusta. Unfortunately, the Karpasia/ Kirpasa peninsula, with its undeveloped beaches and numerous Byzantine monuments, is beyond the scope of an eight-hour journey, especially if two hours have already been devoted to north Nicosia.

Of all the towns in Cyprus, **Famagusta/Gazimagusa** ⑪ (Ammochostos) has been the worst affected by the events of 1974, but earlier in its history it was often hostage to fortune. A town of some sort existed here in Hellenistic and Roman times, but it first achieved prominence when Byzantine settlers arrived from Salamis, after it fell victim to the Arabs during the 7th century.

The Greek name subsequently bestowed on the city, and still used by Greeks today, is Ammochostos, "sunken in sand", after the shifting beaches and sandbars all around. Later, in 1136, Famagusta received an influx of Armenians compulsorily settled here by the Byzantine emperor.

Its golden age was kick-started by the Saracen capture of Acre, the last Crusader stronghold in Palestine, in 1291. The town's population swelled with the influx of thousands of refugee Christians, and thanks to its decent natural harbour and the Pope's ban on trade with the infidels of the Holy Land, the city became spectacularly wealthy from a monopoly in trans-shipping exotic oriental commodities.

A contemporary German traveller, Ludolf von Suchen, left a vivid description of the splendour of

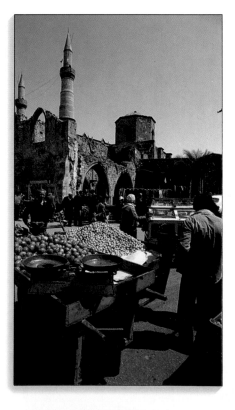

BELOW: fresh produce for sale in the streets of Famagusta.

Famagusta, then the richest – and most ostentatious – city in the world. According to him, the wedding jewellery of a Famagustan merchant's daughter was "worth more than that of the Queen of France"; one citizen, Frangiskos Lakhas, frequently entertained the upper echelons with banquets where precious stones were left on the tables as party favours; and the local loose women were "the most expensive in the world", and could earn a fortune "of at least 1,000,000 gold ducats" at the discreet drop of a handkerchief.

So much vulgarity and riches were naturally a source of envy and jostling for influence, particularly between the Genoese and their main rivals the Venetians. Matters came to a head in 1372, at the coronation of the Lusignan King Peter II, where a scuffle between the Genoese and Venetian escorts degenerated into anti-Genoese riots. The Genoese retaliated by landing troops to ravage the island in general, and Famagusta in particular; it took the Lusignans over 70 years to expel the Genoese, but the damage had been done and Famagusta never recovered its former prominence. The last Lusignan ruler, Queen Caterina Cornaro, abdicated in 1489 at the insistence of the Venetians, who instituted military rule, and decided to make Famagusta their most impregnable stronghold, in advance of the inevitable Ottoman attack.

This came in October 1570, after Keryneia and Nicosia had been taken with little or no resistance. Famagusta proved different, however; the commander of its Venetian garrison, Marcantonio Bragadino, was ingenious and resolute, despite being outnumbered 25 to 1 by the Ottoman forces under Lala Mustafa Paşa. Finally, in August 1571, the 2,000 surviving defenders marched out to surrender to Lala Mustafa, who at first received them with all courtesy and promised them safe passage to Venetian-held Crete.

BELOW: backgammon behind the city walls.

But at some point the parley went sour, and the Ottoman commander – despite the disapproval of his own subordinates – hacked Bragadino's lieutenants to death, and then flayed Bragadino alive in front of St Nicholas cathedral. Thus ended one of the most celebrated campaigns of medieval times.

Despite the high cost of Famagusta's capture, the Ottomans had little use for the walled town, reserving it as a place of exile for disgraced notables, and repairing few of the many buildings damaged by artillery during the long siege. As elsewhere in Cyprus, Orthodox Christians were forbidden residence within the citadel, and were obliged to establish a new settlement outside the walls: **Varosha/Maras ⓬**, which in a few brief years after independence experienced both prosperity and catastrophe. With the emergence of mass tourism, an ugly hotel ghetto of some 4,000 beds sprang up behind the sandy beaches fringing Varosha, making it one of the biggest foreign-currency earners in Cyprus. In mid-August 1974, the Turkish military bombarded Varosha, sending the 40,000 inhabitants into precipitous flight prior to capturing it and sealing most of it off with cordons. Since then this ghost town has remained empty and can only be entered by the Turkish army, and occasional UN patrols. Gardens grow wild, while the buildings slowly decay from the effects of the sun, wind and sand. A number of hotels just outside the dead zone, and north along the coast en route to Salamis, totalling about 2,000 beds, were unaffected by the invasion and still operate under Turkish-Cypriot management. The original Greek-Cypriot owners have yet to receive any compensation.

Map on page 268–9

In Old Famagusta several Gothic churches were converted into mosques following the Ottoman conquest, by the simple addition of minarets. These curious architectural chimeras are still attractive, but overall the walled town's medieval legacy is neglected. Anything surplus to the requirements of tourism is used as car parks, football pitches, or for anchoring washing lines.

The formidable city walls total 3 km (2 miles) in length, and average 15 m (47 ft) in height and 8 m (25 ft) in thickness, with deep moats on the landward sides. It is possible to walk on the walls and to climb up the southwesterly Rivettina bastion, where the Venetians ran up the white flag of surrender. The museum at **Canbulat bastion** (open daily 8am–5pm; entrance fee), formerly the venetion Arsenal, is now a shrine to the Ottoman war hero Cancebeilat Bey. There are many Ottoman artefacts on display as well as the shrine in the tower.

The most impressive single fortification is the northeasterly Citadel, frequently claimed to be the setting for Shakespeare's *Othello*, and therefore known as **Othello's tower**. It's uncertain whether the dark-haired vice-governor Christofero Moro (served 1506–08), who lost his wife here, was the role-model for the tragic figure, or whether it was one of his successors, Francesco de Sessa, known as "Il Capitano Moro", banished from here in 1544 with two subordinates – possibly the basis for the Iago and Cassio characters. Nevertheless, this originally Lusignan fort, redesigned in 1492 by the Venetian engineer Foscarini, remains a plausible and atmospheric venue, used frequently in the past as a film location.

A stroll around Old Famagusta will reveal a series of architectural curiosities.

Elsewhere, in the centre of the old city, spare a glance for the scant remains of the **Palazzo del Proveditore**, the palace of the Venetian Governor in which the Turkish man of letters Namik Kemal was incarcerated for 38 months between 1873 and 1876 for writing a play critical of the sultan. Of the various surviving churches, the smaller among them normally closed, the 14th-century **Sinan Paşa mosque** (formerly the church of St Peter and St Paul) near the Venetian palace is the most substantial. It was built by a merchant, Simone Nostrano, from the profit of a single transaction with a Syrian friend. The building served the Ottomans as a mosque, the English as a potato store, and is now the municipal playhouse.

BELOW:
Othello's tower.

About 200 metres east of the preceding two monuments towers the former cathedral of St Nicholas, now the **Lala Mustafa Paşa mosque**.

Salamis and the Royal Tombs

Leave Famagusta on the most northerly road, passing delightful sandy beaches such as Glapsides and "Silver". After about 8 km (5 miles) a turning heads east to the partially excavated remains of ancient **Salamis** ⑬ (open daily 8am–6pm; entrance fee). The ruins are extensive, scattered over an area of about 5 sq. km (2 sq. miles), so with the limited time at your disposal you'll need your taxi driver to shuttle you between points of interest. The site is fringed

by excellent beaches, and in spring it is splashed bright yellow with flowering mimosa; located near the ticket-booth entrance is a beachfront restaurant well placed for a quick lunch.

Legend has it that Salamis was founded by the Trojan War hero Tefkros, who was exiled by his father King Telamon from his native island Salamina, and brought along his homeland's name – and Bronze Age culture. Thanks to its good natural harbour, the city was for several centuries one of the most important city-kingdoms on the island, until dominated by the Ptolemaic kings. During the Byzantine era, it was renamed Constantia, designated capital of the island and regained its former importance, before devastation by 4th-century earthquakes and 7th-century Arab raids.

Immediately southwest of the site entrance stands the most interesting excavation, the Roman *palaestra*, with its inner courtyards surrounded by columns, and the floors of its east portico tiled with variegated marble. Equally impressive are the monumental baths complex from the 3rd century AD, its various halls still decorated with fragments of mosaics. The best of these, in bays of the southernmost hall, show the river god Evrotas, and a fragmentary battle scene thought possibly to depict Apollo and Artemis fighting against the Niobids.

South of the *palaestra* and baths looms the Roman amphitheatre, dating from the reign of the emperor Augustus, though rebuilt in early Byzantine times. It originally held 15,000 spectators; the rows of seating have been well restored and eight of the 18 are original. If you're ahead of schedule, direct your vehicle to the extreme southeast corner of the site, where the Kambanopetra basilica retains its *synthronon* or bishop's seat, and also some small baths with a brilliant geometric mosaic floor.

BELOW: detail of the Lala Mustafa Paşa mosque (formerly St Nicholas Cathedral) in Famagusta.

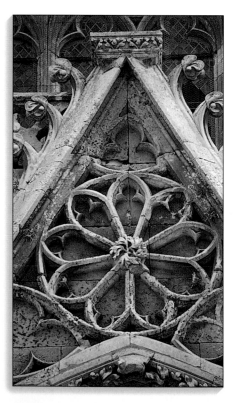

FROM CATHEDRAL TO MOSQUE

The former cathedral of St Nicholas, now the Lala Mustafa Paşa mosque, was erected by the Lusignans between 1298 and 1326 and is often regarded as the supreme Gothic masterpiece on the island.

Built in conscious imitation of the cathedral at Rheims, it lost its twin towers during the 1571 siege, and gained the single minaret afterwards. The west facade, with a huge rose window and gabled porticoes more impressive than those of Nicosia's Selimiye mosque, can be contemplated from the courtyard, where a massive fig tree is believed to be as old as the building. The cathedral and its environs saw many crucial moments of medieval Famagusta. Here the Lusignan rulers underwent honorary coronation as kings of Jerusalem, having already received the crown of Cyprus in Nicosia; here the young widow of the last Lusignan king was forced to sign her abdication, and here too, lashed between the two granite columns pilfered from ancient Salamis, Bragadino was flayed.

Inside the building, two rows of columns support the magnificent vaulting, all is plain and whitewashed in accordance with Islamic doctrine, Koranic calligraphy hangs from the walls and prayer rugs cover old tombstones, the graves long since emptied by an enraged Lala Mustafa.

To gain a fuller understanding of late Bronze Age culture, visit the nearby **Royal Tombs** (open daily; tel: 378-8331; entrance fee), accessible via a side road starting opposite the disused western gate to Salamis. Most of the 150-plus tombs here were plundered in antiquity, but excavations in 1957 uncovered two (numbers 47 and 79) that yielded sensational artefacts confirming Homer's descriptions of Mycenaean funerary rites. These finds included three thrones, a magnificent wooden bed decorated with ivory and silver, pitchers and amphora containing food, jewellery and weapons, all intended to serve the deceased in the next world. Most of the tombs opened towards the east, and were approached by sloping *dhromoi* or ramps; here, archaeologists found chariots, which had carried the biers of dead kings or heroes, and the skeletons of various horses which had been sacrificed – as well as favourite human servants, some discovered bound hand and foot. It seems that these Homeric rituals were being observed as late as the 7th century BC, nearly 500 years after Bronze Age culture on the Greek mainland had faded away.

There is a small site museum, with plans and photographs, as well as a reconstruction of one chariot. The findings from the tombs are in the Cyprus Museum in Nicosia *(see page 256)*, accompanied by photographs and reconstructions.

St Barnabas and the Church of Cyprus

The monastery of the Apostle Barnabas, **Apostolos Varnavas** ⓮ (open daily 8am–7pm; entrance fee), 500 metres beyond the Royal Tombs on the same minor road, commemorates a saint who played a pivotal, and posthumous, role in the history of the Cypriot Orthodox Church. Born in Salamis and brought up in Jerusalem, where he became a follower of Jesus, Barnabas toured Cyprus and

ABOVE AND BELOW: examining the headless statues in the *palaestra* at Salamis.

Map
on pages
268–9

*Richly gilded icon
inside the monastery
of Apostle Barnabas
(Apostolos Varnavas).*

RIGHT: Salamis.
BELOW: the watch-
tower at Kantara
castle.

Asia Minor with the Apostle Paul, and again seven years later with his cousin Mark. He was stoned to death by the Jewish community of Salamis in 75 AD, and buried at an undisclosed location by Mark. Some four centuries later Barnabas appeared in a dream to the archbishop of Salamis, then embroiled in a dispute with the archbishop of Antioch over ecclesiastical precedence, and revealed the location of his tomb. The good bishop dug, and found a catacomb with a skeleton inside, clutching a handwritten copy of St Matthew's Gospel. The authorities in Constantinople were sufficiently impressed by this miracle to declare the Cypriot church autocephalous, independent from Antioch, and divided it into several bishoprics of its own. To the present day, the archbishop of all Cyprus enjoys the the right to carry a sceptre, wear a purple coat and to sign his name in red ink, all in the manner of the Byzantine emperors.

A monastery was founded on the site of the tomb in the 5th century; the present building dates from 1756. It now serves as an ad hoc archaeological museum, most of the items probably rescued from the looted district museum and the Hadjiprodhromou collection in Famagusta. The entrance to the purported tomb of Barnabas is just outside the gate; stairs lead down to ancient rock-cut chambers.

Egkomi and Kantara

On the way back to Nicosia from the monastery, one more possible stop for archaeology enthusiasts is at the excavations of **Egkomi** ❶ (open daily; entrance fee). This early Bronze-Age city, later supplanted by Salamis, was a major copper-exporting port with links to Egypt and Asia before the arrival of migrant Myceneans in the 12th century BC. When archaeologists began excavations here in 1896, they thought they had found the necropolis of Salamis, as there was a skeleton buried under every structure. But this was merely a form of ancestor-worship in what turned out to be a real city, with a clear grid plan of rectangular houses.

If you would like a break from serious cultural sightseeing, you could finish the day by driving 39 km (24 miles) from Salamis to **Kantara castle** ❶ (open daily; entrance fee). The drive up to the castle is not for the faint-hearted, but there are a few spots on the nerve-racking switchbacks that allow cars to get past each other. From the castle you can enjoy a simultaneous view of the north coast and Famagusta bay on the the east coast. It's also a good spot for a picnic. Kantara, the best preserved castle of the three in the Keryneia range, is where Isaac Comnenos surrendered to Richard the Lionheart after the debacle at Tremetousha in 1191; it also saw considerable action during the 13th-century wars between the Holy Roman Emperor and the Lusignan nobility.

From Bogazi/Bogaz a narrow road leads up to a virtually abandoned Kantara village, from where another road leads a further 4 km (2½ miles) to the castle. A long flight of steps leads from the car park through the barbican, massive southeast bastion and barracks, all relatively intact. Above and beyond, the castle is more dilapidated: it was partially dismantled by the Venetians in the 16th century to render it useless to domestic rebels or the Ottomans. ❏

CONTENTS

Getting Acquainted

The Place

Situation The third biggest Mediterranean island, Cyprus is at 34°33–35°34N and 32°16–34°37E at the northeastern end of the Mediterranean.
Area 9,251 sq. km (3,572 sq. miles), with the south under the control of the internationally recognised Republic of Cyprus, and north under Turkish military occupation.
Capital Nicosia (Lefkosia/Lefkosha), with a population of around 225,000, with 190,000 living in the south and an estimated 35,000 in the north.
Population Of the estimated 833,000 people currently living on the island, approximately 616,000 are Greek Cypriots, 210,000 are Turkish Cypriots (not including the 35,000 Turkish occupation troops), 7,000 Armenians, Maronites and several Latin ("Western Christian") minorities.
Languages Greek (southern Cyprus) and Turkish (north).
Religion Greek Orthodox and Muslim.
Time Zone Central European Time: 2 hours ahead of GMT. The switch to Daylight Saving Time occurs at the same time as in other European countries. Darkness falls earlier and more quickly than in northern European countries; twilight lasts for only 30 minutes.
Currency Cyprus pound (CY£), divided into 100 cents. Turkish lira is used in the north.
Weights & Measures Metric.
Electricity 240 volts; flat three-pin plugs. Some hotel rooms have a 110-volt outlet for electric shavers.
International dialling code Republic of Cyprus: 357, **North Cyprus**: 392.

The Climate

Cyprus has a long, hot and dry summer with relatively low humidity; a short spring and autumn; and a mild, wet winter when snow often falls in the Troodos Mountains (but even in December seawater temperatures remain at around 19°C/66°F). The average peak daytime temperature in July and August is 35°C (95°F), and 15°C (59°F) in January. Maximum summer temperatures inland go above 40°C (104°F) and minimum winter temperatures go below freezing in the mountains. Most rainfall is between November and February, when you can expect approximately 9–11 days of rain per

Public Holidays in the Republic of Cyprus

- **1 January** New Year's Day
- **6 January** Epiphany
- **25 March** Greek Independence Day
- **1 April** Greek Cypriot National Day
- **1 May** Labour Day
- **15 August** Assumption
- **1 October** Cyprus Independence Day
- **28 October** Greek National Day, Ochi ("no") Day
- **25 December** Christmas Day
- **26 December** Boxing Day

VARIABLE HOLIDAYS

The Orthodox Church usually celebrates Easter a week or two later than central Europe, so forthcoming dates include:

- **Clean Monday** The first day of Lent, 25 Feb 2003, 9 Feb 2004
- **Greek Orthodox Good Friday** 12 Apr 2003, 27 Mar 2004
- **Greek Orthodox Easter Sunday** 14 Apr 2003, 29 Mar 2004
- **Greek Orthodox Easter Monday** 15 Apr 2003, 30 Mar 2004
- **Pentecost-Kataklysmos** (Festival of the Flood), 2 June 2003, 17 May 2004

ORTHODOX CHURCH HOLIDAYS These have no effect on regular business hours and are often celebrated only in certain regions (these include name days of local holy figures and the patron saints of monasteries). They are often celebrated with processions and festivities:

- **6 January** Coastal regions hold the *Blessing of the Sea*. In the ceremony the bishop plunges a cross into the sea.
- **17 January** *St Anthony's Day*. Services in Nicosia and Limassol in honour of the Egyptian father of monasticism.
- **24 January** *St Neophytos's Day*. A massive procession ending at the cave of this hermit at Tala near Pafos.
- **1, 2 February** *Jesus's Presentation in the Temple*. Pilgrimage to Panagia Chrysorrogiatissa Monastery.
- **23 April** *St George's Day*. Services just about everywhere.
- **29 June** SS *Peter and Paul*.

A large service is held in Kato Pafos, celebrated by the archbishop and other bishops.

- **15 August** *Assumption of the Virgin*. Celebrations conducted in the larger monasteries, with processions taking place all over the island.
- **14 September** *Raising of the Holy Cross*. Large celebrations, particularly in the Stavrovouni Monastery and in Lefkara and Omodos.
- **4 October** *Ioannis Lampadistis* (St John). Service in the monastery at Kalopanagiotis devoted to this local patron saint.
- **18 October** *St Luke's Day*. Celebrated in Nicosia and Palaichori in particular.

The following Orthodox holidays are also worth keeping an eye open for: the *Procession of the Lazarus Icon* through Larnaka, a week before Easter; and the *Festival of the Flood*, with celebrations in Larnaka at Whitsun.

month (winters since 1994–95 have been characterised by below-average precipitation, leading to water shortages).

Best Times to Visit

Cyprus is at its best in springtime, when the island is covered in a carpet of green vegetation and multi-coloured flowers, and the air is fresh. While autumn temperatures are similar (you can still enjoy outdoor lunches, sunbathe and even swim), the intervening summer burns away much of the vegetation and flowers, and the air may be dry and dusty.

Many hotels offer reduced prices in off-peak seasons. In the popular swimming resorts the off-peak season runs from 1 November to 31 March (except Christmas holidays between 20 December and 6 January), and in the Troodos Mountains from 1 October until 30 June.

Government

The Republic of Cyprus has a democratic constitution based on the Zurich Agreements of 1959 and 1960. It grants a great deal of authority to the country's president, who is chairman of the council of state and is directly elected by the Cypriot population for a term of five years.

Since 1960 Cyprus has been an independent republic. Previously the island was a British colony and it remains a member of the British Commonwealth. The Republic of Cyprus also belongs to the United Nations and the Council of Europe. It has been an associate member of the European Union since 1973 and in 1990 applied for full membership, being confirmed by the EU as a candidate member in 1997. In the 1998 presidential elections the conservative Glavkos Clerides narrowly won another term of office. The current president is Tasos Papadopoulos who succeeded Clerides in 2003.

On 20 July 1974, the island was effectively split into two when Turkish troops invaded in response to a Greek-inspired coup against the government of Archbishop Makarios. Today the Republic of Cyprus controls about 63 percent of the country in the south while the Turkish-occupied north consists of about 37 percent.

In 1983, the north unilaterally declared itself to be the independent Turkish Republic of Northern Cyprus, but apart from Turkey no country recognises northern Cyprus as an independent state. In an international context, the "president" of northern Cyprus, Rauf Denktash, is known only as the "Leader of the Turkish Cypriot People". Around 35,000 soldiers from the Turkish mainland are stationed in northern Cyprus and a large number of mainland Turks are now resident there. All settlements in northern Cyprus have been given Turkish place-names. The Republic of Cyprus does not recognise these new names. In the main guide section of this book, the Turkish name is given after the Greek name. This information is included only to help the traveller. It does not represent recognition of the renaming policy.

Numerous initiatives and rounds of negotiations under the auspices of the United Nations have so far yielded no solution to the Cyprus problem. New initiatives launched by the UN, with the support of the United States and European Union, were begun in 2001 and continued in 2002.

Cyprus's pending accession to the European Union in 2004 lends a degree of urgency to the search for a settlement, but entrenched positions on both sides have torpedoed all previous initiatives and there is no compelling evidence that it will be any different this time. Greek Cypriots are prepared to concede a degree of autonomy to their Turkish Cypriot counterparts within a federal state consisting of two provinces but not with shared sovereignty. However, the leadership in the north will contemplate only a loose confederation with a significant degree of independence for their sector.

Business Hours

Republic of Cyprus
Shopping hours
Winter:
Mon/Tues/Thur/Fri: till 6pm
Wed/Sat: till 2pm
Summer:
Mon/Tues/Thur/Fri: till 7.30pm
Wed/Sat: till 2pm
Closing times may be slightly earlier in spring and autumn (about 7pm) and most shops take an afternoon siesta some time between 1pm and 4pm in the summer.

Public Holidays in North Cyprus

- **1 January** New Year's Day
- **23 April** National Sovereignty and Children's Day
- **1 May** Labour Day
- **19 May** Young People's and Sports Day
- **20 July** Peace and Freedom Day (the anniversary of the invasion of the northern part of the island)
- **1 August** Communal Resistance Day
- **30 August** Victory Day (Turkish victory over the Greeks in 1922)
- **29 October** Turkish National Day
- **15 November** Anniversary of the proclamation of the "Turkish Republic of Northern Cyprus"

All museums are closed on 1 January, 19 May, 29 October and 15 November.

In northern Cyprus Islamic rather than Christian holidays are celebrated. The most prominent of these include the end of the month of fasting, Ramadan, referred to as the Sugar Festival *(Seker Bayram)*; the sacrifice festival *(Kurban Bayram)*, which takes place about two months after the end of Ramadan; the Muslim New Year Festival and the birthday of the Prophet. As these holidays are celebrated in accordance with the Islamic (lunar) calendar, their dates shift back 11 days each year.

Place Names

After the 1974 partition of Cyprus into the Republic in the south and Turkish sector in the north, southern Cyprus changed many of its place and street names in a bid to emphasise its Greek roots. For example, the capital of Nicosia is referred to as Lefkosia, Limassol has changed to Lemesos and the transliteration of Larnaca is now Larnaka and Paphos has become Pafos.

All literature and signposting in southern Cyprus or from tourist offices uses the new names.

Business hours

15 Sept–31 May:
Mon–Fri: 8am–1pm, 3–6pm
1 June–14 Sept:
Mon–Fri: 8am–1pm, 4–7pm
You will find that many businesses stay open longer than the official hours.

North Cyprus

Between 15 May and 14 Sept most businesses are open 8am–1pm and 4–7pm Mon–Sat. From 15 Sept to 14 May shops remain open all day, 8am–6pm.

Although banks, shops and businesses are closed on public holidays, in resort and coastal areas shops and certain services may remain open.

Planning the Trip

Passports and Visas

Visas to the island are not required by, among others, nationals of Australia, Canada, Denmark, France, Germany, Ireland, Italy, The Netherlands, New Zealand, Spain, the UK and the US.

In the Republic of Cyprus passports must be valid for at least three months beyond the date of entry; a personal identification card is not sufficient. Children and minors must have their own passports if their names are not entered in their parents' passports.

Any kind of stamp issued in the Turkish Republic of Northern Cyprus found among your travel documents constitutes grounds for denying you entry to the southern part of Cyprus. Although it is possible to enter Turkish-occupied Cyprus directly from Turkey, visitors using this route will be prohibited from entering the southern part of the island. The Republic of Cyprus regards direct entry into the occupied territory as an illegal act. A stamp from the Turkish Republic of Northern Cyprus may even cause you difficulties when trying to enter Greece.

If you plan a future holiday in Greece or southern Cyprus, ask customs officials to stamp a loose sheet of paper instead of your passport – they're used to such requests at Ercan Airport.

Crossing the Border

Currently the only way to visit both the southern and the northern part of the island during the same holiday is to arrive in the former and take a day's excursion into the north. It's impossible to manage this the other way around as officials in the south refuse to recognise entry documents issued in northern Cyprus.

There are four border crossings open between the north and south. The oldest and of most interest to visitors on foot is at the Green Line in Lefkosia. The crossing lies directly to the west of the Venetian Walls, not far from the Pafos Gate, at the old Ledra Palace Hotel.

The procedure for crossing is fairly straightforward, though since the opening of the border in April 2003 there have been crowds of visitors, and consequently there can be queues. Visitors can generally walk straight across. While the police may ask to examine your passport normally they will then allow you to cross. Officially the border opens at 8am and closes for returning visitors at midnight, though no records are kept. Most of the time the police are only interested in goods that you may be carrying upon which duty may be payable.

At the northern end of the crossing you will be asked to fill in a form with your passport number, name and date. This is stamped and given back to you and then you are then to enter the north. The Turkish Cypriot authorities will collect the form when you return south. No fees are payable to enter and there is generally a lack of formalities. The northern authorities do not impose restrictions on how long you stay.

The northern section of Nicosia can easily be explored on foot; but for destinations outside the city the only real option is to take a taxi. Fairly expensive taxis congregate at the border-crossing itself, as well as at Atatürk Square, distinguished by a Venetian column. However, the extended time now allowed visitors may make hiring a car a viability, particularly if you can negotiate a late return. There are a number of car rental agencies near Keryneia Gate. Communal taxis operate throughout the day between Nicosia, Famagusta, Keryneia and Morphou, while very cheap buses and minibuses depart from the communal bus station, a 15-minute walk north-east of the border crossing.

The other border crossings for car drivers are at Agios Dometios in the western suburbs of Nicosia, at Pergamos, 18 km/11 miles north-east of Larnaka, and at Agios Nikolaos very close to Famagusta itself. Both the latter crossings are within the British Sovereign Base area of Dhekelia. Long delays may be encountered on feast days or weekends. Crossing procedures for passengers are very similar to those at Ledra palace and can take southern registered hire cars or private vehicles across. However, you will be asked to take out additional insurance in the north at a rate of CY£3 per day. Check with your hire company first about any restrictions on this practise.

There is no limit on the number of times you may cross to and from the north, and given the ever-changing circumstances that prevail in Cyprus, any of the procedures described above may well change without notice.

Money Matters

Republic The unit of currency in the Republic of Cyprus is the Cyprus pound (CY£), called the *lira* in Greek; UK£1=*circa* CY£0.90. The pound is divided into 100 cents. Cypriot banknotes come in denominations of 1, 5, 10 and 20 pounds, coins in 1, 2, 5, 10, 20 and 50 cents.

While there are no limitations restricting the import of foreign currency, sums of US$1,000/£650 (or equivalent) or more should be declared by travellers upon entering the country. The import or export of Cypriot money is limited to CY£50. It is usually more advantageous to exchange money at a bank or bureau de change in Cyprus than in your own country.

North In the northern part of the island the Turkish lira – the same money in circulation in Turkey – is the official currency; UK£1=*circa* 2,500,000 TL.

Exchange Facilities

Republic In addition to banks, most hotel receptions will exchange

cash and traveller's cheques. Many banks have automated cash dispensers which you can use for withdrawing cash using cash cards, credit cards and cards linked to the Plus and Cirrus networks.

As a rule, banks are open 8.30am–12.30pm Mon–Fri and 3.15–4.45pm on Mon; in July and August opening hours are 8.15am–12.30pm Mon–Fri only. In tourist centres, however, banks frequently operate a special Tourist Afternoon Service between 3.30pm and 5.30pm (Oct–Apr) and 4–6pm (May–Sept) except Monday. Some banks open on Saturday morning. Currency exchange counters at Larnaka and Pafos airports are open following the arrival of foreign flights. All banks are closed on public holidays (including Easter Tuesday) but not 24 December.

Tourist Offices Abroad

UK
Cyprus Tourist Office,
17 Hanover Street,
London
W1S 1YP
Tel: (020) 7569 8800
Fax: (020) 7499 4935
E-mail: ctolon@ctolon.demon.co.uk
www.visitcyprus.org.cy
North Cyprus Tourism Centre,
29 Bedford Square,
London
WC1B 3ED
Tel: (020) 7631 1930
Fax: (020) 7631 1873
E-mail: info@go-northcyprus.com

US
Cyprus Tourism Organisation,
13 E 40th Street,
New York,
NY 10016
Tel: (212) 683 5280
Fax: (212) 683 5282
E-mail: gocyprus@aol.com
www.visitcyprus.org.cy
Northern Region of Cyprus
Tourist Information Office,
1667 K Street, Suite 690,
Washington DC 20006
Tel: (202) 887 6198
Fax: (202) 467 0685.

If you lose your credit card, you should inform your own bank as soon as possible, but you can also contact JCC Payment Services in Nicosia on 22-360820.

North For a visit to the north, you are best off taking one of the main international currencies, such as dollars or pounds sterling, as exchanging money can be less straightforward than in the south. Banks operate only limited hours (generally 8.30am–noon), but there are money exchange houses in all the major centres. These are open longer hours (8am–6pm Mon–Fri with a lunch break, and Saturday mornings), offer a fast, reliable service and do not charge commission.

Foreign money can also be exchanged in many shops (and often for a better rate than at a bank). But it is usually possible to pay for hotel bills, taxis from the airport, souvenirs and meals in overseas cash.

Most hotels and shops will accept major credit cards such as Visa, Mastercard and American Express but expect to pay commission. ATM facilities are available in major towns.

Customs

In addition to limitations on the import and export of Cypriot money (see *Money Matters, page 285*), duty-free goods brought into the country are restricted to:
Republic 2 litres of fortified wines, champagne and aperitifs, plus 2 litres of other wines; 1 litre of spirits (for visitors over 17 years of age); 50 cigars or 200 cigarettes or 250g tobacco (over 17s only); 0.6 litres perfume; 0.31 litres eau de toilette. The total value of other imported goods, such as electronic wares, may not exceed CY£100 (items such as cameras, binoculars and cassette players for personal use, will not normally be subjected to duty).
North 1.5 litres of wine; 1.5 litres of spirits; 400 cigarettes or 100 cigars or 500g tobacco; 100ml perfume; 100ml eau de toilette.

All animals must be quarantined

Specialist Holidays and Packages

Art and Culture
Prospect Music & Arts,
454 Chiswick Road,
London W4 5TT
Tel: (020) 8995 2151
Fax: (020) 8742 1969
Cruises (Cyprus to Egypt)
Argo Holidays,
100 Wigmore Street,
London W1U 3RJ
Tel: (020) 7331 7070
Magnum Travel,
747 Green Lanes,
London N21 3SA
Tel: (020) 8360 5353
Golf
Cyprus Golf Resorts,
PO Box 62290,
Pafos
Tel: 26-642775
Fax: 26-642776
Exclusive Golf Tours,
PO Box 2011,
Thornton Heath CR7 8ZE
Tel: (020) 8679 6571
Hiking
Ramblers Holidays,
Box 43,

Welwyn Garden City,
Hertfordshire
Tel: (01707) 331133
Fax: (01707) 333276
Pafos and Troodos
Mountains:
Waymark Holidays,
44 Windsor Road,
Slough SL1 2EJ
Tel: (01753) 516477
Off the beaten track
Villas and village houses
in quiet, rural western
Cyprus:
Sunvil Holidays,
Sunvil House,
Upper Square,
Old Isleworth,
Middlesex TW7 7BJ
Tel: (020) 8568 4499
Outward bound
Jeep, canyoning and walking
safaris to remote, unspoilt parts of
Pafos district:
Exalt Travel Ltd,
24 Odos Agios Kyriakis,
Kato Pafos
Tel: 26-943803

Scuba-diving
Crusader Travel,
57–58 Church Street,
Twickenham,
Middlesex TW1 3NR
Tel: (020) 8744 0474
Fax: (020) 8744 0574
Diving holidays in Keryneia
in north Cyprus:
Scuba Cyprus Ltd,
22–28 London Lane,
London E8 3PR
Tel: (020) 8986 5636
Fax: (020) 8986 5637
Singles
Solo's Holidays,
54–58 High Street,
Edgware
Middlesex HA8 7EJ
Tel: (020) 8951 2811
Fax: (020) 8951 1051
Tours
Interest and Activity Holidays Ltd,
Hartfield House,
173 Hartfield Road,
London SW19 3TH
Tel: (020) 8251 0208
Fax: (020) 8287 8403

for six months on entering the country, so it is practically impossible for a tourist to bring along a pet.

Health

There are no specific vaccinations required by visitors to Cyprus. Medical care, dentists and chemists are on a par with Europe.

In all cities there are hospitals with English-speaking doctors. It is advisable to take out health insurance, but even tourists who are covered by such insurance (check before your journey whether or not you'll need to take out an additional travel policy) will initially have to pay for doctor's fees and medication, and be reimbursed later; but these sums are fairly low owing to a glut of doctors. Be sure to ask for and keep all receipts and bills for any medical treatment and medicine.

Sun protection is essential and tourists should make sure they have, and use, plenty of suncream. It is

important to compensate for fluid, electrolyte and salt lost through sweating by drinking plenty of bottled water or soft drinks. Generally speaking, most Cypriot dishes are prepared with sufficient salt.

What to Pack

For summer visits to Cyprus, visitors should pack lightweight, cotton clothing and sun protection *(see Health, page 285)*. It is also wise to take some kind of mosquito repellent.

Those planning to spend time exploring the mountainous interior should bear in mind that even in summer temperatures can drop considerably after dark or during storms; and it is advisable to pack a warm sweater, long trousers and rain gear.

Generally, during the winter months you should take warm clothes (and bear in mind the likelihood of snow in the Troodos

Mountains). However, even in winter the sun can be strong enough to warrant protection by wearing sun cream, a hat and sunglasses.

A torch is a good idea for sightseeing, as many monasteries, churches and church ruins are poorly lit and northern Cyprus is prone to power cuts.

Few basins or bathtubs have plugs, so a universal plug may come in useful.

Getting There

By Air

Republic The two main airports in the south are at Larnaka and Pafos. Until the Turkish invasion Cyprus's main airport was Nicosia International Airport (it is currently closed and occupied by the United Nations Force in Cyprus, although its re-opening is always a possibility). Larnaka International Airport has taken over Nicosia's role.

Larnaka International Airport
Tel: 24-643000.
Pafos International Airport
Tel: 26-422833.
 The national airline, Cyprus
Airways, operates direct flights
between Larnaka and London,
Birmingham, Manchester, and major
continental and Middle East cities.
 Most major European and Middle
Eastern airlines fly to Cyprus (usually
only to Larnaka), although some,
such as KLM and Sabena, have route-
sharing agreements with Cyprus Air-
ways. Since the liberalisation of air
travel to and from Cyprus, the
number of operators offering flights
between Europe and the Middle East
has greatly increased.
 The three main airlines to serve
Cyprus from the UK are:
British Airways
52a Leoforos Archiepiskopou
Makariou III, Nicosia
Tel: 22-761166.
Cyprus Airways
50 Leoforos, Archiepiskopou,
Makariou III
Tel: 22-751996.
Helios Airways
22 Nietzche St,
Ria Court 9, 1st Floor,
Larnaka
Tel: 24-815700.
North The north of Cyprus is
becoming an independent destination
in its own right, particularly since the
introduction of specialist tours and
package holidays now being offered
by UK-based tour operators.
 Flying from London to Ercan
airport (tel: 231 7340) in north
Cyprus involves a compulsory
stop-over of about one hour in
mainland Turkey to comply with
international regulations. Ercan is 25
km (16 miles) east of Nicosia/
Lefkosia and visitors arriving on a
package are met by tour
representatives and transported to
their hotels.
 Turkish Airlines (THY) flies into
northern Cyprus from London
(Heathrow), stopping over at Istanbul,
Ankara, Izmir or Adana. Kibris Turkish
Airlines (KTA) also operate services
from London (Stansted), also
stopping over in mainland Turkey,
before proceeding to Ercan.

Turkish Airlines
125 Pall Mall,
London SW1Y 5EA
Tel: (020) 7766 9300
Fax: (020) 7976 1738
Mehmet Akif Cadesi 52,
Lefkosha/Nicosia
Tel: 227 1382/1061/7124
Fax: 228 6152.
The airline also has countless
offices in Turkey.
Kibris Turkish Airlines
Ground Floor,
11–12 Pall Mall,
London SW1Y 5LU
Tel: (020) 7930 4851
Fax: (020) 7839 4004
Atatuok Meydani,
Lefkosha/Nicosia
Tel: 227 3820
E-mail: info@kthy.net
www.kthy.net
Kordonbuyu Cad,
Keryneia
Tel: 815 2513
 It is important to remember that
those who enter Cyprus via the
north cannot extend their journey
into the southern part of the island.
The Republic of Cyprus treats direct
entry into the occupied territory as
an illegal act *(see Passports and
Visas).*

By Boat
Republic Mediterranean cruise
ships often call at the port of
Limassol where there is a thriving
domestic cruise industry operating,
with cruises to Greece, Egypt and
Lebanon currently on offer. However
there are no longer any passenger
ferry services to or from Cyprus.
Cars may be shipped to or from
Cyprus on a car-only ferry service
that operates between Limassol
and the port of Piraeus in Greece
and between the port of Haifa in
Israel.
 The procedure to ship a car,
while cumbersome, generally works
well, though the greatest stumbling
block seems to be the arcane
bureaucracy at the port of Piraeus.
For one, cars are shipped not from
the main passenger port of Central
Piraeus, but from Keratsini, 8 km/5
miles to the west. If that were not
enough, there is no signposting to

help intending dispatchers to locate
the loading area. In Cyprus things
are simpler, though still fairly
paperwork-intensive; this may
change with Cyprus's accession to
the EU in 2004 when customs
formalities between the two fellow
members states should loosen.
 Cars are shipped from the same
port as cruise ships in Limassol
and access to the port is much
simpler than at Piraeus.At either
port it is advisable to meet the ferry
and process your vehicle on arrival,
otherwise you may incur delays and
extra storage charges. Whether
passenger and car ferry services
are re-instituted is anyone's guess,
but for the moment the Republic of
Cyprus is firmly an air-only
destination for visitors without their
own shipping transport.
For information on shipping your
vehicle to from Cyprus contact:
Salamis Lines
PO Box 50531, Limassol
Tel: 25-860100
Fax: 25-342600

North Famagusta is the most
important port, with boat
connections to Syria and Turkey.
The main service is to Mersin on
the southern coast of Turkey.
 In addition to these, shipping
lines operate between the southern
coast of Turkey and Keryneia/Girne
on the northern coast of Cyprus.
The quickest way to cross is by
express service, which takes 3 to 4
hours. Between May and October,
an express service operates three
times a week, departing from
Tasucu, about 11 km (7 miles)
southwest of Silifke, Turkey. A
regular overnight service usually
takes about 8 hours.
 The main boat operator is:
Cyprus Turkish Shipping
3 Bulent Ecevit Bulvari, Famagusta,
tel: 366 5786, fax: 366 7840; or
just right of the harbour gate at
Keryneia/Girne, tel: 815 7885, fax:
815 7884.

By Car
As a rule, the shipping lines also
transport motor vehicles (most
international boat services are by

car ferry). Prices vary considerably, depending on whether it is the peak or off-peak season.

If you and your car do not remain in the country for more than three months, you will not be required to pay any additional tax or duties; should three months be too short a time for you, it is possible to apply at the main customs office in Nicosia for permission to stay in Cyprus for a period of up to 12 months.

Websites

Cyprus Tourism Organization
E-mail: cytour@cto.org.cy
www.visitcyprus.org.cy
Well designed site of the official tourist organisation, with links to airline companies.
The Cyprus Home Page
kypros.org/Cyprus
A comprehensive site covering many aspects of Cypriot life and culture.
Cyprus Guide
www.cosmosnet.net/azias/cyprus
A great site with lots of information.
Republic of Cyprus
The Government's homepage:
www.moi.gov.cy
North Cyprus
Official tourist website for north Cyprus: www.tourism.trnc.net
Hoteliers association:
www.northcyprus.net
General tourist information:
www.northcyprus.co.uk

Practical Tips

Medical Treatment

Republic Pharmacists are well trained to deal with minor ailments and sell almost all brands of medicines, including many over-the-counter drugs that are prescription-only elsewhere. To find out where the nearest pharmacy open after hours is, ask the reception desk at

Embassies and Consulates

Republic
Australia High Commission, corner of Leoforos Stasinou and 4 Odos Annis Komninis, 2nd Floor, 1060 Nicosia
Tel: 22-753001
Fax: 22-766486
Canada Consulate,
1 Odos Lampousas, 1095 Nicosia
Tel: 22-775508
Fax: 22-779905
Ireland Consulate,
Leoforos Armenias & Kalypsos, Flat 301, PO Box 20523, 1660 Nicosia
Tel: 22-333985
Fax: 22-331580
New Zealand Consulate,
35 Odos Agiou Nikolaou, Egkomi, PO Box 24676, 1302 Nicosia
Tel: 22-590555
Fax: 22-590048
South Africa Consulate,
101 Leoforos Archiepiskopou Makariou III, PO Box 21312, 1071 Nicosia
Tel: 22-374411
Fax: 22-377011
UK High Commission, 1 Odos Alexandrou Palli, PO Box 1978, 1587 Nicosia
Tel: 22-861100
Fax: 22-861125
US Embassy,

your hotel, or phone the emergency number below. There are also listings in local papers.

In case of accidents, hospital casualty departments in Cyprus will deal with minor wounds (such as cuts needing stitches or broken bones) free of charge.

If you need to see a doctor, most hotels have access to names and addresses of those who speak English. Most private doctors have visiting hours of 9am–1pm and 4–7pm Mon–Fri. For information on doctors on call during weekends or holidays, there are listings in local newspapers or you can call the following numbers:

Limassol	1425
Larnaka	1424
Nicosia (Lefkosia)	1422

corner of Odos Metochiou and Odos Ploutarchou, Egkomi, 2406 Nicosia
Tel: 22-776400
Fax: 22-780944
North
Because northern Cyprus is not recognised as an independent country, no official reciprocal exchange exists between ambassadors or consuls. But representatives can be found at the following offices:
American Center
Saran 6, Küçük Kaymakli Nicosia
Tel: 22-78295
Australian Representation
Division Güner Türkmen 20 Kösklüçiftlik, Nicosia
Tel: 22-77332
Tues/Thur 9am–12.30pm only.
British Council former embassy chancellery, near the Green Line Mehmet Akif Caddesi 29 Koskluciftlik, Nicosia
Tel: 22-83861
Fax: 22-87054
French Cultural Association
Hasena Ilgas Road, Koskluciftlik, Nicosia
Tel: 228 3328
German Representative
28 Kasim Road, Koskluciftlik, Nicosia
Tel: 227 5161

Pafos   1426
Famagusta
(Agia Napa area)   1423301

North There are dozens of pharmacies and 19 health centres in the north. If you need medical treatment contact your hotel receptionist who will provide an English-speaking doctor. Visitors may obtain free emergency treatment at government hospitals although private doctors charge a consultancy fee. Hospitals in the north are:
Nicosia/Lefkosia,
Government Hospital,
Lekosa Burhan Nalbantoglu
Tel: 228 5441 or 223 2441
Famagusta/Magusa,
Magusa Government Hospital,
Tel: 366 4400 or 366 5328
Keryneia/Girne,
Akçiçek Hastahanes,
Government Hospital,
Tel: 815 2254
Morfou/Guzelyurt,
Cengiz Topel Hospital (Yesilyurt),
Tel: 727 7351

Media

Newspapers and magazines

Foreign publications and other sources of information can be purchased in bookstores, hotels and at newspaper kiosks in both parts of Cyprus. Most UK newspapers are on sale a day after the day of issue.
Republic Two English-language papers are regularly available in southern Cyprus: the *Cyprus Mail* (daily) and the *Cyprus Weekly*. A number of publications in English, containing calendars of events and other information about what's on and where, are available from tourist offices and hotels. These include: the annual *List of Events*; the quarterly *Cyprus Diary of Events*; *Monthly Events*, a CTO bulletin; *Nicosia This Month*; *Larnaka This Month*; *Limassol This Month*, *Time Out*; and *What's On In Pafos*, a monthly brochure.
North In north Cyprus the weekly newspaper *Cyprus Today* is published in English. Other

Emergency Numbers

Emergency services are on these numbers. Operators usually speak good English.
Republic
Ambulance **112**
Police **112**
Fire brigade **112**
Night pharmacies **112**
North
Ambulance **112**
Police **155**
Fire brigade **199**

publications include *Kibris Northern Cyprus Monthly* and *Kuzey Turizm*, published by the TRNC Public Information Office.

Television
Republic In the south, the CYBC 2 television network broadcasts a daily news summary in English at 10.15pm, and carries Euronews from 7am to 1.30pm and midnight to 3am. All television networks in the south (CYBC 1 and 2, Logos, Sigma, Antena, and Greece's ET1) often broadcast programmes and films in English with Greek subtitles. British Forces Broadcasting Service (BFBS) television programmes can be accessed on 89.7 Nicosia, 92.1 West Cyprus, 99.6 East Cyprus, 89.9 Nicosia, 91.7 Limassol, 95.3 Larnaka.
Many hotels and some bars have satellite television, receiving global channels including CNN International, BBC World Television and Sky Television.

Radio
Republic CYBC Radio 1 has daily news broadcasts in English, while Radio 2 (91–1MHz FM) features programmes in English at 10am (weather, currency rates and cultural events), 1.30–3pm (magazine programme with interviews, short talks on Cyprus and music) and 8pm–midnight (starting with news). From June to September the information programme *Welcome to Cyprus* is broadcast between 7pm and 8pm.

The Voice of America and BBC World Service Radio can be picked up. British Forces Broadcasting Service radio is on the air 24 hours a day, with a diet of music, magazine programmes and news.

North Bayrak Radio and Television in north Cyprus provides two TV channels and one radio channel. Most hotels have satellite TV and a number of private radio channels broadcast in English.

Postal Services

Republic Post offices in southern Cyprus are open from 7.30am to 1.30pm Mon–Fri and 3–6pm Thur. The main post offices in Nicosia, Larnaka, Limassol and Pafos stay open in the afternoon (except Wed and Sat) 3–6pm.
A letter sent by airmail to a European country takes about five days to arrive. Stamps can be purchased from hotels, news-stands and some shops as well as post offices.

North Post offices open daily 7.30am–2pm, Mon also 3.30–6pm, and Sat 9am–noon. Because northern Cyprus is not recognised as an independent country, postal authorities in other countries are not permitted to recognise stamps issued by this "country". All mail destined for northern Cyprus must first make a detour through Turkey. In practice this means that, in addition to the address in northern Cyprus, you must write "Mersin-10, Turkey" on the envelope. This does not affect outgoing post, however.

Telecommunications

Telephone
Republic CYTA, the Cyprus Telecommunications Authority, has area administrative offices in the larger towns and cities, but calls cannot be made from them or from post offices. There are a great many CYTA public telephone booths, however, in the centre of towns and villages and in tourist areas. Most

Tourist Offices in Cyprus

Republic
Head Office
19 Leoforos Lemesou,
PO Box 24535, 1390 Nicosia
Tel: 22-337715
Fax: 22-331644
E-mail: cytour@visitcyprus.org.cy
www.visitcyprus.org.cy

Agia Napa
12 Leoforos Kryou Nerou
Tel: 23-721796
Larnaka
Larnaka International Airport
Tel: 24-643576
Plateia Vasileos Pavlou
Tel: 24-654322
Limassol
115A Odos Spyrou Araouzou
Tel: 25-362756
22 Odos A Georgiou A', Potamos
tis Germasogeias
Tel: 25-323211
Limassol Harbour Passenger
Terminal
Tel: 25-571868
Nicosia
11 Odos Aristokyprou, Laïki
Geitonia
Tel: 22-674264

Pafos
3 Odos Gladstonos
Tel: 26-932841
Airport: Tel: 26-423161
Polis
2 Odos Vasileos Stasioikou A
Tel: 26-322468
Platres
Village Square
Tel: 25-421316

North
Famagusta
Fevzı Cakmak Bulvari
Tel: 366 2864
Fax: 366 0684
Keryneia
Yacht Marina
Tel: 815 2145
Fax: 815 6079
Nicosia
Keryneia Gate
Tel: 228 9629
Fax: 228 5625
Ledra Palace
Ledra Palace Gate
Tel: 228 8765
Ercan Airport
Tel: 231 4003
Yeni Erenkoy
Tel 374 4984

of these accept only telecards
(CY£3, CY£5 and CY£10 from CYTA
offices, banks, post offices,
souvenir shops and newspaper vendors), although a few still take 2, 5,
10 and 20 cent coins.

More than 200 countries
worldwide can be dialled direct from
southern Cyprus. Calls made from
hotels cost well in excess of the
standard charge. Reduced rates for
international calls are from 10pm to
8am Monday–Saturday and all day
Sunday.

Mobile phones can operate in
the Republic provided your service
provider has a roaming agreement
with CYTA. For details phone CYTA's
customer service department on
132.

Call direct is a reverse-charge
service that puts you through to
the operator in your own country,
who will connect you once the

person at the other end accepts
the call. This service is cheaper
than collect calls, and you do not
need to go through the operator in
Cyprus.

Numbers to ring are:
Australia 1-800-551157 (Telstra)
Canada 1-800-463 3053
Ireland 1-800-550357
New Zealand 000975
South Africa 0800-990557
UK 0800-890357 (BT)
0500-890357 (Cable and Wireless)
USA 1-800-444 2982 (AT&T)
1-800-321 2982 (MCI)
1-800-488 1357 (Sprint)

Faxes/telexes
There are no public fax or telex
facilities in Cyprus, but most hotels
will be willing to send a fax for you.

For further enquiries about
transmitting within Cyprus phone
192, for overseas 194.

NORTH Telephone connections to
northern Cyprus are conducted via
Turkey. Because of this you must
first dial the Turkish dialling code
00 (90), followed by 392 (the
direct number for northern
Cyprus), then your party's seven-
digit number. To call the north from
the south dial 0139 followed by
the local 7-digit number. To call the
south from the north dial 0123
followed by the local 8-digit
number.

Telephone cards are available
from hotels, large supermarkets
and post offices.

Dialling Codes
Republic of Cyprus 357
North Cyprus from abroad the code
for north Cyprus is
00 90 392 followed by the local
number.
Area codes
Area codes no longer exist. Instead,
there are 8-digit subscriber
numbers.
Those for Nicosia begin with 22;
Agia Napa/Protaras 23;
Larnaka 24;
Limassol/Troodos 25; Pafos/Polis
26;
mobile phones 99.
If phoning from abroad, dial the
country code followed by the
8-digit number.
Country codes
 Australia 61
 Canada 1
 Ireland 353
 New Zealand 64
 South Africa 27
 United Kingdom 44
 United States 1
To telephone from Cyprus, dial 00 +
country code + area code (minus
the initial 0) + subscriber number.

Religious Services

Republic of Cyprus
During the summer, some religious
services are held in English
Agia Napa
Ecumenical Centre, Agia Napa
Monastery
Tel: 24-642858
Larnaka
Anglican: St Helena's Church,

Leoforos Grigori Afxentiou & Agias Elenis
Tel: 24-651327
Catholic: Santa Maria Church, Terra Santa 8
Tel: 24-642858
Limassol
Anglican: St Barnabas Church, 153a Leoforos Archiepiskopou Leontiou I
Tel: 25-362713
Catholic: St Catherine's Church, 259 Odos 28 Oktovriou
Tel: 25-362946
Nicosia
Anglican: St Paul's Church, Leoforos Vyronos
Tel: 22-677897
Catholic: Holy Cross Church, Pyli Pafou (Pafos gate)
Tel: 22-662132
Pafos
Anglican: Chrysopolitissa Church, Kato Pafos
Tel: 26-952486
Catholic: Chrysopolitissa Church, Kato Pafos
Tel: 26-931308
There are also services of the Seventh Day Adventist Church, the Church of God of Prophecy, the Apostolic Church of Jesus Christ, the International Christian Fellowship, the Grace Church and the International Evangelical Church.

These are in addition to Greek Orthodox, Armenian, Maronite and Coptic churches, and there are mosques in Nicosia, Larnaka and Limassol.

North Cyprus
Keryneia
Anglican: St Andrews Anglican Church, Behind Keryneia Harbour
Tel: 815 4329
Sunday services held at 10am in English and communion on Thursdays.
Catholic: Terra Santa Roman Catholic Church,
Ersin Aydin St (opposite the Dome Hotel taxi rank), Keryneia
Mass is held on first and third Sunday of the month at noon.
Tel: 815 2285
Korucam
Maronite: Church of Agios Georgios, Korucam

Mass is held every Sunday. For further details see the church notice board or contact your hotel reception.
Famagusta
Nestorian: Church of George of the Foreigner,
Famagusta old city
Tel: 815 4329
Sunday service at 5pm. Eucharist first Sunday in the month.

Photography

Cyprus provides plenty of interesting subject matter for photographers. Basic rules of courtesy should be observed when photographing people – always ask permission. Film and video camera cassettes may be more expensive in Cyprus than at home.

Photography is strictly prohibited in the areas surrounding military facilities and security zones. These include – but are not limited to – the British military bases at Akrotiri/Episkopi and Dhekaleia; UN Peacekeeping Force in Cyprus (UNFICYP) positions and bases; military installations associated with the Inner-Cypriot Line of Demarcation. Even in the interior, and in seemingly unlikely places, photography may be forbidden because of the existence of a military base or training area, radar or communications sites, even dams.

As a rule, visitors are not allowed to take pictures inside museums. However, you can take snaps in the museums' gardens and at outdoor archaeological sites if no excavations are under way.

Apart from at Stavrovouni, visitors are allowed to take photographs inside monasteries, though usually without flash. Photography is forbidden inside the church at Kykkos Monastery, a rule that is energetically enforced. The same rules of courtesy apply at religious sites as anywhere else: ask permission before snapping pictures of monks or nuns. Keep in mind that these sacred buildings are considered holy places, and that the frescoes and icons can be

damaged by flash photography. Discretion should be employed at all times.

Security and Crime

Cyprus is one of the safest places to visit in the Mediterranean. Crime is low, and in both north and south people are generally relaxed and hospitable. As society is still centred around the family, children are particularly welcomed and catered for. Lone women are rarely harrassed even in tourist areas, and are likely to be given royal treatment in rural villages.

Cyprus police are also hospitable and helpful, and tourists are unlikely to experience anything but the warmest of treatment from the island and its people unless they stray near military zones, take photographs in any prohibited places *(see above)*, or drive on roads marked as no-go areas on a map.

Tipping

As a 10 percent service charge is levied in hotels and restaurants, a tip is not obligatory, although small change is always welcomed. If service is not included a 10 percent tip is standard in restaurants. It is traditional to give taxi drivers 10 percent extra, and porters, tour guides, hairdressers and cloakroom attendants 50 cents to Cy£1 (1–2,000,000 TL).

Etiquette

Cyprus is a relaxed holiday country, so few strict codes of conduct apply.

If you are staying at a luxury hotel, it's wise to wear elegant clothes in the evening as Cypriots are likely to be dressed up to the nines.

When you visit a monastery you should take care to be appropriately attired. People wearing shorts, no shirts, backless tops, very short dresses and swimwear are not admitted (sometimes even women in trousers).

Shoes should be removed before entering a mosque. Make sure a service is not in progress, and don't walk in front of someone who is praying.

Bartering is not really a feature of shopping in Cyprus. You may get small reductions in prices for souvenirs, but if the cost is clearly marked you're unlikely to be able to bargain. In the south hotel prices are generally posted, with little room for reductions, but you may have more luck in the north.

There is not wide social acceptance of gay people in Cyprus, and open displays of affection are not recommended. Recognised gay venues are scarce, and word of mouth is usually the best way to find out where gay people tend to gather.

Getting Around

If you want to travel around within Cyprus, you are probably best off driving. There are no trains in the south or north. A reasonable bus service, which is frequent and inexpensive, links the major towns and sites in both south and north. One of the more characterful ways of seeing Cyprus is by "communal" taxis (called "service" taxis in the south and *dolmus* in the north), which take 4–7 people on main routes – though the driving can be hair-raising!

But if you'd like to venture even slightly off the beaten track, a car is the best way of getting about since public transport is non-existent in remote areas.

The major towns are linked by fairly good roads, and four-lane motorways connect Nicosia with Larnaka, Limassol and most of the way to Pafos; also to Keryneia in the north. Driving at night in the north is hazardous as you're likely to encounter unlit military trucks.

Breakdown Service

If you break down in south Cyprus, a 24-hour towing service is offered by the Cyprus Automobile Association in Nicosia. The association is a member of the Alliance Internationale de Tourisme and Fédération Internationale de L'Automobile, to which all nationally recognised motoring associations belong.
Cyprus Automobile Association
Tel: 22-313233
Fax: 22-313482
Cyprus AA Breakdown Service
Tel: 22-313131 (24 hours)

Speed Limits

Republic
Motorways/dual carriageways
100 kmh (60 mph)
65 kmh (39 mph) minimum
Cities and towns
50 kmh (30 mph)
Country roads (unless otherwise marked)
80 kmh (48 mph)
North
Motorways/dual carriageways
100 kmh (60 mph)
Cities and towns
50 kmh (30 mph)
Country roads (unless otherwise marked)
60 kmh (36 mph)

Minor roads and forest routes are usually unsurfaced, varying from the passable (provided you take care in wet weather) to tracks fit for four-wheel drive vehicles only.

Drivers are advised to wear good sunglasses as glare from the Mediterranean sun can be intense.

Driving

All you need to drive in Cyprus is a valid international or national driving licence, plus Green Card insurance.

Distances are marked in kilometres in the south, whereas in the north signs are in kilometres on major routes and miles (or not at all) on minor roads and forest tracks.

All road traffic signs in the south are written in both Greek and English.

Petrol in the south costs about the same as in central Europe, but is more expensive in the north. All types of petrol and diesel are readily available in the south and in the north.

In the south petrol stations are open 6am–7pm in summer and 6am–5pm in winter Mon–Fri, until 3pm on Saturday. Early closing (2pm) is on Wednesday in the Nicosia district, and Tuesday in Limassol, Larnaka, Pafos and Ammochostos. Many petrol stations are open 24 hours, but not attended throughout that time. They are equipped with vending machines that take CY£1, CY£5 and CY£10 bank notes or credit cards, and operate out of working hours, at weekends and during holidays.

In the north petrol stations open until 9 or 10pm, and regular working hours on Sundays.

Larger petrol stations accept credit cards.

Traffic Regulations

In both parts of Cyprus vehicles are driven on the left side of the road – a practice dating back to when the island was a British colony. Despite this, vehicles approaching from the right always have the right of way, provided there isn't a sign in the vicinity stating otherwise.

Seat belts are compulsory in the front of cars and in the back in cars where they are fitted. Children under five must not sit in the front, and five to 10-year-olds are permitted in the passenger seat only if a child's seat belt is fitted.

Drink-driving laws are similar to those in the UK and North America, with the limit of alcohol in the breath 39mcg and in the blood 90mcg per 100ml. Police operate random breath tests.

When you are going around bends, where visibility is limited, it is common practice to warn any oncoming vehicle by tooting the horn.

Car Rental

Hire cars are often called "Z cars" because their registration numbers, on distinctive red plates, begin with a Z. They can be in a dreadful state (particularly the brakes), so it's worth taking a spin before committing yourself.

All it takes to hire a car in Cyprus is a valid national driving licence. The person renting the car, plus any other driver, must be at least 21 years of age. Drivers under the age of 25 require additional insurance.

Republic In the south there are car rental agencies at the airport and in all main towns and resorts. Many

hotel receptions can provide access to an agency. If you choose one of the international rental companies that maintains an office in Cyprus, reservations can be made in advance from home. The annual hotel guide available from CTO offices contains a list of rental agencies.

Hiring a car for several days will ensure a better rate; the longer you keep the car, the less you'll have to pay per day. Vehicles are rented out grudgingly – if at all – for one day at a time. Rates are generally calculated per day and without any mileage limitations.

Some major car hire companies in the south are:
Astra/Eurodollar tel: 22-775800
Budget tel: 24-629170
Europcar tel: 25-322250
Hertz tel: 22-777411
Petsas tel: 22-662650.

North In the north, there are none of the internationally recognised car hire operators, so you are probably best off arranging hire from home, or using a local company.

Some car hire companies are:
Keryneia
Atlantic Car Rental
Tel: 815 3053, fax: 815 5673
Oscar Rent-a-Car
Tel: 815 5670, fax: 815 3858
Inter Rent Car Rentals
Tel: 815 5000, fax: 815 5003
Celebrity Wheels
Tel: 815 3053, fax: 815 5673
Famagusta
Deniz Rent-a-Car
Mustafa Kemal Blv, G. Magusa
Tel: 366 5479, fax: 366 1376
Fly Rent-a-Car
Salamis Yolu
Tel: 366 6644, fax: 228 2753
Nicosia
Sun Rent-a-Car
Tel: 227 8787, fax: 228 3700
Sur Ltd
K Kaymakli, Tel: 228 1875

Public Transport

Buses

Republic In the Republic of Cyprus buses run infrequently on Sundays. During the rest of the week,

however, the inner city buses in the larger cities operate between 5.30am and 7pm (approximately), with hours occasionally extended throughout the peak tourist season. Long-distance buses also connect all major city centres, departing at roughly one-hour intervals.

In addition, there are numerous small, private "village buses" which transport passengers between country villages and the nearest main town (usually at the start and end of the working day).

For intercity bus information, contact:
Nicosia–Limassol/Limassol–Nicosia
Nicosia–Larnaka/Larnaka–Nicosia
Limassol–Larnaka/Larnaka–Limassol
Larnaka–Protaras–Agia
Napa–Larnaka
Intercity Buses, tel: 22-665814 or 24-643492
Nicosia–Pafos/Pafos–Nicosia
Nea Amoroza Transport,
tel: 66-236822 or 66-236740

North In the north mini-buses and buses operate between all main towns with services finishing at 6pm. The *dolmus*, or shared taxi, is a better option and operates along the same routes *(see page 294)*.

Taxis

Republic Service (communal) taxis are an inexpensive way of travelling between the larger towns in the south. Usually driving with mini-vans, they can take 4–8 people and cost little more than double bus fares. Each person pays a fixed amount, which is not contingent

Bike Hire

Rental agencies in the south often lease motorcycles and sometimes even bicycles, as well as cars.

For information on bike tours through the island, contact:
Cyprus Cycling Federation
1 Odos Kimonos, 2406 Egkomi,
PO Box 24572
Tel: 22-663344
Fax: 22-661150

Sightseeing Tours

Republic of Cyprus Tour operators offer sightseeing tours out of Agia Napa, Larnaka, Limassol, Pafos, Paralimni and Polis. Excursions are half or full-day trips to major places of interest (entrance fees included) in air-conditioned coaches with qualified guides. They can also arrange night tours, dinner at a local restaurant and often folk dancing/music, or boat trips.

Agia Napa

Eman
Leoforos Makariou III 32, PO Box 30073, CY 5340 Agia Napia
Tel: 23-722977
Fax: 23-722978

Limassol

Amathus
Plateia Syntagmatos 2, PO Box 50046, CY 3300, Limassol
Tel: 25-369122
Fax: 25-341695

EAL
Limassol–Ypsonas road, Kato Polemidia, PO Box 1117, CY 3501, Limassol
Tel: 25-390044

GTA Travel
Melios Court, Shop 1, 42 Leoforos Amathous, 3501 Agios Tychonas
Tel: 25-431110
Fax: 25-314954
and
79 Odos Georgios A' Anko Seafront, Shop 1, Potamos Germasogeias

Tel: 25-320800
Fax: 25-320930

Paradise Island
Mitropolitou Kitiou Kyprianou 38, PO Box 50157, CY 3601 Limassol
Tel: 25-357604
Fax: 25-370298

Salamis
Salamis House, Odos Oktovriou 28, PO Box 157, CY 3601 Limassol
Tel: 25-860000
Fax: 25-361981

Sea Island
Ithakis, Neapolis Centre G1, PO Box 4256, CY 3607 Limassol
Tel: 25-583728
Fax: 25-580992

True-Blue
Americanes 2, Athina Court, Flat 22, Patamos tis Germasogeias, PO Box 6832, CY 3310 Limassol
Tel: 25-311353
Fax: 25-311352

Nicosia

Aeolos
Zinas Kanther 6, PO Box 1236, CY 1504 Nicosia
Tel: 22-445222
Fax: 22-447222

Airtour-Cyprus
Airtour CTA, Naxou 4, PO Box 5108, CY 1307 Nicosia
Tel: 22-374282
Fax: 22-375220

National
Louis Tourist Agency, Leoforos

Evagorou 54–8 PO Box 1301, CY 1506 Nicosia
Tel: 22-442114
Fax: 22-461894

Polis Area

Century 21
Siangoutas Court, Cy 8854 Prodromi
Tel: 26-321658
Fax: 26-321693

Pafos

Exalt Tours
Odos Agias Kyriakis 24, Pafos
Tel: 26-943803
Fax: 26-946167

North Cyprus lends itself to independent sightseeing especially by self-drive car. Few travel agents are geared up to providing organised sightseeing tours and the best way of seeing the country on an organised tour is via local reps of UK-based package holiday companies. For details contact your hotel reception or try the following:

Roots Holiday Ltd
Ziya Rizki, Keryneia
Tel/fax: 815 2844
E-mail: rootsh@ebim.com.tr

Kibris Travel Services Ltd
Ortanca Apartments, Flat 2, Floor 1, Puskullu, Keryneia
Tel: 815 7555
Fax: 815 7730
E-mail: kts@cypronet.net

upon how many people are actually in the vehicle.

Service taxis connect Nicosia, Larnaka, Limassol and Pafos, departing Monday to Friday every half hour between 6am and 6pm (in summer 7pm), Saturday and Sunday 7am–5pm (in summer 6pm), no service on public holidays.

As is the case with regular taxis, they will pick up from your apartment or hotel if you are within the city limits and if the taxi has been summoned via the taxi control office. Likewise, on reaching the destination, drivers usually deposit passengers at their front doors.

Service taxis operate only between the four main towns, not to and from either of the airports or between towns and villages. At the airports, new arrivals must use the private taxis outside the terminal. Unfortunately, their rates are higher than those of the much cheaper and almost as speedy group taxis.

Service taxis are operated by Travel & Express. The routes available are:
Nicosia–Larnaka
Larnaka–Nicosia
Nicosia–Limassol
Limassol–Nicosia
Limassol–Larnaka
Larnaka–Limassol

Limassol–Pafos
Pafos–Limassol
The national booking number is 07 77 477 or contact:
Nicosia
Municipal Parking Place, Salaminos (Podcataro Bastion)
tel: 22-730888
Limassol
Othello Building, 22 Odos Thessalonikis, tel: 25-364114
Larnaka
Corner of Odos Papakyriakou and Odos Marsellou, tel 24-661010; or 2 Odos Kimonos, tel 24-662110
Pafos
8 Odos Evagora Pallikaridi, tel: 26-233181

North Several taxi operators can be found in all main towns.
Nicosia
Ankara Taxi, tel: 227 1788
Kombos Taxi, tel: 227 2929
Terminal Taxi, tel: 228 4909
Yilmaz Taxi, tel: 851 2605
Famagusta
Bayram Taxi, tel: 366 8989
Istanbul Taxi, tel: 366 4464
Salamis Taxi, tel: 366 6200
Keryneia
Celebrity Taxi, tel: 821 8995
Dome Taxi, tel: 815 5676
Jet Taxi, tel: 815 4943

Site-seeing by Taxi
Republic If you're interested in taking a sightseeing tour by taxi, it's advisable to choose a private one and come to an agreement beforehand as to how much it will cost, how long it will last and exactly which sights you will be visiting. At the end of such a private tour the driver will expect to receive a tip.

There are set rates for uninterrupted long-distance trips. Currently the base fare is 65 cents, with an additional 22 cents reckoned per kilometre; having the taxi wait for you costs about CY£4 per hour. There is an extra charge of 22 cents for every piece of luggage (weighing more than 12 kg); for each additional piece you'll be expected to pay 22 cents more. Between 10.30pm and 6am passengers pay an extra "night-rate" charge.
North Taxis in the north are unmetered and fixed fares apply. However, it is much better to agree a price before beginning the journey.

Hitching

You won't get great mileage from hitching in the Republic of Cyprus. People in the south will be welcoming, though hitching is not a regular pastime.

In the north, by contrast, there are fewer cars so hitching for many is almost second nature, and is particularly popular with younger travellers.

Where to Stay

Hotels

Republic of Cyprus
The best guide to hotels in the Republic of Cyprus is the annually updated hotel guide issued by the Cyprus Tourist Office, available free at all tourist information centres. The room rates listed in this guide have been determined by the official authorities and hotels that try to demand more than the prices quoted from their guests will be reprimanded (if caught). Moreover, each room must be furnished with a list of rates for overnight accommodation and extra services.

The price for an overnight stay in a simple hotel room is the equivalent to about €25 per person. During the off-peak season (see Best Times to Visit, page 283) many hotels offer price reductions.

Because official control of overnight lodging is fairly tight, private pensions are almost non-existent. This situation is irksome in smaller villages where there are no hotels. (It is no longer possible for tourists to get a room at one of the monasteries without prior arrangement.) This means that excursions must be planned beforehand and must end in larger towns or cities where hotels are available.

However, in a bid to spread some of the economic benefits of tourism

Price Categories

Republic of Cyprus price categories are based on the cost of a double room for one night in the high season.
€= under €50
€€ = €50–125
€€€ = €125–175 and above

away from the coast to the financially strapped villages and countryside, Cyprus is developing an Agrotourism/Rural Tourism initiative. To date, the Cyprus Agrotourism Company has converted some 40 traditional properties, in picturesque village and country locations, for tourist accommodation. The company's guide is available from CTO offices in Cyprus and abroad.

North Cyprus
Before the Turkish invasion, beach tourism – and thus hotels – was mainly concentrated on the eastern coast south of Famagusta (Varosha) and by Keryneia. Today the hotel strip at Varosha lies inside the Turkish ceasefire line and has been abandoned.

The remaining hotels in the north have been taken over by Turkish Cypriot or Turkish management, even though the former Greek operators still claim ownership. In addition there are hotels that were run by Turkish Cypriot proprietors from the start and others that were built shortly after the invasion. Among these are the Saray in Nicosia, the Celebrity and Acapulco near Keryneia, and the Altun Tabya and Kutup in Famagusta.

In the Northern Cypriot Tourist Information Agency brochure you'll find a complete list of hotels and pensions.

Hotel Listings

REPUBLIC

Larnaka
Onisillos Hotel
Onisillou 17
Larnaka
Tel: 24-651100
Fax: 24-654468
E-mail: onisillos@cytanet.com.cy
www.onisillos.com.cy
One of the friendliest and most welcoming places to stay in Larnaka. You have a choice of hotel rooms or self-contained apartments. All are air-conditioned and the hotel is in a quiet part of town handy for the airport. €€

Petrou Apartments
Armenikis Ekklisias 1
Larnaka
Tel: 24-650600
Fax: 24-655122
E-mail:
petroumarios@cytanet.com.cy
www.petrou.com.cy
For self-caterers these large fully
equipped apartments in central
Larnaka are great for a stay of a
few days. Air-conditioning is
standard and the manager also
rents out cars at competitive prices.
€

Sun Hall
Leoforos Athinon,
Larnaka
Tel: 24-653341
Fax: 24-652717
This is a good resort hotel in the
city, with 112 rooms and a sea
view. €€

Limassol
Chrielka
Olympion 7
Tel: 25-358366
Fax: 25-358279
E-mail:
chrielkasuites@cytanet.com.cy
High quality business-style hotel
suites and mini-apartments
characterise this exceptional
accommodation choice close to the
centre of Limassol. There is also an
in-house pool though the central
beach is very close by. €€

Curium Palace
Vyronos 2
Tel: 25-363121
Fax: 25-359293
Still within the central precinct of
Limassol is the well-priced and very
comfortable four-star Curium Palace
with its cool, inviting marble-paved
lobby. There is a wide range of
guest facilities including outdoor
freshwater pool, restaurant and bar.
€€

Kapetanios Hotel
Pan. Symeou 6
Tel: 25-586266
Fax: 25-591032
E-mail: kapetdev@spidernet.com.cy
Fully renovated, the Kapetanios is
another mid-range and very
comfortable choice for visitors
wanting to stay in central Limassol.

Price Categories

Republic of Cyprus price
categories are based on the cost
of a double room for one night in
the high season.
€   = under €50
€€ = €50–125
€€€ = €125–175 and above

You'll find it just beyond the zoo on
the east side of the old town. €€

Nicosia
Classic
94 Odos Rigainis
Tel: 22-664006
Fax: 22-360072
E-mail: classich@logos.cy.net
www.classic.com.cy
A modern, air-conditioned hotel with
57 rooms, in the Old City, ideal for
the main shopping and restaurant
areas. €€

Cyprus Hilton
Leoforos Archiepiskopou
Makariou III
Tel: 22-377777
Fax: 22-377778
E-mail: hiltoncy@spidernet.com.cy
www.hilton.com
With 300 rooms, the Hilton is the
largest and also the best hotel in
Nicosia. It has an indoor and a
heated outdoor swimming pool, as
well as other sports facilities and
shops, children's playground and
floodlit tennis court. €€€

Castelli Hotel
Ouzounian 38
Tel: 22-712812
Fax: 22-680176
E-mail: hinnicres@cytanet.com.cy
A distinctly classy business-style
hotel right in the centre of Nicosia
and on the edge of the old town.
The Castelli boasts an excellent in-
house Polynesian restaurant and
each of its comfortable rooms are
well equipped for Internet
connectivity. €€€

Pafos–Polis
Agapinor
26 Odos Nikodemos Mylonos,
Ktima (Nea Pafos)
Tel: 26-233927
Fax: 26-235308

E-mail: agapinorhotel@cytanet.com.cy
www.agapinorhotel.com.cy
If you want to be away from the
coast and amid the action in the
heart of Ktima, you can't get much
closer than this central 73-room
hotel. €

Amarakos Inn
Kato Akourdalia
Tel: 26-633117
Fax: 22-313374
E-mail: amarkos@markos.com
www.amarkos.com
Some 23 km (14 miles) north of
Pafos on the cooler Akamas Heights
plateau is another agrotourist
complex. This one has large air-
conditioned apartments in a cluster
of low, stone and wood buildings.
There's a pool and restaurant too.
€€

Axiothea Hotel
Ivis Mallioti 2
Tel: 26-932866
Fax: 26-945790
Commanding possibly the best view
in the whole of Pafos, the Axiothea
("Worthy View") is a relaxing, low-
key hostelry without the frills, but
with a superb view over Pafos. The
large lobby area is perfect for
watching the sun set over the sea
below. €€

Coral Beach
Coral Bay, near Pegeia,
12 km (8 miles) north of Pafos
Tel: 26-621601
Fax: 26-621742
E-mail: manager@coral.com.cy
www.coral.com.cy
A luxurious 5-star hotel with 421
top-grade rooms, good restaurants,
excellent sports and other facilities,
and both indoor and outdoor
swimming pools. It is convenient for
the beach at Coral Bay. €€€€

Kings
38 Leoforos Tafon ton Vasileion,
Kato Pafos
Tel: 26-233497
Fax: 26-245576
E-mail: kingshot@cytanet.com.cy
www.kings.com.cy
Popular with travellers who
don't want to stay at one of Pafos's
big resort hotels. It has 27 rooms
and a location convenient for the
Tombs of the Kings archaeological
site. €€

Kiniras
Archiepiskopou Makariou III 91
Tel: 26-941604
Fax; 26-942176
E-mail: info@kiniras.cy.net
www.kiniras.cy.net
Kiniras, in Ano Pafos is a
traditionally renovated pension
with its own very popular
restaurant. All rooms are well
appointed and rates include a
hearty breakfast. €€

Loxandras Inn
Kathikas
Tel: 99-608333,
Fax: 25-335739;
E-mail: gandronikou@cytanet.com.cy
www.gmbds.com/lox.htm
Part of the CTO agrotourist chain,
this cosy inn is made up of two
high-ceilinged one-bedroomed
apartments and a larger studio. All
are grouped around a large
courtyard. Facilities are of a high
standard. Kathikas is 21 km (13
miles) north of Pafos. €

Nicki Holiday Resort
Polis
Tel: 26-322226
Fax: 26-322155
E-mail: manager@nickiresort.com
www.nickiresort.com
Handily located between Polis and
Latsi is this very pleasing low-key
resort complex. The rooms are very
tastefully decorated with TVs that
have local and satellite stations.
The pool is very inviting. An in-
house restaurant completes the
picture. €

Park Mansions
16 Odos Pavlou Melas,
Ktima (Nea Pafos)
Tel: 26-245645
Fax: 26-246415
One of Cyprus's accommodation
gems, this is an old Venetian-style
mansion now converted into a
characterful hotel with 25 rooms. It
also has a swimming pool. €€€

Troodos Mountains
Edelweiss
Pano Platres
Tel: 25-421335
Fax: 25-422060
E-mail: edelweiss@cytanet.com.cy
As its name implies, this hotel
looks like a typical Austrian Alpine

hotel, set down in the Troodos. With
22 rooms it stands on the main
street in Platres. €

Forest Park
Pano Platres
Tel: 25-421751
Fax: 25-421875
E-mail: forest@cytanet.com.cy
www.forestparkhotel.com.cy
Set amid the forests outside
Platres, this 137-bed hotel is
considered to be the best in the
mountains. Good facilities, it also
has a heated outdoor swimming
pool. €€€

Jubilee Hotel
Troodos Village
Tel: 25-420107
Fax: 22-673951
E-mail: jubilee@cytanet.com.cy
Near the summit of Mt Olympus is
this very laid back country style inn
with wooden floors and richly
upholstered sitting rooms. Great for
a mountain break and very handy
for the walking trails. There's a
good bar and an in-house
restaurant. €

Minerva Hotel
Kaledonion 6
Platres
Tel: 25-42173
Fax: 25-421075
E-mail: minerva@globalsoftmail.com
One of the cosiest and prettiest
places to stay in Platres itself. The
two star Minerva is made up of two
parts: the main hotel and the
delightful annexe at the back with
rooms boasting four-poster beds.
Each room has private facilities and
phone.

Mountain Rose
Pedoulas
Tel: 22-952727
Fax: 22-952555
A jovial and informal place with a
popular restaurant, it has 20 rooms
and is situated on the hilly main
street in Pedoulas. €

Polyxeni's House
Kalopanagiotis
Tel: 22-497509
Fax: 22-354030
In the northern slopes village of
Kalopanagiotis, the two-bedroomed
Polyxeni's House will accommodate
up to four persons. It has a
kitchenette and large bathroom,

while guests can wine and dine in
peace in the quiet courtyard. €€

Rodon
Agros
Tel: 25-521201
Fax: 25-521235
E-mail: swaypage.com/rodon
A largish communally owned and
run establishment in the rather
under-rated but flourishing village of
Agros, Rodon is an excellent choice
and is always busy. Large, comfy
rooms and extensive guest
facilities, including two pools,
tennis court, excellent restaurant
and bar. €

NORTH

Famagusta
Blue Sea
Dipkarpaz
Tel: 372 2393
Fax: 372 2255
E-mail: bluesea@northcyprus.net
No frills accommodation situated
on isolated headland 65 km (40
miles) from Famagusta and
appealing to those seeking an
ethnic experience or an overnight
stay to explore the Karpaz
Peninsular. €

Iskele
Bogaz Iskele
Tel: 371 2559
Fax: 371 2557
E-mail: bogazhotel@interema.net
Unpretentious yet comfortable
40-roomed hotel with beach across
the road. About 4 km (2 miles)
from Famagusta and comfortably
placed for exploring Karpas
Peninsular. €–€€

Palm Beach
Deve Limani
Tel: 366 2000
Fax: 366 2002
E-mail: bilferpalmbeach@
superonline.com
www.bilferhotel.com
Pleasant refurbished beachfront
hotel of 108 rooms set in lush
gardens with freshwater swimming
pool. Facilities include Turkish
Bath, tennis courts and casino.
Situated on the edge of Varosha and
2.5 km (1½ miles) from the old
walled town. €€€

Portofino Hotel
Fevzi Çakmak Bulvarı 9
Tel: 366 4392
Fax: 366 2949
E-mail: reservation@portofino-hotel.cyprus.com
www.portofino-hotel.cyprus.com
Perhaps the most convenient hotel choice in Famagusta, the Portofino Hotel, has been renovated in recent times and is now a very cosy spot to stay for a few days. It's on the south side of town just outside the city walls. €

Salamis Bay Conti Resort Hotel
Famagusta
Tel: 378 8201
Fax: 378 8209
E-mail: salamis@interema.net
www.salamisbayconti.com
Large modern hotel complex overlooking private beach with wealth of facilities including indoor pools, shopping mall, sports and entertainment, Turkish Bath, casino and mini-club. Ideal for exploring Salamis ruins. €€€

Theresa Hotel
Yenierenköy
Tel: 374 4266
Fax: 374 4009
E-mail: theresahotel@hotmail.com
www.theresahotel.com
This rather isolated hostelry is 7 km (4 miles) east of Yenierenköy on the northern side of the Karpas panhandle. It caters for 36 guests who tend in the main to be hikers and nature lovers. All rooms have bathroom and fan, while there is a convenient in-house restaurant. €

Keryneia area
Acapulco Holiday Village
Catalkoy
Tel: 824 4110
Fax: 824 4455
E-mail: acapulco@clubacapulco.com
www.clubacapulco.com
Large holiday complex of hotel rooms and bungalow accommodation just 8 km (5 miles) east of Keryneia with direct access to sandy beach. Popular with families. €€€

British Hotel
Eftal Acka Sok,
Yat Limani
Tel: 815 2240
Fax: 815 2742

E-mail: british@northcyprus.net
Small and simple 18-roomed family-run bed and breakfast hotel in enviable harbourside location within spitting distance of fine restaurants and bars. €

Chateau Lambousa
Maresal Fevzi Cakmak Cad,
Lapta
Tel: 821 8751
Fax: 821 8761
E-mail: info@celebrityhotelonline.com
www.celebrityhotelonline.com
Spacious Moorish style property. 45 nicely furnished rooms set in tranquil gardens and with relaxed atmosphere. Car hire handy if exploring, as this hotel is 18 km (11 miles) west of Keryneia. €€€

Dome Hotel
Kordonboyu Street,
Keryneia
Tel: 815 2453
Fax: 815 2772
E-mail: thedome@kktc.net
Long established hotel in central Keryneia, right on the seafront, with traditional and welcoming atmosphere. 160 comfortable rooms, swimming pool, lively casino and excellent food. Popular with returning British clientele. €€€

Ergenekon Hotel
Kyreneia Harbour
Tel: 815 4677
Fax: 815 6010
E-mail: ergenekon@iecnc.org
www.ergenekon-hotel.com
On the west side of the picturesque Kyreneia harbour the Ergenekon is a perennial budget to mid-range favourite with visitors. It is open all year and the rooms are bright and cheery. €

Keryneia Jasmine Court
Naci Talat Cad,
Keryneia
Tel: 815 1450
Fax: 815 1488
E-mail:
jasminecourt@northcyprus.net
Swanky modern holiday resort in central Keryneia consisting of studios and self-catering suites arranged round large pool. The casino is reputed to be one of the biggest in Europe. Suitable for singles, couples and families. Several bars and restaurants. €€€

Keryneia Oscar Resort
16 Hasan Esat Isik Sok,
Keryneia
Tel: 815 2363
Fax: 815 3980
E-mail: oscar@northcyprus.net
Modern resort-type complex of hotel rooms, villas and self-catering studios with plenty of sports and entertainment facilities; popular with couples and families, and within walking distance of Keryneia Harbour. €€–€€€

Resort Dedeman Olive Tree
Catalkoy
Tel: 824 4200
Fax: 824 4209
E-mail: olivetree@northcyprus.net
Lively hillside complex of attractive whitewashed bungalows arranged round a large pool with swim-up bar appealing to families and couples, with option of quieter hotel rooms facing well-kept lawns. €€

Price Categories

North Cyprus price categories are for a double room for one night in the high season. Discounts are available during off season.
€ = under €35
€€= €35–75
€€€ = €75 and above

Riverside Holiday Village
Alsancak
Tel: 821 8906
Fax: 821 8908
Attractive self-catering units of one- and two-bedroomed villas arranged around large lap pool in rural location, just 10 km (6 miles) west of Keryneia. Pleasant children's pool with water slides and quieter adult pool. €–€€

Nicosia
Royal
19 Kemal Asik Cad
Tel: 228 7621
Fax: 228 7580
E-mail: royalhotel@northcyprus.net
Tall modern glass-fronted hotel with 46 rooms with indoor pool, gymnasium and car park. €€

Youth Hostel Addresses

Hostels in the Republic:
Agia Napa
23 Odos Dionysiou Solomou
Tel: 22-442027/23-723113
Larnaka
27 Odos Nikolaou Rossou
Tel: 24-621188
Nicosia
5 Odos Hadjidaki
Tel: 22-674808

Saray
Ataturk Medani
Tel: 228 3115
Fax: 228 4808
E-mail: saray@northcyprus.net
The Saray's central location
and excellent views over north
and south Cyprus from the
rooftop terrace and restaurant
compensate for the
uninspiring 1959 tower block
edifice. €€

Youth Hostels

Access to youth hostels depends
on possession of an International
Youth Hostel Card. Currently
the price for an overnight stay
is between €5 and €12 per
person. Reservations are
recommended. For general
information on hostels in Cyprus,
contact:
Cyprus Youth Hostels Association
PO Box 21328, 1506 Nicosia,
Cyprus, tel: 22-670027.

Camping

REPUBLIC

There are seven licensed camp
sites in the south of Cyprus. Rates
are the same at all of them:
currently about €2.50 per person
each day with an additional charge
of €2.50 per caravan or tent.

Each camping area has its own
sanitary facilities and a grocery
shop or restaurant.

With the exception of the camp
site located in the Troodos
Mountains, all camp sites are
situated along the coast.

Pafos
37 Leoforos Eleftheriou
Venizelou
Tel: 26-232588
Troodos
In a pine forest in the mountains
near Troodos, on the
Troodos–Kakopetria road,
open Apr–Oct
Tel: 25-420200

Agia Napa Camping
West of the town. Open: Mar–Oct,
tel: 23-721946.
Feggari Camping
Near Coral Bay, 11 km (7 miles)
northwest of Pafos. Open: all year
round, tel: 26-621534.
Forest Beach
About 8 km (13 miles) east of
Larnaka. Open: June–Oct,
tel: 24-644514.
Governor's Beach Camping
About 20 km (12 miles) east of
Limassol. Open: all year round,
tel: 25-632878.
Polis Camping
Along the town beach in a small
stand of eucalyptus trees.
Open: Mar–Oct; tent rental
possible, tel:26-321526.
Troodos Camping
About 1 km (2 miles) northeast of
the town in the midst of a pine
forest. Open: May–Oct, tel: 25-
420124.
Zenon Gardens Camping
At Geroskipou about 5 km (3 miles)
east of Pafos. Open: Apr–Oct,
tel: 26-242277.

Although it is illegal to camp
anywhere you happend to find a
suitable spot, during the summer it
is common – among tourists and
natives alike.

NORTH

In the northern part of the island
camping in the wild is allowed, but
there are restrictions on lighting
fires in forests and restricted areas.
Riviera Beach Bungalows
15 Neset Ikiz St, Karaoglanoglu,
Keryneia

Tel: 822 2877
Fax: 822 2062
E-mail: riviera@future.com.tr
www.rivierahotel-northcyprus.com
Relaxing and friendly camping
facilities by the beach with selection
of bungalows, terraced restaurant
and swimming pool.

Marinas

REPUBLIC

Yachting crews wanting to break their
cruise across the Mediterranean Sea
can take advantage of the marinas
near Larnaka and Limassol. Both
are equipped with repair facilities
and supplies (petrol, diesel,
electricity, drinking water, laundry
and sanitary facilities).
Larnaka
Located in the bay of Larnaka (34°
55'N–30° 38'E) with 210 mooring
slips
Tel: 24-653110/3
Fax: 24-624110
Limassol
Located east of the city (34°
42'N–33° 11'E); operated by the St
Raphael Hotel; 227 mooring slips
Tel: 25-321100
Fax: 25-329208
Radio Cyprus broadcasts the
weather report on channels 15, 24,
26 and 27.

NORTH

Keryneia
50–60 mooring bays include
electricity, laundry, storage fees,
Captain Service, technical
assistance.
Tel: 815 3587
Fax: 815 6079

Where to Eat

Eating Out

Republic of Cyprus

In southern Cyprus there is a dearth of the kind of simple, traditional tavernas that are common in Greece, which serve memorably tasty local food and make eating out one of the highlights of a holiday. Just as much of Cyprus's tourism "product" is aimed squarely at the mass sector, with little consideration for independent travellers, so much of the food on offer takes a bland "international" approach, usually heaped up with that limp and greasy legacy of the British – the ubiquitous chip. Despite the fact that the markets are overflowing with a wide variety of vegetables, in nearly every restaurant the emphasis is on meat dishes. Vegetarians can opt for a range of side-dishes.

Meze

You can't stay in Cyprus without sampling the traditional *meze*. Available in both the south and north, it's served to two or more people – and worth starving yourself the rest of the day for. *Meze* is a cascade of as many as 30 little dishes (a good bet if you have small children as there's bound to be something they like!) that run the gamut of meat, vegetable, seafood and dessert items on the menu. The dishes come in wave after wave, usually in something like this order: Greek salad, *halloumi, loúntza, kalamári* rings, *sheftaliá* and *souvlákia* pieces, *afélia, stifado* and lamb chops served with olives, *tahíni, taramosalata* and *talattouri*.

That's the downside, and since the downside represents most of what you will encounter, it is best to be armed and ready for it. The upside is that Cyprus does actually have a tradition of fine cuisine, a mix of Greek, Turkish and Middle Eastern influences. And the island really is that well-worn cliché; a cornucopia of fresh fruit and vegetables, which retain something that European supermarket shoppers may remember with wistful fondness – taste. Finally, there is a growing niche market of real tavernas dishing up the genuine cuisine of Cyprus at levels that range from homely to sophisticated.

Seafood represents a special case. Fish is relatively scarce in the eastern Mediterranean, due to a combination of naturally low populations in these nutrient-poor waters and overfishing. It tends to be expensive and much of what you see is imported frozen. There are, however, fishing harbours dotted around the coast and the fish the boats catch often go straight onto the table of the nearest seafood restaurants. Watch out, however, for owners who display fresh fish for you to select, then take something from the freezer after you've gone back to your table, keeping the genuine items for their favoured regular customers!

Included in the prices listed on every menu is a 10 percent service charge. It is customary to leave the waiter a little something extra, too.

The best place to eat if you're looking for a relatively authentic and inexpensive meal is in a traditional taverna, and the best introduction to Cypriot cuisine is the *meze (see left)*. Washed down with local wine from the barrel, a *meze* at the right time and place is a real delight.

Price Categories

Republic of Cyprus prices are based on the cost of a meal for one person without drinks.
€ = under €10
€€ = €10–15
€€€ = €15 and above

Popular Snacks

Street vendors aren't as prevalent in Cyprus as they are in Greece, so you're more likely to pick up snacks in a café. These are the most popular:
Eliópitta Olive turnover
Takhinópitta Sesame turnover
Kolokótes Pastry triangle stuffed with pumpkin, cracked wheat and raisins
Soudzoúko Almond strings dipped in molasses
Pastelláki Sesame, peanut and syrup bar
Börek Meat/cheese turnover
Aïráni (ayran in the north) Refreshing herby yogurt drink with mint or oregano
Pide The north's answer to pizza, usually served with soup (*çorba*). Standard toppings include cheese, egg, mince and sausage, or combinations of these.

North Cyprus

Restaurants in the northern part of the island offer pretty much the same fare and national dishes – with the addition of a few specifically Turkish specialities. However, both the wine produced in the south as well as southern-brewed beers are not available in the north, where you'll have to choose from an assortment of imported Turkish brands.

In line with the predominance of Muslims on the northern part of the island, beef and lamb are eaten rather than pork.

What To Eat

National Specialities

Afélia: pork marinated with coriander.
Bread: an indispensable component of every meal.
Fish: usually deep-fried.
Fruit: apples, pears, little local bananas, cherries, grapes, figs, melon, citrus fruits, papaya, peaches, almonds, apricots, avocados, pomegranates and strawberries (usually very early in the year).

Greek salad (horiátiki salata): salad composed of cucumber, tomato, pepper, olives, feta cheese and herbs.

Gúvec (Turkish): vegetable stew with meat.

Halloúmi: cheese made from either sheep's or cow's milk which tastes especially good when fried; spiced with peppermint (Turkish: helim).

Hiroméri: smoked ham.

Húmus: cold chickpea purée.

Keftedes: fried meatballs (Turkish: köfte).

Kléftiko: lamb gently cooked for a long time until very tender.

Kolokási: root vegetables.

Kolokithákia: courgettes either stuffed or fried, as a side-dish.

Koukiá: broad beans, either as soup or raw in salad.

Koupépia (dolmadakia): stuffed vine leaves (Turkish: dolma).

Loúntza: ham, served in sandwiches and fried with halloumi.

Makarónia tou Fournou (pastítsio): macaroni casserole made with ground meat.

Oil: the local olive oil is especially tasty and used liberally – though not excessively – in the preparation of many foods.

Olives: marinated exquisitely with garlic, coriander, lemon and thyme.

Pastourmas: garlic sausage (Turkish: sucuk, but with the omission of pork).

Pilaf: coarsely ground wheat grains and vermicelli cooked in chicken broth and served with a selection of different vegetable side-dishes (Turkish: bulgur).

Pitta: flat, hollow rounds of bread filled with different sheftaliá or souvláki and vegetables.

Sheftaliá: grilled sausage made of ground meat.

Soúvla: lamb roasted on a spit, popular fare at family picnics.

Souvlakia: grilled meat kebabs (Turkish: i kebab).

Stifado: beef or rabbit prepared with lots of onions – reminiscent of goulash.

Tahíni: sesame sauce with lemon and garlic (Turkish: terator).

Talattouri: yogurt prepared with cucumber and peppermint, similar to tzatziki (Turkish: cacik).

Taramosalata: cod's roe with lemon, potato purée, onions and oil.

Trahanas: coarsely ground wheat grains dried with yogurt and added to soups together with halloumi.

Vegetables: artichokes, asparagus, various kinds of lettuce, potatoes, mushrooms, aubergine, courgettes and celery

Desserts

Báklava: puff pastry filled with nuts and soaked in syrup.

Dáktila ("finger"): finger-shaped strudel pastry filled with a nut-cinnamon mixture and soaked in syrup.

Glykó sto koutáli: fruit or walnuts marinated in syrup and served with a glass of water as a welcome titbit for guests.

Honey: very aromatic. Often served with yogurt and almonds.

Kourabiédes: see Festive Fare page 302; this delicacy is also available in shops at Christmas.

Koulourákia: a ring-shaped cookie sprinkled with sesame seeds.

Loukoumádes: deep-fried balls of choux pastry served in syrup.

Loukoúmia: a famous culinary speciality from Geroskipou, near Pafos, cubes of gelatin flavoured with rose water and dusted with powdered sugar.

Paloúses: a kind of pudding made from grape juice and flour; it is the basis for soutsoúko.

Drinking Notes

Visitors to Cyprus will find plenty of both non-alcoholic and alcoholic drinks to choose from. Coffee is prepared in the traditional Turkish way: boiled in a little pot with sugar added upon request and poured into a cup with the steeped coffee grounds. For those who prefer something a bit less fierce, Nescafé is usually available.

Tapwater is generally safe to drink, although it can be rather brackish in the north. Mineral water is readily available.

An especially delicious treat is a glass of freshly squeezed orange juice, sold by numerous street vendors.

In addition to beer, a number of excellent wines, local brandies and fruit liqueurs are offered. These are not only significantly cheaper than other, imported spirits, but are often of very high quality. Alcohol is usually drunk only with meals by the locals, so late-night revelries in the steet are likely to be frowned upon.

Wine

In the south Arsinoe, Palomino and White Lady are palatable dry whites. Bellapais, a medium-dry sparkling wine, comes in white or rosé. Aphrodite is a cheap medium white. For reds, Othello is a full-bodied, Cabernet Sauvignon-type, while Hermes is a heartier dry wine. There are also several versions of Commandaria, a dessert red like Madeira. In villages, your best choice is definitely the cheap local barrel wine, which is often very good.

In the north most wine is imported from Turkey, so the choice is less extensive. Play safe with Turasan and Peribacasi.

Beer

In the south KEO lager is a good all-day beer, though deceptively strong at 4.5 per cent (drink the bottle version as the draught is insipid in comparison). In the north the Turkish brand you're likely to encounter is Efes, or the Austrian lager Gold Fassl.

Spirits

As well as ouzo (or, more likely, raki in the north), locals tend to go in for brandy, the best brand of which is Three Kings. A popular aperitif, both with Cypriots and holidaymakers, is brandy sour: brandy spiked with lime or lemon juice and Angostura bitters.

Price Categories

Republic of Cyprus prices are based on the cost of a meal for one person without drinks.

€ = under €10
€€ = €10–15
€€€ = €15 and above

Soutsoúko: a long chain of almonds strung together, dunked in *paloúses* (*see above*) and then dried – very popular.
Sütlac (Turkish): a pudding made of milk, rice and rose water.

Restaurants

REPUBLIC

Agia Napa
Limelight
Dionysiou Solomou 10
Tel: 23-721650
In a town where dining can be hit and miss, you're more likely to hit than miss at Limelight. The main feature is the open barbecue on which suckling pig or lamb are cooked to a fine turn along with fish, chicken and lobster. €
Potopoieion to Elliniko
Theodosi Pieridi 2
Tel: 23-722760
More of a musical mezes joint than a restaurant, this cosy place appeals to visitors looking for something a little more genuine. Food is served *mezes* style and is usually accompanied by ouzo, zivania or wine of your choice. There is live music at nights. €€
Tsambra
Dionysiou Solomou 9
Tel: 23-722513
Also a decent choice in Agia Napa, this place offers a shaded courtyard where you can dine in relative peace and quiet by day and night. Variations on port dishes feature prominently. €

Coral Bay
Saint George
Agios Georgios (north of Coral Bay)
Tel: 26-621306
A deceptively unattractive-looking restaurant that occupies a stunning

location on the cliff above Agios Georgios harbour, and serves great seafood fresh off the boats. €€

Foini
Phini Taverna
Foini village
Tel: 25-421828
A delightful village taverna in one of the prettiest mountain villages (although with a slightly stuffy image as an "artist's haven"), serving good traditional food. €

Kakopetria
Maryland at the Mill
Kakopetria village
Tel: 22-922536
You may get vertigo climbing to the dining room of this astonishingly high, wood-built restaurant. Its mountain trout and other fresh dishes are excellent. €€

Kathikas
Araouzos
Main street
Tel: 26-632076
This may well be the most authentic village taverna in Cyprus (Kathikas lies midway between Pafos and Polis). A wickerwork covering softens the stone floor, and there's no menu, just whatever the family feels like rustling up that day. €

Larnaka
Archontiko
24 Leoforos Athinon
Tel: 24-655905
Cypriot food in a picturesque old building beside the seafront Foinikoudes Promenade. Next door is the associated Archontissa steakhouse. €€
Kamares Restaurant
Hrysoupoleos 24a
Tel: 24-364400
Not too many visitors find Kamares (Arches) Restaurant – so called because of the ancient aqueduct nearby, but it is a top class place that appeals mainly to Cypriots. Dishes are imaginative, well priced and well presented – best of all they are genuine. €
Varoshiotis Seafood Restaurant
Piyale Pasha 7
Tel: 24-655865

Poised right above the water on Larnaka's south foreshore, this is a great place for a relaxing lunch or slow fish dinner. Professional and attentive service, wide ranging menu and excellent draft wine. €€

Limassol
Blue Island
3 Leoforos Amathoundos
Tel: 25-321466
One of Limassol's classiest restaurants, serving French and international cuisine in a formal setting, although there is also a vine-shaded patio for outdoor dining. €€€
Karatello
Vasilissis 1
Tel: 25-820464
A touch of modernistic pizzazz characterises this buzzing bistro-style restaurant in a converted carob warehouse in Limassol's old town. You create your own meal combination from a checklist with options for vegetarians and carnivores alike. €€
Old Neighbourhood Taverna
Ankara 14
Tel: 25-376082
Get away from the tourist strip and visit a cluster of great eateries near the Old Fort. The Old Neighbourhood is one of these. Dine outside on grills and Cypriot specialities such as

Festive Fare

Weddings *Réssi* (wheat with meat), *pastítsio, kleftiko,* cucumber, tomato, chips for each well-wisher and *kourabiedes* (shortcrust pastry filled with almonds).
Easter lamb *Soúvla*, Easter Soup (made of parts from the head of a calf or lamb and vegetables, served with garlic bread), eggs dyed red, and *flaoúnes* (turnover made from a yeast dough and filled with eggs, cheese and raisins).
Christmas *Vassilópitta* (cake made from yeast dough, spread with egg and generously strewn with sesame seeds and almonds).

afelia or *kleftiko*. Very low-key and very friendly. €

Rizitiko Tavern
Tzamiou 4-8
Tel: 25-348769
Another place nearby is the Rizitiko offering a menu of decidedly Cypriot origin. It's a small place with only two to three tables on the street, so get in early. Best for evening dining when most of the traffic and crowds have dispersed. €

Porta
17 Odos Genethliou Mitela
Tel: 25-360339
Fancy eating in an atmospherically renovated donkey stable? Well, this is the place. Designer class and good taste have also been added at this restaurant in the old Turkish quarter. €€

Vassilikos
Odos Agiou Andreas
Tel: 25-375972
A violinist accompanies your meal at this fine Cypriot restaurant, specialising in *meze*. It also has a garden terrace. €€

Nicosia

Aegeon
40 Odos Ektoros
Tel: 22-433297
The Famagusta Gate area has developed a reputation for being smart, stylish and pricy. Aegeon, however, has managed to keep to its simple family-taverna origins. €€

Arhondiko
27 Odos Aristokyprou,
Laïki Geitonia
Tel: 22-680080
Laïki Geitonia can seem just a little too twee to be true. Yet it's undeniably romantic to eat here surrounded by lanterns and serenaded by Greek music. €€

Arheon Gefsis
Stasandrou 29
Tel: 22-452830
Fancy some ancient Greek food? Look no further than Arheon Gefsis (Taste of the Ancients) where traditional ancient Greek food has been revived in this original dining venue. Olives, chickpeas, beets, nuts, figs and honey all feature on the occasionally improbable-looking menu. €

Armenaki
15 Odos Sans Souci
Tel: 22-378383
As its name implies, this is an Armenian restaurant and, although a simple place at heart, is popular with well-heeled Nicosians. €

Axiothea
14 Odos Axiotheas, Nicosia
Tel: 22-430787
A superbly traditional restaurant jammed up against the barricades of the Green Line. The food is good and authentically Cypriot, and there is convivial seating in the narrow street outside. €

Erodos
Patriarchou Grigoriou 1
Tel: 22-752250
The call of muezzin in the nearby Omeriye mosque often startles first-time diners at this busy little and very atmospheric bar-cum-restaurant in the heart of Nicosia's old town. There is an extensive menu and drinks list and meal portions are large. Great for evening dining. €€

Konatzin
10 Odos Delfi
Tel: 22-776990
Serves a great vegetarian *meze* in the fine setting of a converted mansion with a garden. €€

Plaka
8 Odos, Stylianou, Egkomi
Tel: 22-352498
The restaurant occupies the centre of the old village square of now suburban Egkomi, spreading its terrace among the flowers and bushes. €€

Xefoto
6 Odos Aeschylou,
Laïki Geitonia
Tel: 22-666567
Xefoto has three faces: a breezy outside terrace; a stylish café-restaurant on the ground floor; and a more intimate spot upstairs. It serves a well-considered interpretation of Cypriot cuisine. €€

Pafos

Argo
Pafias Afroditis 21
Tel: 26-933327
This is one of those places where the service and food is still family-style and where locals as well as

visitors come back regularly. The best-known dish is the twice weekly *kleftiko* (Tuesday & Saturday) though the filling mousaka is a top choice on any day . €

Cavallini
65 Leoforos Poseidonou, Kato Pafos (near the Amathus Hotel)
Tel: 26-964164
With a relaxed environment, this excellent Italian restaurant offers an upmarket approach and fine cooking. €€€

Demokritos
1 Odos Dionysou, Kato Pafos
Tel: 26-933371
Prides itself on being Kato Pafos's oldest taverna, having opened in 1971. Traditional Greek and Cypriot dance accompanies dinner. €€

Fettas Corner
33 Odos Ioannis Agrotis, Ktima
Tel: 26-237822
A gem virtually untouched by tourists. An unpromising location and unforced atmosphere are the setting for genuinely great Cypriot food. €€

Nicos Tyrimos
71 Odos Agapinoros, Kato Pafos
Tel: 26-942846
Pafos's fishermen themselves come to eat at this excellent, family-owned seafood taverna, where airs and graces are left at the door. €€

Pelican
102 Leoforos Apostolou Pavlou (Pafos Harbor)
Tel: 26-946886
Probably the best of a line of harbour-front tavernas that are popular because of their atmosphere and location, but where quality is often indifferent. €€

The Royal Oak
Kato Akourdalia
tel 26-633117
Out of Pafos and in the Akamas Heights are a few places worth seeking out. This is one. It's in an old stone building and serves typical country fare such as sausages, *afelia* and *ofto* (oven baked meat packages). It belongs to the Amarakos Inn. €

Pedoulas

To Vrysi
Pedoulas Village Centre.
Tel: 22-952240

Price Categories

North Cyprus prices are based on the cost of a meal for one person without drinks.
€ = under €10
€€ = €10–15
€€€ = €15 and above

Otherwise known as Harry's Spring Water Restaurant, this unusual looking place is one of the best restaurants in the mountains. €€

Pegeia
Peyia Tavern
1 Leoforos Markou Kyprianou
Tel: 26-621077
Grilled meats are the speciality here in this rustic place, accompanied by side dishes and village wine. €
Vineyard
Coral Bay Road
Tel: 26-621994
Good home-cooked food is served at this modern taverna set among scented fields outside Pegeia. €

Pissouri Bay
Simposio
Pissouri Beach
Tel: 25-221158
All the restaurants at Pissouri Beach are more expensive than need be, and Simposio is no exception, but the Cypriot *meze* and the setting here are both well worth experiencing. €€

Platres
Kalidonia
Pano Platres
Tel: 25-421404
Cypriot food tastes great on a summer evening when served in this unpretentious place. €

Polis
Alekos Restaurant
Makariou 20
Tel: 26-323381
This place is a real find and a rarity in Cyprus. A restaurant that serves up home-cooked food at budget prices. The garden beans with lamb or the black-eyed beans are as filling as they

are scrumptious. Complimentary house wine for each pair of diners makes the deal so much more rosy. €
Archontariki Restaurant-Tavern
Makariou 14
Tel: 26-321328
Dine on top class fare in an old stone house or in the relaxing garden at Arhontariki. The service is smooth and professional and the whole ambiance lends to lingering. Menu items are original with interesting spins on chicken and octopus. €
Old Town
Polis-Paphos Road
Tel: 26-322758
Another of Polis's garden café-restaurants, with an extensive menu. There are both meat and vegetarian dishes. €€

Protaras
Anatolia
Agios Elias
Tel: 23-831533
Despite the Turkish name, the speciality in this taverna is Cypriot *meze*. €€
Spartiatis
Konnos Beach
Tel: 23-831386
Seafood fresh from the nearby harbour, as well as a selection of traditional Greek dishes, amid a quiet, romantic atmosphere. €€

Troodos
Linos Inn Taverna
Tel: 22-923161
Kakopetria
One of the more imaginative restaurants in the whole of Cyprus. The setting is very pleasing – an old stone house with rough wooden tables – while the menu includes items such as ostrich and salmon. A good beginner's choice is the 'Cyprus plate' consisting of a variety of Cypriot *mezedes*. €
Psilo Dendro Restaurant
Aïdonion 13
Platres
Tel: 25-421350
Open only until late afternoon, the Psilo Dendro does trout best as the whole property is a trout farm. Located right at the end/start of

the popular Kaledonia trail, time your walk to arrive here at lunchtime. €
Village Tavern
Leoforos Makariou
Platres
Tel: 25-422777
Tucked away on the west side of Platres the Village Taverna has earned its spurs through a combination of solid and palate-pleasing Cypriot mountain fare with kleftiko and stifado earning top marks. Unusually for Cypriot restaurants there is well-priced draft house wine available. €

Zygi
Apovathra
Seafront,
Zygi village
Tel: 24-332414
Stands out for quality in a waterfront village where seafood tavernas are common, but not all of them good. €€

NORTH

Bellapais
Abbey Bell Tower
Tel: 815 7507
Warm and welcoming restaurant with an authentic Turkish corner full of photographs and artefacts and open fireplace. In summer enjoy Abbey and mountain views from the outdoor terraces. €€–€€€
Tree of Idleness
Tel: 815 3380
Friendly atmosphere, huge outdoor terraces and views of the famous abbey make this a popular choice with coach parties. Try delicious grills, thick yoghurt, mixed salads and finish off with a platter of fresh fruit. €€

Degirmenlik
Baspinar Restaurant
Tel: 232 3345
Mountainous rural location popular with locals, especially at weekends. Everything from kebabs, quail and kofte. Built over a former underground stream, which fed 35 water mills in the

area with the purest of water; some believe that it was linked to the Taurus Mountains on the Turkish mainland by an underground tunnel. €€

Famagusta

Cyprus House Restaurant
Fazıl Polat Paşa Bulvarı
Tel: 366 4845
A kind of 'theme' restaurant with belly dancing and succulent kebabs meeting in almost equal proportions. The outside dining area is very appealing and the food is well cooked and very filling. Another good choice for a town where dining choices can be a bit thin on the ground. €

D & B Café
Namik Kemal Meydani 14
Tel: 366 6610
Trendy café serving a good choice of sandwiches, salads and kebabs. Popular in the summer when food is served at outdoor tables. €

La Verandah
Namik Kemal Meydani
Tel: 367 0153
Hamburgers, kebabs, salad and other fast food are served on delightful shaded terrace in Famagusta's central square, with views of the cathedral and old Venetian Palace. €

Petek
5 Yesil Denis Sok
Tel: 366 4870
The trendiest patisserie in town well-known for its huge selection of calorific Turkish cakes. €

Sindoma
Canbulat Yolu 1
Tel: 366 5356
Cosy and friendly restaurant serving wide range of Turkish food including ubiquitous kebabs, tasty pilaf and fresh salads. Popular with tourists and locals. €

Viyana Restaurant
Liman Yolu Sokak 19
Tel: 366 6037
Unassuming, very casual and hearty characterise the style at the Viyana Restaurant where grills and kebabs feature prominently on the menu. The leafy courtyard is very welcoming after a hard day walking

Famagusta's streets as is an ice-cold beer with your meal. €

Karaman

Hideaway
Below Edremit on the Karaman road from Karaoglanoglu
Tel: 822 2620
West of Keryneia with panoramic views of the coastline this family-run restaurant offers mixed Cypriot and European cuisine in a friendly atmosphere. €–€€

Jashan
Karaman Road
Tel: 822 2514
Jashan means "celebration" in Urdu. Smart, spacious restaurant serving Indian specialities, which include a good range of curries, breads and rice. €€–€€€

Keryneia

Address Restaurant & Brasserie
Ali Aktas Sokak 13
Tel: 822 3537
Widely held to be Keryneia's top dining choice, the menu here reflects a beguiling Turkish-French mélange of past and fish dishes, while the locale – at Karaoglanoglu to the west of Keryneia - is particularly fetching, being right on the sea. Worth a visit for a splurge. €€

Akpinar Café
Philecia Court, opposite the Ataturk Statue near Dome Hotel
Tel: 815 2058
Pleasant patisserie popular with tourists and locals where delicious pastries, ice creams and snacks and selection of fruit teas and alcoholic drinks are served on a wide terrace. €

The Brasserie
Efeler Sok
Tel: 815 9481
Drift back in time at the former Manifold House, a colonial home

Price Categories

North Cyprus prices are based on the cost of a meal for one person without drinks.
€ = under €10
€€ = €10–15
€€€ = €15 and above

once owned by a wealthy Scotsman. Dark oak-panelled bar, open fireplaces, grand piano and comfortable armchairs complete the ambiance. Specialities include Lobster Newburg and breast of duck. Open evenings only. Closed Sunday. €€–€€€

Café Chimera
Yacht Harbour
Tel: 815 4394
This is a place for a gut-busting breakfast, all day snacks and sophisticated European evening meals in a prime position at the eastern end of the harbour. €

Guthrie's Bar
Bellapais
Tel: 0523 865 8262
Restauranteurs Deirdre Guthrie and Justin McClean run a rather loose deal here offering light English-style lunches to all and sundry, while offering customised private meal deals to evening diners for parties of up to eight. Bookings are essential. €€

Kyrenia Restaurant
Türkmen Caddesi 2
Tel: 815 1799
A rather improbable kind of restaurant: dining here is rather like dining in someone's front room and the table service is like what you would expect from an old friend. Known also in Turkish as the Pasabahçe Restaurant, this dining choice is something of an institution in town. Simple food, but lovingly prepared in the old-fashioned way. €

Niazi's
Opposite The Dome Hotel
Tel: 815 2160
Everything from full kebab and hefty meze to charcoal grilled specialities and extensive wine list in this spacious and established restaurant in a central Keryneia location. €–€€

Onar Restaurant
Onar Village Complex
Keryneia–Nicosia road
Tel: 815 5850
Wonderful hilltop location in which to sample delicious European and Turkish cuisine with buffet nights and live music on Friday and Saturday. €€

Nicosia
Annibal
Saraçoglu Meydanı
Tel: 227 1835
As elsewhere in the Turkish-dominated north, kebabs feature on the menu of this busy and ever-popular restaurant just outside the walls of the old town. It's not flash but honest, good value and always full of hungry kebab aficionados. €

Biyer
Mehmet Akif Cad, Nicosia
Tel: 228 0143
Atmospheric restaurant popular with local businessmen and discerning tourists in new part of Nicosia. Try the full *meze* washed down with excellent local wine. €€–€€€

Yusuf Usta Oçakbasi Restaurant
Bahçeli Sokak 2
Tel: 228 9852
Hard up against the Green Line barricades is this small and unassuming eatery that serves up filling and exceptionally well-prepared kebab style dishes. Given that you can now dine in the north at night it's a great choice for an evening meal at half the price of the south. €

Attractions

Monasteries

Republic of Cyprus
There are 12 Greek Orthodox monasteries still in operation on the island today, all of them in southern Cyprus.

Generally speaking, the monasteries do not maintain specific visiting hours. However, prospective guests should respect the midday pause and plan their visits outside this time. Frequently the monks must unlock the churches, and when this is the case it is customary to leave a small donation for the monastery after you have completed your tour. The most courteous way to do this is not to hand your donation directly to the monk himself, but to leave it either on the plate provided for this purpose at either the entrance to the church or near the iconostasis (the screen that separates the altar from the nave).

Out of respect, visitors should avoid pointing to icons or standing with their backs turned towards them or with their hands clasped behind their back.

(For further information regarding appropriate behaviour when visiting a monastery, refer to the section *Photography, page 290*.)

The most important monasteries in Cyprus are:
Agios Georgios Alamanos 20 km (12 miles) northeast of Limassol, not far from the road to Larnaka, near Governor's Beach.
Agios Irakleidios in the village of Politiko, about 24 km (15 miles) from Nicosia.
Agios Minas near Lefkara.
Agios Neofytos 10 km (6 miles) north of Pafos.

Kykkos in the Troodos Mountains, northwest of Pedoulas.
Machairas in the eastern foothills of the Troodos Mountains, about 40 km (25 miles) south of Nicosia.
Panagia Chrysorrogiatissa 2 miles (3 km) south of Panagía village.
Stavrovouni west of Larnaka; be warned that women are not permitted to enter.
Trooditissa 5 km (3 miles) northwest of Platres. Open only to members of the Greek Orthodox church.

Churches

Republic of Cyprus
As many of the most beautiful Byzantine churches are situated in rather remote areas, only a few can be reached directly by public transport.

To minimise damage to their interior decorations and contents, most of the churches are kept closed; if you want to look around them you must first collect the key. Usually a local in the coffee house in the nearest village will help. After your visit, it is customary to give a small tip to the person responsible for the keys.

Nine churches in the Troodos Mountains have been added to the UNESCO list of the buildings important to the cultural heritage of mankind. For a full list of these, *see page 241*.

Other important churches in southern Cyprus are:
Arkhángelos Mikhail In the village of Pedoulas.
Agia Paraskeví In the village of Geroskipou, about 3 km (2 miles) east of Pafos.
Agii Apostóloi In the village of Perachoria, 17 km (10 miles) from Nicosia.
Agioi Varnavas & Hilariou In the village of Peristerona, about 27 km (17 miles) west of Nicosia.
Agios Ioánnis In Nicosia, directly next to the new palace of the archbishop.
Panagia Angelóktisti In the village of Kiti, 11 km (7 miles) west of Larnaka.

North Cyprus

There are numerous Orthodox churches in the northern part of Cyprus that are worth visiting. Unfortunately though, since the Turkish invasion of 1974, most of them have been vandalised, and priceless icons, frescoes and mosaics have been stolen or destroyed. Today, most of these churches are, with good reason, permanently closed; some have been converted into mosques and others are currently used as sheep-cotes. Churches and monasteries still open for public viewing include:
Arabahmet Mosque in Nicosia.
St Barnabas Monastery near Famagusta.
Bellapais Monastery near Keryneia.
Agios Mámas Church near Morphou/Guzelyurt.

Buildings of Historic Interest

North Cyprus
The Eaved House
8 Kutuphane Sok, Nicosia
Tel: 227 7547
A beautifully restored 17th-century Ottoman house with wide eaves, this L-shaped two-storey building encloses a tranquil square courtyard. Now used as a cultural and arts centre. Open daily in summer 9am–2pm and in winter 9am–1pm and 2–4.45pm.
Lusignan House
1 Yenicami Sok, Nicosia
Delightful 15th-century mansion with Gothic arch and entrance door. Former home of a Russian family who occupied it during the 1950s. Restored in 1997 it contains some furniture from the Ottoman period. Open daily in summer 9am–2pm

and in winter 9am–1pm and 2–4.45pm.
Museum of Barbarism
Off Mehmet Akif Cad, Nicosia.
A chilling reminder of barbaric acts committed during inter-communal fighting pre-1974 between Greek and Turkish Cypriots displayed in graphic detail. The museum is the former home of a Turkish Cypriot army officer whose family were slaughtered in the bathroom by EOKA terrorists in 1963. Open 8am–1pm and 2–5pm. Admission charge.

Ecology

North Cyprus
Karpas Peninsula A trip to the Karpas Peninsula, also known as the "pan handle" of Cyprus, is just about practical for tourists crossing from the south to the north on an

Arts Festivals in Cyprus

Republic of Cyprus
Nicosia International Arts Festival
A two-week programme of art exhibitions, theatre, music and dance. It takes place in June at various venues in the city, particularly the Famagusta Gate Cultural Centre.
Limassol International Arts Festival
For 10 days in June and July the city's Municipal Gardens are the venue for a programme of music, song and dance by both international and local artists.
Curium Drama Festival
Throughout July and August the 2,000-year-old Theatre at Kourion stages classical and modern theatre. There is also classical and modern music, ballet, and a sound-and-light show.
Musical Sundays
During March, April and May, in the morning or late-afternoon, performances of folk music, dance and jazz and classical music can be seen in Larnaka (opposite the Municipal Hall), Limassol (Municipal Gardens) and Pafos (Castle Square or Central Kiosk).

Ancient Greek Drama Festival
There's nothing quite like the spectacle and atmosphere of watching a Greek play by candlelight on a balmy summer evening in an open-air ancient theatre. A festival of popular works is staged from June to August in some of the old theatres, such as the Kourion and Pafos Ancient Odeon. Though they are performed in the original ancient Greek, they're surprisingly easy to follow (and a précis of the plot is provided in English if you're struggling!). For exact dates and venues, see the *Monthly Events* guide available from tourist offices.
Pafos Festival
A full programme of theatre, music and dance takes place from June to September at the Ancient Odeon and in the Pafos castle area.
Larnaka Festival
A month of dance, theatre and music performed by both local and international artists in the courtyard of the Larnaka Medieval Fort and Patticheion Municipal Amphitheatre takes place during July.

North Cyprus
North Cyprus International Bellapais Music Festival
Bellapais Abbey is the venue for this annual festival which brings together musicians from all over the world. It takes place 21 May–24 June.
International Spring Concert
A full programme of classical music organised by the Friends of Music Association of North Cyprus takes place at Bellapais Abbey 1–20 May every year.
Famagusta International Festival
This outdoor music festival with local and international artistes is held between 27 June and 19 July in the old town of Famagusta.
Guzelyurt Orange Festival
Competitions, concerts, folk dancing and an opportunity to taste the famous Guzelyurt oranges at the town of the same name can be enjoyed at this festival 15–22 May.

All towns and some villages hold local festivals at various times in the year. For further details contact the tourist office.

extended day trip. However, for those who arrive direct in North Cyprus, a trip to the Karpas Peninsula offers lovely remote beaches, wild donkeys and quiet villages.

There are several historic churches and monasteries that, in spite of being in ruins, are worth visiting, such as Apostolos Andreas Monastery, Ayios Trias Basilica, Ayios Philion, and Kantara Castle with its spectacular views of the Karpas Peninsula.

The drive from Keryneia takes the best part of half a day, particularly if you are stopping en route, so it is best to include an overnight stay at one of the few basic hotels on the peninsula near Dipkarpaz. For better comfort you might consider a hotel at Bogaz or Famagusta.

North Cyprus Herbarium
Alevkaya
Tel: 232 3422
Botanists and anyone with a keen interest in gardening might enjoy a visit to this herbarium to see pressed flowers and orchids and other flora. Set in a glorious location at Alevkaya, it is signposted 8 km (5 miles) off the Keryneia-Famagusta mountain road opposite the slip road leading to

Gambling

Northern Cyprus is a haven for anyone keen to know the latest racing results from Newmarket or yearning for a flutter on roulette tables. No passport is needed and entrance is free. Some casinos offer free refreshments and minimum bets are as low as 50p. Casinos can be found at the following hotels:
Celebrity, Kyrenia
Club Acapulco, Catalkoy, Keryneia
Club Keryneia, Keryneia
Club Lapethos, Lapethos
Dome, Keryneia
Grand Rock, Keryneia
Jasmine Court Hotel, Keryneia
Limani, Kyrenia
Palm Beach, Famagusta
Sabris Orient, Nicosia

Buffavento Castle. Open daily 8am–4pm. Outside these hours the forester on duty will open the doors.
Turtle Headquarters
Algadi Beach
Tel: 815 5135
The coast of North Cyprus is the habitat of the loggerhead and green turtles, classified as vulnerable and endangered respectively. Every year between June and September they come to lay their eggs on the beaches and once the young have hatched they make a perilous night-time journey towards the sea. Many hatchlings do not survive the rigours of nature and pollution. Tourists can visit the Turtle Headquarters from 6pm after 1 June to see what is on the agenda that day, watch slides, spot turtles or even adopt one. A tagging scheme is in process so you can get news of the whereabouts of your own special turtle. In Keryneia contact The Grapevine Restaurant on 815 2496.

Sites for Children

Republic
Luna Parks These permanent fun fairs can be found in all major towns in the south. Most are open all year round until 8pm weekdays and later at the weekend. Admission is free, but rides can add up! For the best head for Tivoli Luna Park, Elia Papakyriakou 10, Egkomi.

For the more daring, Skycoasters at Agia Napa, just by the Luna Park, features some heart-stopping rides; and there's a go-karting track at Nicosia Luna Park.
Waterworld Agia Napa Water chutes galore, log rolling, river trips and geysers are just some of the delights of Waterworld; 5 km (3 miles) from Agia Napa along the Agia Thekla Road. Open daily Mar–mid-Nov 10am–6pm.
Limassol Zoo Municipal Gardens, 28 Odos Aktovriou. Open daily 9am–7pm.
Glass-bottomed boats A great way to see marine life at Agia Napa, Larnaka, Limassol, Latsi and Pafos harbours. Daily throughout the summer.

Ostrich Farm Park Said to be Europe's largest ostrich farm (with exhibition and playground), where children can have their photograph taken on an ostrich egg! Agios Giannis Malountas, about 25 minutes from Nicosia. Open summer daily 9am–8pm, winter daily 9am–6pm.

North Cyprus
Octopus Aqua Park
45 Besparmak St, Catalkoy
Tel: 853 9764
Neat complex for families, consisting of pool bar and pub restaurant for grown ups and climbing frames and towers, swings, pool and slides for the children.

Culture

Music, Theatre and Dance

Republic

The main location for cultural events such as art exhibitions, classical music concerts, ballet, opera and theatre is Nicosia (the one city with the venues to put on such shows regularly). Limassol, Larnaka and Pafos have their own cultural programmes and venues, with less-frequent events sprinkled throughout the tourist season.

For listings, the Cyprus Tourist Organisation publishes a *Diary of Events* for the year, plus a *Monthly Events* guide.

Venues

Larnaka
Municipal Theatre
Tel: 24-665794
Larnaka Fort
Tel: 24-630576
Occasionally hosts concerts and theatre.

Limassol
Municipal Theatre
Tel: 25-396126
Limassol Castle
Tel: 25-305419
Occasionally hosts concerts and theatre.
Kourion Odeon
Tel: 25-932453
A great place to see classical Greek plays, as well as Shakespeare.

Nicosia
Municipal Theatre,
Odos 4 Leoforos Mousieou
Tel: 22-680026
Classical music, dance and opera, as well as classic and modern plays in both Greek and English are performed here.

Famagusta Gate Cultural Centre,
Pyli Ammochostou
Tel: 22-430877
Art exhibitions and experimental theatre.
British High Commission,
1 Odos Alexandrou Palli
Tel: 22-861100
Chamber music and other events are occasionally featured.

Pafos
Markideon Theatre
Tel: 26-932571
Ancient Odeon,
Harbour Archaeological Area
Tel: 26-940217
Classical Greek plays, as well as Shakespeare and modern opera, are occasionally performed here.
Pafos Fort, Harbour
Tel: 26-232841
Occasionally hosts concerts and theatre.

Cinema

Latest releases in English are shown at cinemas in the main towns of both the Republic and north Cyprus.

For times and programmes contact the following:

Nicosia
Galleria Cinema Club
Tel: 227 7030

Keryneia
Galleria Cinema Club
Tel: 815 9433
Lemar Cineplex
Tel: 822 3565

Famagusta
Galleria Cinema Club
Tel: 365 1270

Folk Festivals

An important part of Cyprus's cultural life is covered by festivals, some of which are island-wide and some local.

January
Epiphany: on 6 January, coastal towns hold a traditional procession, known as the Blessing of the Sea. The local bishop throws a crucifix

Youth Card

Available to anyone aged 13 to 26, the Youth Card costs the equivalent of €10 for a year and is valid in 29 countries. It entitles you to reduced prices on theatre and cinema tickets, air and taxi fares, books, clothes and sports goods. It is available from youth agencies such as Student Travel Centre, 24 Rupert Street, London W1V 7FN, tel: (020) 7434 1306 or the Cyprus Youth Board, 41 Odos Themistokli Dervi, Nicosia, tel: 22-304162.

into the water, and youngsters dive in after it.

February/March
Carnival: 50 days before Orthodox Easter is "Clean Monday", the start of Lent. Carnivals are held in many towns and villages the week beforehand. The biggest and most colourful is in Limassol, where the Carnival King's arrival is the signal for masquerades and feasting, culminating in a float procession on the final Sunday.

March/April
Orthodox Easter: this is the biggest Orthodox festival of the year and it is well worth witnessing. Following morning Mass on Holy Thursday, it is traditional for housewives to paint eggs red. In the evening all the icons in the church are draped in black.

On Good Friday the sepulchre is decorated with flowers, and a procession of flower-bedecked images of Christ makes its way through the streets during Mass at 9pm. Parishes compete for the best-decorated sepulchre and most beautiful procession. In the village of Kathikas in Pafos, the priest walks the streets laden with a cross.

On Easter Saturday the black drapes come off the icons and the congregation rap their seats to express their joy and chase the demon of Hades away. Housewives bake Easter breads, pastries and *flaoúnes* (cheese pies). At midnight, dressed in their best Easter clothes, they gather for Mass. Then bonfires are lit and effigies of Judas are thrown onto them. Everyone goes home by candlight to eat the Easter feast of traditional *mageirítsa* soup (made of lamb's offal), and to crack the red eggs.

On Easter Sunday and Monday it is customary to roast lamb outdoors on the spit or in big clay ovens, and celebrations may continue all day long with games in the church yard or village square. Villages that retain these traditions include: Paralimni, Agia Napa, Deryneia (Ammochostos district), Akaki, Geri and Tseri (Nicosia area), Aradippou and Pervolia (Limassol), Neon Chorion, Geroskipou, Pegeia and Pafos.

May

Anthestiria: flower festivals are held in Pafos, Limassol and several other Republic towns, celebrating spring's return with processions and re-enactments of the ancient Greek myths.

June

Feast of Saint Paul: on the 28th and 29th, the Bishop leads a procession through Pafos, carrying an icon of St Paul.

July

Kataklysmos (Festival of the Flood): Noah's Ark and the Great Flood are recalled, especially in Larnaka and Limassol, with three days of fairs and water-throwing contests.

August

The month of the village festival, when relatives and friends get together for a drink, a dance and a song – this is a chance to get a flavour of true Cypriot life. Festivities can include folk music and dance, exhibitions of agricultural products, flowers, folk art, photography, painting, silverware and (particularly in Lefkara and Omodos) embroidery.

September

Limassol Wine Festival: the city's Municipal Gardens are filled with throngs of people drinking free wine from stalls set up by the island's many wineries. There is also folk dancing, fairground stalls, amusements and food.

Shopping

Souvenirs

Republic of Cyprus

Typical souvenirs from Cyprus, aside from the local wine, spirits and *halloumi* cheese, include various Cypriot handicrafts such as lace, leather goods, pottery, glassware, woodcarvings and embroidery.

Many towns are known for a specific product, for example ceramics from Kornos, Koloni, Lemba and Foini; high-quality embroidered lace from Lefkara and Omodos; hand-blown glassware from Omodos; silver jewellery from Lefkara; basketry from Liopetri, Sotira and Geroskipou; woven wares and tapestry from Fyti; silk products and Cypriot (Turkish) Delight *(Loukoúmia)* from Geroskipou. Good-quality gold jewellery and leather goods can be very reasonably priced.

Two handicrafts that travelled with the Greek Cypriot refugees in their flight from the north to south after 1974 and are now produced in the south are *lefkonika* woven cloth (from Lefka) and the pottery cats of Lapithos.

In addition to the numerous privately operated souvenir shops, the national **Cyprus Handicraft Service** maintains branches in the old parts of Nicosia, Limassol, Larnaka and Pafos. At its workshop in Nicosia visitors can watch various craft items of a notably high quality being made. The shops open 7.30am–2.30pm Monday–Friday, Thursday 3–6pm (closed afternoons during July and August). The CHS has several branches that offer craftwork at fixed prices:

Nicosia

186 Leoforos Athalassis (workshop and shop)
Tel: 22-305024
Laïki Geitonia
Tel: 22-303065

Larnaka

Odos Kosma Lysioti
Tel: 24-630327

Limassol

25 Odos Themis
Tel: 25-305118

Pafos

64 Leoforos Apostolou Pavlou
Tel: 26-940243
August is a good time to pick up handicrafts in Pafos, when the Pafos Folkloric organises exhibitions of local specialities, some of which are for sale.

Monasteries and abbeys are sources of souvenirs. Icons range from simple little pieces to superb works, often made with gold-leaf imbued paint, made by Father Kallinikos at Stavrovouni Monastery. Nuns at some of the convents keep bees and sell excellent honey.

North Cyprus

In the shops in Keryneia and Niocosia in north Cyprus look for fake designer clothes such as Levis and Armani (although quality varies). There is attractive basketware at Edremit on the road to Karaman and jewellery which is weighed before a price can be negotiated.

Other good buys in supermarkets in Keryneia, Famagusta and Nicosia include olive oil, Turkish delight, Turkish coffee and vacuum-packs of hellim cheese.

Green Jacket Bookshop

20 Temmuz Cad, Keryneia
Tel: 815 7130
Fax: 815 7130
The best place in the north to buy guide books, maps, postcards and gifts, crafts and souvenirs.

Food

Cyprus does not go in for the huge supermarkets of central Europe, (though there are at least two hypermarkets in Nicosia) but there are many corner stores and small supermarkets in main towns. In the Republic, food is usually labelled in English as well as in Greek.

Each town also has a central market hall, an excellent source of meat, fruit and vegetables. Once a week (for example, on Saturday in Pafos) there will also be a lively adjacent street market. Though northern shops and markets are less opulent than in the south, there are good market halls at Keryneia and north Nicosia.

Fruit is plentiful and delicious throughout Cyprus (in the south all of it is home grown), with many (such as strawberries and melons) appearing long before they do in central Europe.

Outdoor Activities

Bird watching

There are around 100 bird species on the island and many more on the migratory path from Europe to Africa.

Republic One of the highlights of the year is the arrival of 10,000 flamingos, which winter on the salt lakes. Details are available from the **Cyprus Ornithological Society** 4 Odos Kanaris, Nicosia Tel: 22-420703. **Birdwatching Society** Tel: 26-270447 or 25-232487

North One of the best places for bird-watching is at Zafer Burnu and Zeytin Burnu on the very tip of the Karpas Peninsula.

Other habitats for migratory species, such as the great black-headed gull, include Bafar lagoon

Cyprus's Flora

Of the 130 plants endemic to Cyprus, nearly half grow close to the peak of Mount Olympus. From February to April the Cyprus crocus pops its head through the melting snow. By April lowland areas are a sea of wild flowers, from small blue irises, crocuses and tulips to poppies in red, yellow and purple. Roadsides are bright with buttercups, crown daisies, marigolds and huge wild fennel. Metre-high stems of white asphodel signal spring, and in June and July dense dwarf broom carpets the top of Olympus. After a lull in summer, the red of the vines in autumn is a glorious sight. *(See also pages 100–101.)*

and Ergazi Reservoir half way between Bogaz and Kantara Castle. At Silver Plaj, just south of Salamis is the best natural wetland of north Cyprus where flamingos and white-fronted geese can be seen in winter and many other migrant water birds can be seen in spring.

The Besparmak mountain range near Keryneia is the habitat of many species year-round, including Bonelli's eagle, Cyprus wheatear and blue-rock thrush.

For further information contact the Society for the Protection of Birds and Nature on tel: 815 7337.

Cycling

Republic Given the mountainous terrain of the hinterland, a cycling holiday in Cyprus will probably appeal only to the dedicated cyclist. But for those who do not enjoy struggling up steep inclines, opportunities abound for exploring the countryside away from the main roads.

In the Troodos Mountains, in particular, there are earth and sand tracks through remote, wooded areas offering shade – but do not set off without plenty of drinking water.

Cycle hire facilities exist in most tourist resorts, but more ambitious cyclists would do better to bring their own bike.

You need a good level of fitness and cycling skill before trying mountain biking seriously, but in the Troodos Mountains and Akamas Peninsula in the west you'll get all the action you can handle.

Mountain bikes can be hired in Platres, Pafos, Polis and other resort towns.

Various non-racing activities and events, which welcome participants, are organised by: **Cyprus Cycling Federation** 1 Odos Kimonos, 2406 Egkomi, PO Box 24572 Tel: 22-663344 Fax: 22-661150 **Limassol Cycling Club** PO Box 56142, Limassol Tel: 25-585980

Dog Walking

North North Keryneia Animal Rescue Centre is set in a beautiful hillside location 16 km (10 miles) east of Keryneia above Arapkoy village. This charity, recognised by the RSPCA, is home to more than 100 dogs and 40 cats and positively welcomes visitors who would like to walk rescued dogs in the shadow of the Besparmak Mountains. If you are an animal lover you can help by buying T-shirts, hats and leads or sponsor your own mutt or moggie and receive details of its progress.

For further details contact: Paul Chaplain at the Rescue Centre, tel: 0533 863 1950 or e-mail the secretary at christineoktekin@ hotmail.com. Open daily 9am–1pm.

Fishing

Most coastal resorts have fishing boats from which you can try your hand at catching sea fish. It is also possible to go angling in some of the inland reservoirs, which stock 17 species (including trout, bass and carp). You'll need a licence from the Fisheries Department (or one of its district offices in Larnaka, Limassol and Pafos). The department sells a booklet with details of all fish found in the reservoirs:

Fisheries Department
13 Aiolou Street, Nicosia
Tel: 22-303526
Fax: 22-365955

Golf

Republic There are two golf courses in the Pafos area, both of them 18-hole and par 72:
Secret Valley Golf Club
Tel: 26-642774
Fax: 26-642776
Tsada Golf Club
Tel: 26-642774
Fax: 26-642776
The Elias Country Club, near Limassol, also has a golf course, as well as offering horse riding, archery and bowling.
Elias Country Club, Pareklisia
Tel: 25-636000
Fax: 25-635300

Hiking

Republic of Cyprus

The Cypriot authorities produce two leaflets on walks and nature paths on the Akamas Peninsula and in the Troodos Mountains. As well as outlining the itinerary, they also contain information on flora to be found en route. A map of walking routes in both regions is given on the inside back cover of this book.

Akamas Peninsula Situated in the westernmost part of Cyprus, this peninsula, named after Akamas, the son of the Greek hero Theseus, offers wonderful opportunities for hiking (as well as swimming). There are two fairly well-trodden nature trails – the Aphrodite and Adonis trails – but the region is never crowded with visitors. *(See also pages 218–19.)*

Troodos Mountains These mountains offer active visitors many inviting hiking opportunities in summer. Even during August, daytime temperatures do not rise above 27°C (80°F). It is possible to set off along either an undeveloped path or on one of the official trails that have been marked by the Cyprus Tourism Organisation (CTO), among which four are classified as nature trails. The point of departure for any hike is Troodos itself, where you'll find hotels, a youth hostel, restaurants and souvenir shops.

The trail named **Persephone** runs for about 3 km (2 miles) southeast to a scenic viewpoint; the **Atalante** trail runs about 10 km (6 miles) northwest, making its way past Mount Olympus and finally ending at an abandoned chromium mine last used in 1974. If you follow the asphalt road at the mine for about 3 km (2 miles), you'll eventually find yourself back in Troodos.

To reach the **Kaledonia** trail beside the Kryos Potamos (Cold River), hikers must first gain the road that leads to the summer palace of the president, located to the southwest of Troodos. From here the path follows the Cold River for 1.5 km (1 mile) downhill to the picturesque Kaledonia Waterfalls. At the Psilodendro fish restaurant, a 45-minute walk south of the falls, you can treat yourself to fresh trout. If you're too tired to walk the trail back to Troodos, use the restaurant's phone to order a taxi.

Another walk, the **Artemis**, leads

Spectator Sports

The following spectator sports regularly take place in the Republic:
Cyprus Motor Rally
This exciting annual spectacle takes place in September, following a gruelling course through much of the central and western areas of the island, including the mountains. Results count towards the European Championships. Details from The Cyprus Automobile Association, tel: 22-313233.
Cycling
The main cycling organisation holds international road racing and mountain bike contests in spring and autumn.
Cyprus Cycling Federation
Tel: 22-663344

Football
CTO carry details of fixtures.
Horse racing
Nicosia's race course holds regular meetings.
Nicosia Race Club
Tel: 22-379566
Kite flying at Pafos
Every year the Pafos Municipality organises a kite flying competition in the first or second week in March. It takes place in the castle area. Details from the Municipality, tel: 26-911900.
Tennis
Nicosia hosts an international Davis Cup tournament in May.
Cyprus Tennis Federation
PO Box 22393, Nicosia
Tel: 22-666822
Fax: 22- 668016

Sports Information

For details of indoor and outdoor sporting facilities in southern Cyprus, the Cyprus Tourism Organisation publishes a six-page leaflet.

through the forest around Mount Olympus and runs for about 5 km (3 miles). It starts and finishes a short distance from the Prodromos–Mount Olympus road junction.

It is not possible to climb to the top of the mountain – at 1,951 metres (6,505 ft) the highest point on the island – as the British operate an air surveillance radar station here.

Those planning an extended hike in the Troodos region and wishing to stay overnight should bear in mind that in August, the peak holiday season for Cypriots, all accommodation is generally booked solid well in advance.

North Cyprus
Hiking in the north is pleasurable if basic rules are observed. Bring proper walking shoes or boots, take your own water, a hiking stick and keep away from military areas.

Post Offices display maps of hunting areas and you should be aware of the hunting season which starts on the last Sunday in October and continues every Sunday for 12 weeks. The Mountain Climbing Sport Association (mobile: 0542 851 1800) organises walks of all levels, usually of about three hours duration, throughout the year.

A basic walking trail leaflet may be obtained from the tourist office. A useful publication detailing walks of different levels is *Walks in North Cyprus* from the Green Jacket Bookshop in Keryneia.

Horse Riding

Republic of Cyprus
There are a number of riding centres with trained instructors that offer lessons for both beginners and advanced riders. These include:

Amathus School of Riding,
Pareklisia
Tel: 25-320339
Elias Horse Riding Centre,
Pareklisia
Tel: 25-325000 ext 317
George's Ranch
near Agios Georgios, Pegeia
Tel: 26-621790.
Lapatsa Sports Centre
Nicosia
Tel: 22-621201/2/3
Or contact the central horse riding body:
Cyprus Equestrian Federation
PO Box 24860, Nicosia
Tel: 22-472515 or 22-349858.

North Cyprus
Riding schools with instructors are available at:
Tunac Riding School
Karaoglanoglu
Tel: 822 2868
Riding facilities for residents and non-residents are available at:
Merit Cyprus Gardens
Iskele, Famagusta
Tel: 371 3450
Fax: 371 2370
E-mail:
cyprusgardens@northcyprus.net
Mare Monte Hotel
Keryneia
Tel: 821 8310
Fax: 821 8887
E-mail: maremonte@northcyprus.net
Riverside Holiday Village
Alsancak
Tel: 821 8906
Fax: 821 8908
E-mail: riverside@northcyprus.net

Quad Biking

A novel way of seeing the country is by hiring a quad bike. Tours of various duration with English speakers can be organised into the mountains of north Cyprus.

Contact Quad Bike Safari at Lapta on tel: 821 2594.

Skiing

Republic of Cyprus
Snow falls heavily in the Troodos Mountains in winter: it is not for nothing that the nickname of Mount

Olympus is *khionistra* – "chillblain". There are three ski lifts and four runs at Mount Olympus. You can rent ski gear at the Cyprus Ski Club Hut, and also in the village of Troodos. For further details contact:
Cyprus Ski Club
Nicosia
Tel: 22-365340.

Watersports

Throughout the summer watersports enthusiasts will have no difficulty renting the necessary equipment (surf-boards, water-skis, pedal boats, dinghies, yachts, motor boats and so on) at any of Cyprus's more popular beaches.

In the north, windsurfing, sea kayaks, pedaloes and water-skiing facilities are available at most hotel beaches.

Diving
Republic All of the bigger resorts have diving schools with trained professional (PADI) instructors. More experienced divers can do their own thing but must have a permit. Using underwater spearguns is not permitted, nor is collecting sponges or archaeological artefacts. For more information, contact:
The Cyprus Federation of Underwater Activities
PO Box 1503, 1510 Nicosia
Tel: 22-454647

North Dives for novices and experienced divers can be organised at 18 sites along the coast around Keryneia. They vary between 12 and 42 metres (40 and 140 ft) and provide good opportunities for viewing various marine life and artefacts dating back thousands of years. Of special interest for experienced divers only is the Wreck Site, best done after a visit to the Shipwreck Museum at Keryneia Castle. You can book a special interest holiday from home *(see page 286)* or contact:
Keryneia Diving Centre
Canbulat Sok, Keryneia
Tel/fax: 815 6087
Mobile: 0542 853 7377

Scuba Cyprus
Kazim Ozalp Sok, Alsancak,
Keryneia
Tel: 822 3431
Mobile: 0542 8514924

Sailing
Republic With Cyprus's temperate
climate, sailing is pleasant right
into winter. Several companies offer
chartered yachts for licensed
sailors or skippered boats for non-
sailors or those with less
experience:
Interyachting
PO Box 4292, Limassol
Tel: 25-725533
Fax: 25-720021
Navimed
Nicosia,
Tel: 22-591202
Fax: 22-591203
The Old Salt Yachting Co
PO Box 57048, Limassol
Tel: 25-337624
Fax: 25-337768
Sail Fascination Shipping
27 Nikiforou Foka, PO Box 50257,
Limassol
Tel: 25-364200
Fax: 25-352657

North Day boat trips can be
organised from any of the operators
based in the old harbour at
Keryneia and the new port at
Famagusta.

Swimming
Republic There are numerous
inviting beaches on Cyprus, some
more frequented than others.
During summer the beaches on the
southern coast are busiest. Agia
Napa, Protaras and Paralimni, as
well as the those close to Larnaka,
Pafos and Limassol, are especially
crowded. Most tourist hotels are
also concentrated in this area.
   There are a number of beautiful
beaches, which are less developed,
in the area around Polis. The
tavernas and pubs thereabouts are
consequently less touristy than
those at other, more developed
spots and tend to offer more
traditional native cuisine (although
Polis is catching up fast on the
development front).

The sandy beach of Coral Bay
extends from the northwest of
Pafos; adjacent to this is a cliff-
lined, wildly romantic stretch of
shoreline called Cape Drepanon,
near Agios Georgios. If you're
looking for relatively untouched,
rarely frequented beaches try the
Chrysochou Bay between Cape
Arnaoutis (at the western tip of the
island) and Polis (at the centre of
the bay shore).
   Although nude bathing is strictly
prohibited, going topless – both on
the beaches and at hotel swimming
pools – is tolerated. You can go
nude sunbathing and swimming if
you are prepared to hike into the
Akamas Peninsula to get away from
the maddening crowds at the
pocket-handkerchief-sized beaches
in this area, or if you can afford to
hire a speedboat at nearby Latsi to
get you there in style.

North In terms of natural beauty,
the beaches in the northern part of
the island beat those in the south.
There are splendid bays and sandy
beaches around Keryneia and in
the east, in close proximity to
Salamis. Many of the best spots
have been commandeered by hotels
and provided with sanitary facilities
such as showers and toilets. They
charge admission onto the beach
for people who are not hotel guests.
   Another inside tip for those in
search of unspoilt beaches is the
Karpasia Peninsula, jutting out to
the northeast, which is graced by
many inviting coves and beaches
(even if many of them have become
"nesting grounds" for dumped black
plastic rubbish bags and their
odoriferous contents).

Language

Language Tips

In the southern part of the island
the official language is Greek,
although visitors should have no
trouble communicating in English
due to the fact that until 1960
Cyprus was a British colony and the
British still maintain military bases
on the island. German and French
are spoken by an increasing
number of people in the tourist
industry.
   In northern Cyprus, Turkish is the
official language. Turkish Cypriots
who have been living in the country
since before 1974 can, for the most
part, still understand both Greek
and English, while young people
learn English at school. German is
also spoken by many people working
in the tourist industry.
   One of the blessings of Cyprus is
you need never speak a word of
anything but English. But a
frustration is that if you do venture
to ask for something in Greek or
Turkish you're more than likely to be
answered in English. As a lasting
legacy of the colonial period,
English is considered to be the
language of sophisticated discourse

Numbers

1/*éna*/(bir)
2/*dío*/(iki)
3/*tría*/(üç)
4/*téssera*/(dört)
5/*pénte*/(bes)
6/*éxi*/(alti)
7/*eftá*/(yedi)
8/*ochtó*/(sekiz)
9/*enniá*/(dokuz)
10/*déka*/(on)
100/*ekató*/(yüz)
1000/*chília*/(bin)

in both sectors of the island, and the route to career advancement.

If you know some Greek already, beware – Cypriot Greek can be a far cry from the language spoken on the mainland. In fact, until recently Cypriots could only hold virtually incomprehensible conversations with a Greek-speaker from Athens. About 15 percent of vocabulary is unique to Cyprus, and the distinctive Cypriot accent may make the words you know incomprehensible to the traveller who has learned Greek elsewhere.

Places and Facilities

English/Greek/(Turkish)
bank/*i trápeza/(banka)*
envelope/*to fákelo/(mektup zarfi)*
letter/*to gramma/(mektup)*
letter box/*to grammatokivótio/ (posta kutusu)*
money/change/*ta leftá/ta chrímata/ta psìlá/(para/bozuk para)*
petrol station/*to pratírio venzínis/(petrol ofisi/benzin istasyonu)*
police/*i astinomía/(polis)*
post office/*to tachidromío/ (postane)*
postcard/*i kárta/(kartpostal)*
stamps/*ta grammatósima/ (posta pulu)*
telephone/*to tiléfono/(telefon)*

Useful Words/Phrases

English/Greek/(Turkish)
Bon appetit/*kalí órexi /(afiyet olsun)*
Cheers!/*(stín) yá mas!/(serefe!)*
excuse me or sorry/*signómi/(affedersiniz)*
Good evening/*kalí spéra* (from midday)*/(iyi aksamlar)*
Good morning/*kalí méra* (up to midday)*/(gün aydin)*
Good night/*kalí nichta/(iyi geceler)*
Goodbye/*adío* or *yía sas/(allaha-ismarladik)*
Hello/*kalí méra/(merhaba)*
How are you?/*ti kánete?/ (nasilsiniz?)*
...Very well/*kalá/(iyiyim)*
How much is...?/*póso káni?/(kaç para?)*

Pronunciation Tips

In the south
ai = e as in egg
oi/ei/y = i as in India
ou = ou as in tour
In the north
s = sh
ç = ch
g = y

How?/*pos?/(nasil)*
I don't understand/*den katalavéno/(anlamiyorum)*
I'd like.../*thélo/(istiyorum)*
I'd like to pay now/*thélo na plipíso/(ödemek istiyorum)*
It's cheap/*íne ftinó/(ucuz)*
It's expensive/*íne akrivó/(pahali)*
It's good/*íne kaló/(iyi)*
It's nice/*íne oréo/(güzel)*
No/*óchi/(hayir)*
Okay/*endáxi/(tamam)*
Please/*parakaló/(lütfen)*
Thank you/*efharistó/(tesekkür ederim)*
Tomorrow/*ávrio/(yarin)*
We'd like to see some folk dances/*théloume na doume laikóus chórous (oyun havasi görmek istiyoruz)*
We'd like to go to a coffee house/*théloume na páme s'éna kafenío/(bir kahvehane'ye gitmek istiyoruz)*
What's that?/*ti íne aftó?/(bu ne?)*
What's your name?/*pos se léne?/(adin ne?)*
When?/*póte?/(ne zaman?)*
Where can I find...?/*pou ipárchi edó...?/(burada nerededir...?)*
...Cypriot music?/*...i kypriakí mousikí?/(...kibris'den müzik?)*
Where is a beach?/*pou ipárhi paralía?/(Nerede sahil vardir?)*
Where?/*pou?/(nerede?)*
Who?/*piós?/(kim?)*
Why?/*yatí?/(niçin?)*
Yes/*né/(evet)*
Yesterday/*chtes/(dün)*

Food

Fruit
apple/*to mílo/(elma)*
banana/*i banána/(muz)*
broad beans/*ta koukiá/(bakla)*
cherries/*ta kerásia/(kiraz)*

fig/*to síko/(incir)*
fruit/*ta froúta/(meyve)*
grapes/*ta stafília/(üzüm)*
musk melon/*to pepóni/(kavun)*
orange/*to portokáli/(portakal)*
peach/*to rodákino/(seftali)*
pear/*to achládhi/(armut)*
plums/*ta damáskina/(erik)*
pomegranate/*to ródi/(nar)*
strawberries/*i fraoules/(çilek)*
watermelon/*to karpoúsi/(karpuz)*

Vegetables
artichoke/*i anginára/(enginar)*
asparagus/*to asparagos/ (kuskonmaz)*
aubergine/*i melitzána/ (patlican)*
cabbage/*to rambi/(lahana)*
carrots/*to karóto/(havuç)*
celery/*to sélino/(kereviz)*
courgettes/*to kolokitháki/ (kabak)*
cucumber/*to angoúri/(salatalik)*
garlic/*o skórdos/(sarmisak)*
green beans/*ta fasolákia/(taze fasulye)*
green/red pepper/*to pipéri/(biber)*
navy beans/*ta fasólia/(kuru fasulye)*
olives/*i eliés/(zeytin)*
onion/*to kremídi/(sogan)*
peas/*ta bizélia/(bezelye)*
potatoes/*i patátes/(patates)*
Romaine lettuce/*to maroúli/ (marul salatasi)*
spinach/*to spanáki/(ispanak)*
tomato/*i tomáta/(domates)*
vegetables/*ta hórta* or *ta lachaniká/(sebze)*

Miscellaneous
bread/*to psomí/(ekmek)*
butter/*to voútiro/(tereyagi)*
cheese or sheep's cheese/*to tyrí* or *i féta/(peynir* or *beyaz peynir)*
chicken/*to kotópoulo/(pilic)*
egg/*ta avgá/(yumurta)*
fish/*to psári/(balik)*
honey/*to méli/(bal)*
hors d'oeuvre/*to orektikó/ (çerez)*
ice-cream/*to pagotó/(dondurma)*
meat/*to kréas/(et)*
oil/*to ládi/(yag)*
pasta/noodles/*ta makarónia/ (sehriye)*
pepper/*to pipéri/(biber)*
rice/*to rízi/(pilav)*

ripe/órimos/(olgun)
salad/i saláta/(salata)
salt/to aláti/(tuz)
soup/i soúpa/(çorba)
vinegar/to xídi/(sirke)

Drinks

aniseed brandy/i ouzó/(raki)
beer/i bíra/(bira)
bottle/i boukála/(sise)
brandy/to brandy/(keskin içki)
cup/to flintsáni/(fincan)
glass/to potíri/(bardak)
juice/o chimós/(meyva suyu)
lemon/to lemóni/(limon)
milk/to gála/(süt)
mineral water/i sóda/(maden suyu/soda)
Nescafé/to nescafé/(nescafé)
orangeade/i portokaláda/(limonata)
refreshments/to anapsiktikó/(alkolsüz icki)
sugar/i zachari/(seker)
without sugar/skétos/(seker siz)
sweet/glikís/(çok sekerli)
tea/to tsai/(çay)
Turkish/Greek coffee/o ellinikós kafés/(kahve)
water/to neró/(su)
wine/to krasí/(sarap)

Architectural Words

fresco/i tichografía/(fresk)
church/i eklisía/(kilise)
mosaic/to psifídoto/(mozaik)
mosque/to tzamí/(cami)
temple/o naós/(tapinak)

Directions

right/dexiá/(sag)
left/aristerá/(sol)
straight on/ísia/(dogru)
go back/píso/(geri)
Where does this road go?/Pou pái aftós o dromos?/(Nereye bu yol gidiyor?)
From where/when does the bus go?/Apó pou/póte févgi to leoforío?/(Otobüs nerede/ne zaman gidiyor?)
How much is a ticket/the entrance fee?/Pósa íne to isitírio/i ísodos?/(Bilet/giris kaçedir?)
When does the archaeological museum open?/where is...?/Póte

íne anichtó to archeologikó mousío?/Pou ine...?/(Arkeoloji müzesi ne zaman açik? ...nerede?)

Driving Terms

petrol/ì venzíni/(benzin)
oil/to ládi/(yag)
tyres/to lásticho/(lastik)
insurance/ì asfália/(sigorta)
Can you repair it, please?/sas parakaló na diorthósete aftó?/(lütfen bunu tamir edin?)
I'd like to rent a car/motorbike/bicycle/thélo na nikiáso éna aftokínito/mía motosiklétta/éna podílato/(bir otomobil/motosiklet/bisiklet kiralamak istiyorum)

General Terms

ashtray/to tasáki/(kül tablasi)
matches/ta spírta/(kibrit)
cigarettes/ta tsigára/(sigara)
battery/i bataría/(pil)
film/to film/(filim)
spoon/to koutáli/(kasik)
fork/to piroúni/(çatal)
knife/to machéri/(biçak)
teaspoon/to koutaláki/(çay kasik)
plate/to piáto/(tabak)
soap/to sapoúni/(sabun)
newspaper/i efimerída/ (gazete).

Further Reading

Good Companions

The Aphrodite Plot by Michael Jansen. A factually parallel novel based around the events of 1974, and the Colonel-inspired coup against President Makarios that led directly to the Turkish invasion. The author was an American correspondent who covered the crisis. Did the Americans and British give the nod to the invasion? Was the CIA behind it all?
British Cyprus by W Hepworth Dixon. A classic travelogue first published in 1887.
Bitter Lemons by Lawrence Durrell completed his trilogy of Greek island books, describing it as "a somewhat impressionistic study of the moods and atmosphere of Cyprus during the troubled years 1953–6." He lived in the village of Belapais to finish the book.
Hostage to History: Cyprus from the Ottomans to Kissinger by Christopher Hitchens. A study of misconduct of the Geat Powers, the book comes up to date with the island's bid for EU membership.
The Cyprus Conspiracy by Brendan O'Malley and Ian Craig. Tales of intrigue and double dealing by London and Washington are unearthed in this investigation into Western interference in the island.
Cyprus: From Constitutional Conflict to Consitutional Crisis 1957–1963 by Diana Weston Markides. 2001. An academic look at the festering problems that are widely recognised as being almost insurmountable hurdles to the realisation of a solution to the Cypriot problem. Written starkly and honestly, this account pulls no political punches.
Cyprus: Images of a Lifetime by Reno Wideson. 1992. In this large-format book, the author/photographer uses several decades of his sensitively shot pictures to take a

nostalgic look back at the Cyprus that has vanished. His colour photography captures an innocent time before overdevelopment and bitter division.

The Cyprus Imbroglio by Clemet H Dodd. If you've overdosed on the Greek Cypriot viewpoint of the Cyprus issue, try this fairly dry and academic analysis of the politics and history that divide the island. While taking a fairly clear pro Turkish-Cypriot stance, the book nonetheless provides plenty of room for constructive thought.

Exerpta Cypria by Claude Delaval. First published in 1908, this is a fascinating series of excerpts from writers who have turned their pens – or styluses – on Cyprus from AD 23 to 1849.

The Isle of Discord by Ioannis Stefanidis. 1999. This quite recent analysis from a Greek point of view is a scholarly look at the apple of discord that has to date permeated the whole process of solution, author Stefanidis highlights the constant stumbling blocks that have thwarted all reconciliation attempts to date.

Journey Into Cyprus by Colin Thubron, who trekked nearly 1,000 km (600 miles) through the island. He wrote, "The nervous cohabitation which I witnessed in 1972 was, I now realise, the island's halcyon time – and this is the record of a country which will not return."

Other Insight Guides

Other Insight Guides that cover eastern Mediterranean destinations include *Greece*, *Greek Islands*, *Crete*, *Turkey*, *Istanbul* and the *Turkish Coast*.

Insight Pocket Guide: Rhodes has tailor-made tours and recommendations to make the best use of short-stay visitors' time. With a fold-out map. Other Pocket Guide titles include *Athens*, *Corfu*, *Crete*, and *Istanbul*.

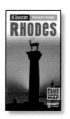

Insight Compact Guide: Cyprus is one of a series of nearly 100 portable, fact-packed guides intended for use on the spot. Other Compact Guides include *Athens*, *Greece*, *Rhodes*, *Turkey*, and *Turkish Coast*.

Feedback

We do our best to ensure the information in our books is as accurate and up-to-date as possible. The books are updated on a regular basis, using local contacts, who painstakingly add, amend and correct as required. However, some mistakes and omissions are inevitable and we are ultimately reliant on our readers to put us in the picture.

We would welcome your feedback on any details related to your experiences using the book "on the road". Maybe we recommended a hotel that you liked (or another that you didn't), as well as interesting new attractions, or facts and figures you have found out about the country itself. The more details you can give us (particularly with regard to addresses, e-mails and telephone numbers), the better.

We will acknowledge all contributions, and we'll offer an Insight Guide to the best letters received. Please write to us at:

Insight Guides
PO Box 7910
London SE1 1WE
United Kingdom
Or send e-mail to: **insight@apaguide.co.uk**

ART & PHOTO CREDITS

INSIGHT GUIDE
CYPRUS

Cartographic Editor **Zoë Goodwin**
Design Consultants **Klaus Geisler, Carlotta Junger, Graham Mitchener**
Picture Research **Hilary Genin, Monica Allende**

Index

Numbers in italics refer to photographs